Great Hotels
and Motels
at Half Price
Across America

Great Hotels and Motels at Half Price Across America

Neil Saunders

Foreword by
Elysa Lazar

Madison Books
Lanham • New York • London

To Olivia & Graham

Published by Madison Books
4720 Boston Way
Lanham, Maryland 20706

3 Henrietta Street
London WC2E 8LU, England

Distributed by National Book Network

Library of Congress Cataloging-in Publication Data

Saunders, Neil, 1952-
   Great hotels and motels at half price across America / by Neil Saunders ;
    Foreword by Elysa Lazar.
    p. cm.
    1. Hotels–United States–Directories. 2. Motels–United States–Directories. I. Title.
   TX907 . 2. S28 1995
   647 . 947301–dc20   95-31321
                                                           CIP

ISBN 1-56833-058-8

Contents

State Listings

Foreword

With all the traveling I've done over the years, the bane of my life always seems to be having to pay full price—or close to it—for hotel rooms. Even when corporate rates, weekend specials, and other promotions are available, the discounts offered sometimes amount to very little and may not be worth the effort. Yet consider the bargain fares offered by all the airlines...the super deals you can get on car rentals...the budget packages for ski trips, golf vacations, and all kinds of other special tours. Of all the travel costs involved in exploring this great country of ours, accommodations remain an expensive proposition.

That's why I'm so excited about this invaluable new travel guide. **Great Hotels and Motels at Half Price Across America** will save you hundreds of dollars when you travel. We all owe a huge debt of gratitude to Neil Saunders. He has painstakingly compiled a directory of more than 1,600 hotels and motels throughout the United States that each offer a 50 percent discount off the regular room rate. Book a room at any of these places and you can relax in the knowledge that at checkout time your bill will be cut in half.

What I particularly like about **Great Hotels and Motels at Half Price Across America** is the extraordinary variety of places to stay that Saunders has included. I travel extensively, and my needs vary greatly. When I'm on the road for business, I usually look for reliable hotels with comfortable rooms and excellent business facilities. You can imagine my delight in seeing so many old favorites in the pages of this guide. But when it comes to going on vacation with my family, amenities such as swimming pools, tennis courts, and restaurants suddenly become a lot more important. And I'm happy to report that **Great Hotels and Motels at Half Price Across America** passes with flying colors on this front, too. I found no shortage of ocean-front hotels, resort lodges, and places that cater specially to kids—and even to pets! Finally, what would life be without an occasional romantic weekend for two? I want whirlpools, saunas, four-poster beds, fireplaces, and candlelit restaurants. Two thumbs up again! Neil Saunders has liberally sprinkled country inns, Victorian B&Bs, and some of America's grandest hotels among his listings.

On my desk sits a small bookshelf with an "elite" group of books that I keep close at hand at all times. Most are essential reference works—my Webster's dictionary, thesaurus, local phone book, and the like. The latest addition is **Great Hotels and Motels at Half Price Across America**. Take it from me, you're going to want to find a handy place for your copy, too. And if my experience is anything to go by, it will quickly become a well-thumbed book.

Elysa Lazar

Elysa Lazar, a nationally recognized travel expert, is a consumer correspondent for CNBC and a regular contributor on "Live with Regis & Kathie Lee" WNBC's "Today in New York," has appeared on hundreds of programs including "The Oprah Winfrey Show" and "Sally Jesse Raphael." Elysa has been called "The World's Smartest Shopper" by **Redbook**. Among her many travel books are **Elysa Lazar's Outlet Shopper's Guide**, **Museum Shop Treasures**, and **Shop by Mail**. Although she lives in New York City, much of her time is spent at hotels and motels in various parts of the United States.

Introduction

In many respects this is a typical travel accommodation guide, but there is one major difference: at every single one of the hotels, motels, and other properties listed here, you can stay for 50 percent off the regular rate at any time of the year.

From personal experience I know what a wonderful feeling it is to see your hotel bills cut in half. A few years ago, I became a member of one of the largest travel clubs in the nation. Since then wherever my travels around the United States have taken me, I have saved 50 percent on all my accommodation costs. In fact, this national program impressed me so much that I began to wonder why it could not be made available to a broader audience. After more than a year of gentle cajoling, I finally persuaded this exclusive travel club to offer the program, albeit in a slightly more limited form, to the millions of travelers looking for reasonably priced overnight accommodations. And so was born **Great Hotels and Motels at Half Price Across America**.

By purchasing a copy of this guide, you automatically become a Quality Services International® (QSI®) cardholder entitled to a 50% discount at the properties listed within the guide. (You will find your discount card at the back of this book.)

Since variety is the spice of life, my goal in selecting the more than 1,600 properties featured in this guide was to ensure that there would be something for everyone: clean, comfortable motels for families traveling on a tight budget; attractive, conveniently located hotels with such amenities as fax machines, computers, and secretarial services for business people; hotels that cater to children, with large rooms, kitchen facilities, baby-sitting services, video rentals, and kids' menus; hotels for the health conscious, with exercise equipment, jogging tracks, swimming pools, and saunas; and deluxe accommodations, such as country inns, historic B&Bs, resort hotels, lodges, and spas, for those who like to travel in style. Since pet owners increasingly want to travel with their canine or feline companions, I even included a sizable number of hotels and motels that welcome dogs and cats (although you should always check in advance, because some properties have size and weight restrictions).

Today, spending nights away from home can take many different forms: a midweek break, a weekend getaway, an anniversary celebration, a trip to attend a graduation, or a visit to see grandparents. Gone are the days when travel for most people was largely confined to a conventional one- or two-week vacation. With **Great Hotels and Motels at Half Price Across America**, all kinds of other possibilities may now open up. In fact, if you stay just one night at a hotel or motel listed inside, you will save more than enough money to repay the cost of this guide.

Whenever you decide to take advantage of the 50 percent savings offered by any of the properties listed in the guide, be sure to follow the simple instructions below:

1. Make your hotel or motel selection.

2. Call the hotel or motel, using either the local or toll-free telephone number provided in the listing, between 2 and 30 days in advance, and ask for the reservations department.

3. Identify yourself as a QSI®/ENCORE® cardholder before asking the reservationist about availability for the date(s) you want to stay. Verify the QSI/ENCORE rate and ask for a confirmation number.

4. Present your QSI/ENCORE card (at the back of this book) with your credit card and confirmation number when you check in, and 50 percent will be automatically deducted from the regular room rate.

Although almost all of the places listed in this guide offer year-round savings every day of the week, a few do "black out" certain dates. Most of these dates occur during holidays (such as New Year's Eve) or major local events (such as the Indy 500 in Indianapolis), when hotels or motels are likely to be fully booked months in advance. These and any other restrictions are noted in parentheses at the end of each listing. Of course, QSI will not be liable for the actions and omissions of any property.

It's worth emphasizing that the regular rate—often referred to as the "rack" rate by the travel industry—on which the 50 percent discount is based, is the highest rate a hotel or motel is allowed to charge for a room. This rate should be posted on the back of each hotel room door.

Each listing indicates the normal price range of the property with a dollar sign system, similar to those used in restaurant reviews. These prices are for two people sharing a hotel room; if additional adults occupy the room, you may be required to pay an extra charge. Children sharing the same room as their parents usually stay free. A key to these symbols is located on page XV.

The listings are arranged alphabetically, first by state, then by city, and finally by property. Each listing includes the name and street address of the property, followed by a local telephone number and sometimes a toll-free 800 telephone number. (The majority of these toll-free numbers are for the specific hotel or motel and not for the nationwide hotel chain. Do not use any other toll-free numbers, such as those for the central reservations offices of chain hotels, since only the property itself can accurately determine space availability.) Each listing also contains a brief line or two of general information about the particular property, usually indicating the number of stories (if more than two), the nearest interstate or other major highway, nearby places of interest, and any other notable features.

The listings conclude with a list of symbols indicating the amenities available at each hotel (see Amenity Symbols key on page XV).

For each state, I have also included a short introductory section, spotlighting the major cities and sites with recommendations on what to see and do during a visit. An accompanying map pinpoints the locations of these places.

I am particularly grateful to Stephanie Krupin, who labored long, hard, and very successfully to make my words look attractive on the page. Special thanks also go to my wife, Ingrid, for her seemingly unlimited supply of patience and support, and to my children, Olivia and Graham, who hopefully will grow up to be intrepid travelers, just like their Mummy and Daddy.

And, finally, to everyone who uses this guide: I hope it truly stimulates your desire and interest to travel.

Key to Listings

Rate System

Remember that when using your QSI®/ENCORE® card, you pay **half** of these rates:

$	=	$35-50
$$	=	$51-79
$$$	=	$80-150
$$$$	=	$151 or more

Amenity Symbols

Parking on Premises	P	Exercise Facility	
Restaurant on Premises		Tennis Courts	
Free Breakfast		Golfing on Premises	
Bar/Lounge		Whirlpool/Sauna	
Non-Smoking Rooms		Pets Allowed	
Business Center	B	Airport Nearby	
Outdoor Swimming Pool		Airport Transportation	
Indoor Swimming Pool			

Sample Listing

Charleston ——————————— location
——————————— nightly rate (see above)

$$$ **CHARLESTON MARRIOTT**——— name of property
4770 Marriott D———————— street address
(803) 747-1900 or
(800) 228-9290 —————————— telephone number(s)
9-story hotel off I-26 ———————— brief information

——————————— amenities (see above)

Alabama

*T*he spirit of the "Old South" still pervades Alabama. Antebellum mansions, moss-draped trees, and lush, unspoiled countryside are still very much in evidence.

Surprisingly, **Birmingham**, the state's principal city, was not founded until after the Civil War, in 1871. Today it's a busy commercial center, the South's biggest iron and steel producer, and the home of a diverse array of cultural and tourist attractions, including Birmingham Botanical Gardens, Birmingham Museum of Art, Red Mountain Museum (noted for its geologic exhibits), Birmingham Zoo, and Arlington Antebellum Home and Gardens (one of the finest examples of its kind in the South).

One of Alabama's most fascinating cities is **Huntsville**, the site of NASA's George C. Marshall Space Flight Center, which has played an integral role in the development of America's space program since its opening in 1960. At the U.S. Space and Rocket Center, billed as the largest space museum in the world, you can see a full-size exhibit on the space shuttle as well as an extensive collection of rocketry and many other hands-on displays.

One of the oldest settlements in the state is **Mobile**, with a history stretching back to 1702. Alabama's only major seaport, the city is famous for its graceful old mansions, its annual Mardi Gras celebration (second only to that of New Orleans), and its fabulous 37-mile Azalea Trail, best enjoyed in late March and early April.

Also well worth visiting are **Auburn**, home of Alabama's largest and most notable university and an engaging series of historic districts, and **Dothan**, site of an annual Peanut Festival and an opera house built in 1915 that is still in use today.

Auburn

$$$ AUBURN UNIVERSITY HOTEL
241 S College St
(205) 821-8200 or
(800) 228-2876
6-story hotel next to
Auburn University
(excl home football weekends)

🕪 🍸 🚭 ≋ 🍴 🚌 🅿

Birmingham

$$ CIVIC CENTER INN
2230 10th Ave N
(205) 328-6320
Off I-20/I-59 next to
Civic Center

🖥 🚭 ≋ ✈ 🏠

$$$$ THE TUTWILER
2021 Park Place N
(205) 322-2100 or
(800) 845-1787
Historic 1914 downtown hotel

🕪 🚭 🍴 🅿

Dothan

$$ RAMADA INN
3001 Ross Clark Cir
(205) 792-0031
Near US 231

🕪 🍸 🚭 ≋ 🚌 🏠

Huntsville

$$$ HUNTSVILLE HILTON
401 Williams Ave
(205) 533-1400 or
(800) 544-3197
4-story hotel in historic district opposite Civic Center

🕪 🍸 🖥 🚭 ≋ 🔌 🍴
🍽 🚌 🏠

$$$ HUNTSVILLE MARRIOTT
5 Tranquility Base
(205) 830-2222 or
(800) 228-9290
7-story hotel off I-565 next to
US Space and Rocket Center

🕪 🍸 🚭 ≋ ≋ 🍴
🚌 🏠

$$$ RADISSON SUITE HOTEL
6000 Memorial Pkwy S
(205) 882-9400
3-story hotel off US 231

🕪 🍸 🖥 🚭 ≋ 🔌 🍴
🚌 🏠

$$$ RESIDENCE INN BY MARRIOTT
4020 Independence Dr
(205) 837-8907 or
(800) 331-3131
All-suite motel near
downtown and US Space
and Rocket Center

🖥 🚭 ≋ 🔌 🍴 🍽
🚌 🏠

$$$ SHERATON INN AIRPORT
1000 Glenn Hearn Blvd
Box 20068
(205) 772-9661 or
(800) 241-7873
6-story hotel off I-565 in
airport complex

🕪 🍸 🚭 ≋ 🍴 🍽 🍴
✈ 🚌 🏠

Madison

$$$ HOWARD JOHNSON PARK SQUARE INN
8721 Hwy 20 W
(205) 772-8855
Hotel off I-265 near airport

🕪 🍸 🚭 ≋ 🍴 ✈ 🏠

Mobile

$ CHOICE INN
1724 Michigan Ave
(800) 352-3297
Hotel off I-10

🛏 🍽 🚭 🏊

$$ CLARION HOTEL
3101 Airport Blvd
(205) 476-6400 or
(800) 982-9822
20-story hotel off I-65

🛏 🏊 ✈ 🚌

$$ HOLIDAY INN DOWNTOWN
301 Government St
(205) 694-0100
16-story hotel in restored
building in historic district

🛏 💻 🚭 🏊 🚌 🏠

$$ HOLIDAY INN EXPRESS
255 Church St
(205) 433-6923
Restored hotel off I-10 in
historic district, close to
Convention Center

💻 🚭 🏊

Oxford

$$ HOLIDAY INN
US 78 and Hwy 21 S
(205) 831-3410 or
(800) 465-4329
Opposite Quintard Mall
(excluding race weeks)

🛏 🍽 🚭 🏊 🛁 🍴 ✈
🚌 🏠

$ OXFORD DAYS INN
1 Recreation Dr
(205) 835-0300
Hotel off I-20 near Talladega
International Speedway
(excluding race weeks)

🍽 💻 🚭 🏊 🍴 ✈
🚌 🏠

Arizona

or most visitors, the principal attraction of Arizona is its spectacular scenery. This is the land of the Grand Canyon, Monument Valley, the Painted Desert, and the San Francisco Peaks. Equally enticing are the state's rich Native American roots, for Arizona was originally peopled by some of America's most sophisticated prehistoric settlers. Today, one-quarter of Arizona is composed of tribal reservations, including those of the Apache, the Hopi, and the Navajo.

At the very heart of Arizona is **Phoenix**, capital of the state and center of the American Southwest. A vibrant, cosmopolitan city, it offers a dazzling array of sights and experiences: from the Heard Museum, one of America's most outstanding collections of native culture and art, to the Desert Botanical Garden, where you can see some of the world's most exotic plants in an extraor-

dinary natural setting.

Phoenix's sister cities of **Scottsdale**, famous for its luxurious shopping, **Tempe**, host of the annual Fiesta Bowl, and **Mesa**, a popular resort area, are not to be missed, too.

Arizona's other big city is **Tucson**, which enjoys a dramatic desert setting amid four mountain ranges. Among its sightseeing highlights are the Arizona-Sonora Desert Museum, Mission San Xavier Del Bac (which dates back to 1783), and Saguaro National Monument.

Other recommended stops around the state include **Flagstaff**, gateway to the Grand Canyon and the scenic drive through Oak Creek Canyon to Sedona; **Lake Havasu City**, a resort community now boasting the relocated London Bridge among its attractions; and **Sierra Vista**, a horse breeding center nestled in the Huachuca Mountains.

Apache Junction

$$$ GOLD CANYON RANCH RESORT
6100 S Kings Ranch Rd
(602) 982-9090 or
(800) 624-6445
Resort hotel in foothills of
Superstition Mts, 8-unit adobe-
style villas, summer kids camp

Chandler

$$$ SHERATON SAN MARCOS GOLF RESORT
1 San Marcos Place
(602) 963-6655
1912 hotel listed on National
Register of Historic Places

$$$ WYNDHAM GARDEN HOTEL
7475 W Chandler Blvd
(602) 961-4444
4-story hotel off I-10

Flagstaff

$$$$ COUNTRY CLUB CONDOS
2380 N Oakmont Dr
(520) 526-4287 or
(800) 424-7748
1-, 2-, and 3-bedroom condos
off I-40 in residential neighbor-
hood (no weekend reservations
more than 3 days in advance)

Kingman

$$ HOLIDAY INN
3100 E Andy Devine Ave
(520) 753-6262
Hotel off I-40 near downtown

Lake Havasu City

$$$ LONDON BRIDGE RESORT
1477 Queens Bay Rd
(520) 855-0888 or
(800) 624-7939
Hotel off I-40 on banks of Lake
Havasu next to English Village
and relocated London Bridge

Mesa

$$$ ARIZONA GOLF RESORT
425 S Power Rd
(602) 832-3202 or
(800) 528-8282
150-acre resort complex with
mountain views (reservations
must be made within 30 days
of arrival)

$$$ SHERATON MESA HOTEL
200 N Centennial Way
(602) 898-8300
12-story downtown hotel
near business district

Phoenix

$$$ DOUBLETREE SUITES
320 N 44th St at Van Buren
(602) 225-0500
6-story all-suite hotel near
Desert Botanical Garden and
Phoenix Zoo

🔟 🍸 🚭 🏊 🛗 🍴 🚶
🏧 🚌

$$$ HOTEL WESTCOURT
10220 N Metro Pkwy E
(602) 997-5900 or
(800) 858-1033
5-story hotel off I-17 at
Metrocenter shopping and
entertainment complex

🔟 🍸 🚭 🏊 🛗 🍴 🚶

$$ KNIGHTS INN AIRPORT
2201 S 24th St
(602) 267-0611
Hotel off I-10 near airport

🍴 🚭 🏊 🏧 🚌 🛎

$$$ LEXINGTON HOTEL AND CITY SQUARE SPORTS CLUB
100 W Clarendon
(602) 279-9811 or
(800) 272-2439
Multistory hotel with full-size
basketball court and nightclub

🔟 🍸 🍴 🚭 🛗 🍴
🚌 🛎

$$$ LOS OLIVOS EXECUTIVE HOTEL
202 E McDowell Rd
(602) 258-6911 or
(800) 776-5560
3-story hotel in downtown
business district

🔟 🚭 🏊 🍴 🚶

$$ PHOENIX AIRPORT DAYS INN
3333 E Van Buren
(602) 244-8244 or
(800) 528-8191
Hotel near airport

🔟 🍸 🚭 🏊 🍴 🏧
🚌 🛎

$$$$ PHOENIX AIRPORT HILTON
2435 S 47th St
(602) 894-1600
4-story hotel off I-10
near airport

🔟 🍸 🚭 🏊 🍴 🏧 🚌

$$$ QUALITY HOTEL
3600 N 2nd Ave
(602) 248-0222
Multistory hotel in financial
district opposite Park Central
shopping mall

🔟 🍸 🚭 🏊 🏧 🚌 🛎

$$$ RAMADA INN METROCENTER
12027 N 28th Dr
(602) 866-7000
4-story hotel off I-17 near
Metrocenter shopping and
entertainment complex

🔟 🍸 🚭 🏊 🛗 🛎

$$$ ROYAL PALMS INN
5200 E Camelback Rd
(602) 840-3610
48-acre Spanish-style resort
on southern slope of
Camelback Mountain

🔟 🍸 🚭 🏊 🛗 🚶 🍴
🚌 🛎

$$$ SAN CARLOS HOTEL
202 N Central Ave
(602) 253-4121 or
(800) 528-5446
1928 downtown hotel listed
in National Register of
Historic Places

**$$$ WYNDHAM GARDEN
HOTEL NORTH**
2641 W Union Hills Dr
(602) 978-2222
Hotel off I-17

**$$$ WYNDHAM GARDEN
HOTEL AIRPORT**
427 N 44th St
(602) 220-4400
7-story hotel near airport

Scottsdale

**$$$$ MARRIOTT'S MOUNTAIN
SHADOWS RESORT**
5641 E Lincoln Dr
(602) 948-7111 or
(800) 228-9290
70-acre resort complex at
foot of Camelback Mountain

**$$$$ REGAL MCCORMICK
RANCH**
7401 N Scottsdale Rd
(602) 948-5050
Luxury Southwestern-style
resort with rooms and villas
overlooking Camelback Lake

**$$$$ RESIDENCE INN BY
MARRIOTT**
6040 N Scottsdale Rd
(602) 948-8666
(800) 331-3131
All-suite hotel with
Southwestern-style decor

Sierra Vista

$$$ RAMADA INN
2047 S Hwy 92
(520) 459-5900
3-story hotel near historic
Fort Huachuca

$$$ SIERRA SUITES
391 E Fry Blvd
(520) 459-4221
Motel near historic
Fort Huachuca in busy
commercial district

Tempe

**$$$ COUNTRY SUITES BY
CARLSON**
1660 W Elliot Rd
(602) 345-8585 or
(800) 456-4000
3-story all-suite motel near
foothills of South Mountain

$$$ PARAMOUNT HOTEL
225 E Apache Blvd
(602) 967-9431
7-story hotel opposite
Arizona State University and
near Old Town Tempe

$$$$ RESIDENCE INN BY MARRIOTT
5075 S Priest Dr
(602) 756-2122 or
(800) 331-3131
All-suite hotel, many rooms
have fireplaces (discount on
studio suites only)

🖥️ 🚫 🏊 🛏️ 🍴 🚶 🚌 🛖

Tolleson

$$ ECONO LODGE
1520 N 84th Dr
(602) 936-4667
Motel off I-10 west of Phoenix

🚫 Ⓟ 🏊 🛖

Tucson

$$$ DOUBLETREE HOTEL
445 S Alvernon
(520) 881-4200
Multistory hotel next to
Randolph Park

🔊 🍸 🚫 🏊 🍴 🚶 🛖

$$ HOLIDAY INN AIRPORT
4550 S Palo Verde Blvd
(520) 746-1161 or
(800) 465-4329
Multistory resort-style hotel
off I-10

🔊 🍸 🚫 🏊 🛏️ 🍴 🚶 🚌 🛖

$$$ HOTEL PARK TUCSON
5151 E Grant Rd
(520) 323-6262 or
(800) 257-7275
4-story all-suite hotel next to
Tucson Medical Center

🔊 🍸 🖥️ 🚫 🏊 🛏️ 🍴

$$$ PLAZA HOTEL AND CONFERENCE CENTER
1900 E Speedway Blvd
(520) 327-7341 or
(800) 843-8052
7-story hotel off I-10
opposite University of Arizona

🏊 🛏️ Ⓟ

$$$$ QUALITY INN UNIVERSITY
1601 N Oracle
(520) 623-6666 or
(800) 777-2999
Hotel off I-10 near downtown
and University of Arizona

🍸 🚫 🏊 🚌 🛖

$$ RAMADA DOWNTOWN TUCSON
475 N Granada
(520) 622-3000
Multistory downtown hotel off
I-10 near Convention Center
and University of Arizona

🔊 🍸 🚫 🏊 🚌 🛖

$$$ TUCSON EAST HILTON
7600 E Broadway
(520) 721-5600 or
(800) 648-7177
7-story hotel in financial
district with scenic views of
Catalina Mountains

🔊 🍸 🚫 🏊 🍴 🚌

Arkansas

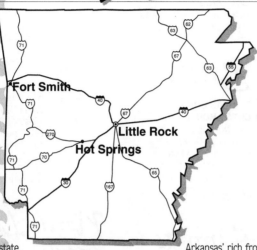

*T*he state made famous by Bill Clinton is an appealing mixture of fashionable resorts, dense forests, open prairie, rolling hills, quick flowing rivers, and historic frontier sights. Recreational opportunities abound, including boating, fishing, and duck hunting, a particular Arkansas favorite.

Located in the heart of the state, **Little Rock** functions both as capital and principal city. Nicknamed the "City of Roses" because of the distinctive flowers that dot its residential districts, Little Rock has much to offer. Historically, there is the Quapaw Quarter, with its ornate Victorian mansions, and the Old State House, a magnificent example of Doric architecture. The Arkansas Arts Center is a major cultural highlight, and kids won't want to miss the Little Rock Zoo and the Museum of Science and Industry.

At **Fort Smith**, you can relive Arkansas' rich frontier history by clambering around the remains of the two forts established in the early nineteenth century or by exploring a series of fascinating museums and historic homes.

If it's rest and relaxation you're after, head for **Hot Springs**, the health and pleasure resort famous for the bubbling mineral waters that flow naturally from the ground. Be sure to drive through Hot Springs National Park and sample these extraordinary displays of nature for yourself. The city of Hot Springs itself has plenty of attractions, including the interesting Mid-America Museum, myriad shopping possibilities, and sporting pursuits such as golf.

No trip to Arkansas would be complete, however, without a trip to its great natural treasure, the Ozarks, a heavily forested region of towering hills and plunging valleys cut by crystal clear streams.

Benton

$$ **DAYS INN BENTON**
1501 Interstate 30
(501) 776-3200
Motel off I-30 near downtown

Fort Smith

$$ **THOMAS QUINN
GUEST HOUSE**
815 North B St
(501) 782-0499
Restored 1863 hotel in
historic district, all rooms
individually furnished

Hot Springs

$$$ **HOLIDAY INN
LAKE HAMILTON**
4813 Central Ave
(501) 525-1391
7-story hotel overlooking
lake, boat docks available

Jonesboro

$ **PARK INN**
1421 S Caraway
(501) 935-8400
Hotel in business district

Little Rock

$$ **CAMELOT HOTEL**
424 W Markham
(501) 372-4371 or
(800) 937-2789
Downtown hotel off I-30
next to Convention Center

$$ **HOLIDAY INN CITY CENTER**
617 S Broadway
(501) 376-2071
12-story downtown hotel off
I-630 near Convention Center
and State Capitol

North Little Rock

$$ **HOLIDAY INN**
111 W Pershing Blvd
(501) 758-1440
Multistory hotel off I-40

California

America's most populous state, California is also full of spectacular natural attractions: from the immense redwood forests in the north to the huge expanses of barren desert in the south, from the dramatically rugged and rocky coast in the west to the towering snow-capped mountains in the east.

No city epitomizes the state more than **San Francisco**, beautifully situated at the head of a narrow peninsula and surrounded by water on three sides. Allow plenty of time to explore the city's manifold delights, including Golden Gate Park, Chinatown, Nob Hill, and Fisherman's Wharf among others. Then venture a little further afield to discover the many exciting destinations surrounding the city, such as **Berkeley**, **Oakland**, **Palo Alto**, and **San Jose**.

If possible, take a spectacular drive down the coast on fabled Route 1 to **Los Angeles**, California's other—and vastly different—major metropolis. The sheer size of this sprawling city is difficult to comprehend, but before you leave be sure to investigate some of its most distinctive parts: **Hollywood**, **Beverly Hills**, **Santa Monica**, **Anaheim** (site of the legendary Disneyland), **Long Beach**, and **Pasadena** to name but a few.

Your California odyssey should also include trips to **San Diego**, home to one of the finest zoos in the world and a truly gorgeous shoreline; the state capital of **Sacramento**, with its magnificent Capitol building and other historic neighborhoods; **Palm Springs**, the exclusive desert resort famous for its luxurious shopping and fabulous golf courses; **Monterey**, with its breathtaking peninsula and colorful waterfront; and **Santa Barbara**, a shining jewel overlooking the Pacific Ocean, noted for its Spanish heritage.

Agoura Hills

$$$ RADISSON HOTEL
30100 Agoura Rd
(818) 707-1220
Hotel in Santa Monica
Mountains near Malibu Beach
(excluding Jun 23-24)

Alpine

$$$$ COUNTRY SIDE INN
1251 Tavern Rd
(619) 445-5800
Motel off I-8 with antiques
in the rooms

Anaheim

$$ ANAHEIM CARRIAGE INN
2125 S Harbor Blvd
(714) 740-1440 or
(800) 345-2131
3-story motel with free shuttle service to Disneyland

$$$ ANAHEIM CONESTOGA HOTEL
1240 S Walnut
(714) 535-0300 or
(800) 824-5459
Hotel with Old West theme,
free shuttle service to
Disneyland

$$$$ ANAHEIM HILTON AND TOWERS
777 Convention Way
(714) 750-4321 or
(800) 222-9923
14-story hotel, lobby with
marble fountain and hanging
sculpture, free shuttle service
to Disneyland (tower rooms
not available)

$$$ ANAHEIM INN AT THE PARK
1855 S Harbor Blvd
(714) 750-1811 or
(800) 421-6662
14-story hotel next to the
Convention Center, free
shuttle service to Disneyland

$$$ ANAHEIM INTERNATIONAL INN AND SUITES
2060 S Harbor Blvd
(714) 971-9393
3-story hotel with rural
French-style decor, free
shuttle service to Disneyland

$$$ ANAHEIM JOLLY ROGER INN HOTEL
640 W Katella Ave
(714) 772-7621 or
(800) 446-1555
Multistory hotel opposite
Disneyland, one unit has a
private pool

$$$$ ANAHEIM MARRIOTT
700 W Convention Way
(714) 750-8000
19-story hotel next to
the Convention Center

$$$ ANAHEIM PARKSIDE INN AND SUITES
2145 S Harbor Blvd
(714) 971-5556 or
(800) 322-7268
Hotel near Convention
Center, free shuttle
service to Disneyland

$$$ ANAHEIM PLAZA HOTEL
1700 S Harbor Blvd
(714) 772-5900 or
(800) 228-1357
Multistory hotel opposite
Disneyland

$$$ ANAHEIM RAMADA
1331 E Katella Ave
(714) 978-8088 or
(800) 228-0586
Hotel near Anaheim Stadium,
free shuttle service to
Disneyland

$$$ ANAHEIM TRAVELODGE PARK SOUTH
2171 S Harbor Blvd
(714) 750-3100 or
(800) 221-6385
Motel near Disneyland with
free shuttle service

$$ BROOKHURST PLAZA INN
711 S Brookhurst St
(714) 999-1220 or
(800) 909-1220
Hotel off I-5

$$$ CAROUSEL INN AND SUITES
1530 S Harbor Blvd
(714) 758-0444 or
(800) 854-6767
Multistory motel opposite
Disneyland with rooftop pool

$$ CONVENTION CENTER INN
2017 S Harbor Blvd
(714) 740-2500 or
(800) 521-5628
3-story motel next to
Convention Center, free
shuttle service to Disneyland
(excluding Dec 31)

$$$ CROWN STERLING SUITES
3100 E Frontera St
(714) 632-1221 or
(800) 433-4600
7-story all-suite hotel, free
shuttle service to Disneyland
and Knott's Berry Farm

$$$ DESERT PALM INN AND SUITES
631 W Katella Ave
(714) 535-1133
Hotel opposite Convention
Center and near Disneyland

$$$ GRANADA INN
2375 W Lincoln Ave
(714) 774-7370 or
(800) 648-8685
All-suite hotel

$$$$ GRAND HOTEL
1 Hotel Way
(714) 772-7777 or
(800) 421-6662
10-story hotel opposite
Disneyland

$$ RODEWAY INN
800 S Beach Blvd
(714) 995-5700
Hotel near Knott's
Berry Farm

$$ SUPER 8 MOTEL
915 S West St
(714) 778-0350 or
(800) 248-4400
3-story motel near Disneyland
with free shuttle service

$$ VALENCIA INN
2630 W Lincoln Ave
(714) 821-3690
3-story hotel

Arcadia

$$$$ EMBASSY SUITES
211 E Huntington Dr
(818) 445-8525
7-story all suite hotel off
I-210 near Santa Anita race-
track (excluding Dec 29-31)

Arcata

$$$ HOTEL ARCATA
708 9th St
(707) 826-0217 or
(800) 344-1221
Restored 1915 hotel with
individually furnished rooms

$$ NORTH COAST INN
4975 Valley W Blvd
(707) 822-4861
Hotel off US 101 near
Redwood National Park

Arroyo Grande

**$$$ BEST WESTERN CASA
GRANDE INN**
850 Oak Park Rd
(805) 481-7398
Hotel off US 101 near
Pismo Beach

Artesia

**$$ RAMADA INN ARTESIA
CERRITOS**
17510 S Pioneer Blvd
(310) 924-6700
Hotel near Cerritos
Performing Arts Center

Bakersfield

$$ BEST WESTERN INN
2620 Pierce Rd
(805) 327-9651 or
(800) 424-4900
Hotel near downtown
and airport

$$$ RIO BRAVO RESORT
11200 Lake Ming Rd
(805) 872-5000 or
(800) 282-5000
Spacious resort next to Lake
Ming with Sierra Nevada
Mountains as backdrop

$$$ SHERATON INN
5101 California Ave
(805) 325-9700
Hotel in business district
with landscaped garden with
stream and pond

Baldwin Park

$$$ SAN GABRIEL VALLEY MARRIOTT
14635 Baldwin Park
(818) 962-6000
10-story hotel off I-10, free
shuttle service to West Covina
Plaza Mall (max 5-night stay)

Berkeley

$$$ BERKELEY MARINA MARRIOTT
200 Marina Blvd
(510) 548-7920
Multistory hotel off I-80,
some rooms with bay views

Beverly Hills

$$$$ THE BEVERLY RODEO HOTEL
360 N Rodeo Dr
(310) 273-0300 or
(800) 356-7575
Hotel next to shopping district with French Renaissance
decor, 2 penthouse suites
(discount on deluxe and superior accomodations only)

Buena Park

$ COMMONWEALTH AIRPORT INN
8180 Commonwealth Ave
(714) 521-8888
Motel near Knott's Berry Farm

$$$$ EMBASSY SUITES HOTEL
7762 Beach Blvd
(714) 739-5600
4-story all-suite hotel near
Knott's Berry Farm, free
shuttle service to Disneyland

$ FARM DE VILLE MOTEL
7800 Crescent Ave
(714) 527-2201
Motel opposite
Knott's Berry Farm

$$$ HOLIDAY INN BUENA PARK
7000 Beach Blvd
(714) 522-7000 or
(800) 522-7006
5-story hotel with free shut-
tle service to Knott's Berry
Farm and Disneyland

Burbank

$$$ BURBANK AIRPORT HILTON AND CONVENTION CENTER
2500 Hollywood Way
(818) 843-6000
9-story hotel off I-5
near airport

Burlingame

$$$ DAYS INN-SAN FRANCISCO AIRPORT
777 Airport Blvd
(415) 342-7772 or
(800) 451-6641
5-story hotel near airport,
some rooms feature bay views

$$$ DOUBLETREE HOTEL SAN FRANCISCO AIRPORT
835 Airport Blvd
(415) 344-5500
8-story hotel near airport,
some rooms have bay views

Calabasas

$$$ COUNTRY INN AT CALABASAS
23627 Calabasas Rd
(818) 222-5300
4-story motel off US 101
(max 3-night stay)

Camarillo

$$$$ COUNTRY INN AT CAMARILLO
1405 Del Norte Rd
(805) 983-7171
3-story motel off US 101
(max 3-night stay)

$$$ DEL NORTE INN
4444 Central Ave
(805) 485-3999
3-story motel off US 101
(max 3-night stay)

Campbell

$$$$ CAMPBELL INN
675 E Campbell Ave
(408) 374-4300 or
(800) 582-4300
Motel, some rooms have
fireplaces, 16-mile jogging
and bicycle path nearby

$$$$ PRUNEYARD INN
1995 S Bascom Ave
(408) 559-4300 or
(800) 582-4300
3-story motel within
Pruneyard Shopping Center,
some rooms have fireplaces

Canoga Park

$$ BEST WESTERN CANOGA PARK MOTOR INN
20122 Vanowen St
(818) 883-1200
Hotel off US 101 with 24-hour bowling alley

Cardiff by the Sea

$$$ COUNTRY SIDE INN
1661 Villa Cardiff Dr
(619) 944-0427
Motel off I-5 near beach

🛏 📺 🚫 🏊

Carlsbad

$$ SUN COAST INN
3700 Pio Pico Dr
(619) 720-0808 or
(800) 890-8890
Hotel off Hwy 5

🚫 🏊 🏊 P ✈

Cathedral City

$$$$ DOUBLETREE RESORT PALM SPRINGS
67-967 Vista Chino
(619) 322-7000 or
(800) 637-0577
350-acre resort complex
off I-10 near airport

🛏 🍸 🚫 🏊 🛗 🍴 🚶
🚴 🚌 🏠

Chatsworth

$$$ 7-STAR SUITES HOTEL
21603 Devonshire St
(818) 998-8888 or
(800) 782-7872
3-story motel, one unit
has suntan booth

🚫 🏊 🛗

$$$$ SUMMERFIELD SUITES HOTEL
21902 Lassen St
(818) 773-0707 or
(800) 833-4353
3-story all-suite hotel

🚫 🏊 🍴 🚶 🏠

Chico

$$$ HOLIDAY INN
685 Manzanita Ct
(916) 345-2491
5-story hotel opposite North
Valley Plaza Shopping Center

🛏 🍸 🚫 🏊 🛗 🚌 ✈
🏠 P B

Chula Vista

$$ ALL SEASONS INN
699 E Street
(619) 585-1999 or
(800) 873-INNS
Motel off I-5, free local
shuttle service

📺 🚫 🏊 🛗

$$$ DAYS INN SAN DIEGO
225 Bay Blvd
619-425-8200
Off I-5 just 10 minutes
from the San Diego Zoo

🛏 🏊 🚫

Claremont

$$$ GRISWOLD'S INN AND ENTERTAINMENT CENTER
555 W Foothill Blvd
(909) 626-2411 or
(800) 854-5734
17-acre resort hotel with
dinner theater, post office
and shops (max 5-night stay)

🛏 🍸 🚫 🏊 🚌 🏠

$$ RAMADA INN AND TENNIS CLUB
840 S Indian Hill Blvd
(909) 621-4831
Hotel off I-10 in foothills of
San Gabriel Mountains

🛏 🍸 📺 🚫 🏊 🚶
✈ 🚌

Colton

$$ **PATRIOT INN AND SUITES**
2830 Iowa Ave
(909) 788-9900
Hotel off I-215

Commerce

$$ **RAMADA INN**
7272 Gage Ave
(310) 806-4777
4-story motel off I-5

$$$ **WYNDHAM GARDEN HOTEL**
5757 Telegraph Rd
(213) 887-8100
7-story hotel off I-5 in Citadel
business complex

Compton

$$ **BEST WESTERN WILLOW TREE INN**
1919 W Artesia Blvd
(310) 537-6700 or
(800) 548-8733
Hotel off 91 Freeway

Concord

$$$ **CONCORD HILTON**
1970 Diamond Blvd
(510) 827-2000 or
(800) 826-6688
11-story hotel off I-680

Corona

$$ **CORONA TRAVELODGE**
1701 W 6th St
(909) 735-5500
Motel off 91 Freeway

Corte Madera

$$$ **MARIN SUITES HOTEL**
45 Tamal Vista Blvd
(415) 924-3608
All-suite hotel off US 101
(max 5-night stay)

Costa Mesa

$$$ **ANA MESA SUITES**
3597 Harbor Blvd
(714) 662-3500
Hotel off I-405

$$$ **COUNTRY SIDE INN AND SUITES**
325 Bristol St
(714) 549-0300 or
(800) 322-9992
4-story hotel near John
Wayne Airport, some rooms
have fireplaces

$$ **RAMADA LIMITED**
1680 Superior Ave
(714) 645-2221 or
(800) 345-8025
3-story motel near John
Wayne Airport, free shuttle
service to beach and harbor
at Newport Beach

$$$ RESIDENCE INN BY MARRIOTT
881 Baker St
(714) 241-8800
All-suite hotel near John Wayne Airport, many rooms have fireplaces

$$$ WYNDHAM GARDEN HOTEL
3350 Ave of the Stars
(714) 751-5100
6-story hotel off I-405 opposite Orange County Performing Arts Center and near South Coast Plaza Shopping Center

Culver City

$$$ RAMADA HOTEL LAX AIRPORT
6333 Bristol Pkwy
(310) 670-3200
12-story hotel off I-405 near Fox Hills Mall shopping center

$$$ WYNDHAM GARDEN HOTEL
5990 Green Valley Cir
(310) 641-7740
8-story hotel off I-405 near Fox Hills Mall shopping center

Del Mar

$$$ DEL MAR HILTON NORTH SAN DIEGO
15575 Jimmy Durante Blvd
(619) 792-5200
3-story hotel off I-5 near Del Mar racetrack

$$$ DOUBLETREE CLUB HOTEL DEL MAR
11915 El Camino Real
(619) 481-5900
5-story hotel off I-5

Desert Hot Springs

$$$ DESERT HOT SPRINGS SPA HOTEL
10805 Palm Dr
(619) 329-6495 or
(800) 843-6053
Hotel with 8 natural hot mineral pools, offering therapy massages, facials, and body wraps

Diamond Bar

$ RADISSON INN
21725 E Gateway Dr
(909) 860-5440
6-story hotel

Dunsmuir

$ SHASTA ALPINE INN
4221 Siskiyou Ave
(916) 235-0930 or
(800) 880-0930
Motel off I-5 in pretty forest setting

El Cajon

$ HACIENDA BUDGET HOST
588 N Mollison Ave
(619) 579-1144
Motel off I-8

El Segundo

$$$ DOUBLETREE CLUB HOTEL-LAX AIRPORT
1985 E Grand Ave
(310) 322-0999
7-story hotel in business
park near beach

Escondido

$$$ CASTLE CREEK INN RESORT AND SPA
29850 Circle R Way
(619) 751-8800 or
(800) 253-5341
Resort hotel off I-15 overlooking Castle Creek Country
Club, near Lawrence Welk
Theatre and Museum

$$ PALMS INN
2650 S Escondido Blvd
(619) 743-9733
Motel off I-15 near San Diego
Wild Animal Kingdom

$$$ SHERIDAN INN HOTEL
1341 N Escondido Blvd
(619) 743-8338 or
(800) 258-8527
Motel off I-15, near Lawrence
Welk Theatre and Museum

Fallbrook

$$ BEST WESTERN FRANCISCAN INN
1635 S Mission Rd
(619) 728-6174
Motel next to Camp Pendleton

Fountain Valley

$$ FOUNTAIN VALLEY INN
9125 Recreation Cr
(714) 847-3388 or
(800) 826-1964
Hotel off Hwy 405

Fremont

$$$ RESIDENCE INN BY MARRIOTT
5400 Farwell Pl
(510) 794-5900 or
(800) 331-3131
All-suite motel off I-880,
some rooms have fireplaces

Fresno

$$$ FRESNO HILTON
1055 Van Ness Ave
(209) 485-9000 or
(800) 649-4955 (CA)
9-story hotel in downtown
business district

$$$ HOLIDAY INN
CENTRE PLAZA
2233 Ventura St
(209) 268-1000
9-story hotel next to
Convention Center

$$$ PICCADILLY INN AIRPORT
5115 E McKinley
(209) 251-6000 or
(800) HOTEL-US
Hotel near airport

$$$ PICCADILLY INN SHAW
2305 W Shaw Ave
(209) 226-3850 or
(800) HOTEL-US
Hotel next to Convention
Center and Piccadilly Square
shopping center

ℱullerton

$$ DAYS INN
1500 S Raymond Ave
(714) 635-9000
Hotel with free shuttle
service to Disneyland and
Knott's Berry Farm

$$$$ FULLERTON MARRIOTT
2701 E Nutwood Ave
(714) 738-7800 or
(800) 228-9290
6-story hotel on campus of
California State University-
Fullerton

$$ HERITAGE INN
333 E Imperial Hwy
(714) 447-9200 or
(800) 843-0616
4-story motel in
commercial district

$$$ HOLIDAY INN FULLERTON
222 W Houston
(714) 992-1700
Hotel with free shuttle
service to Disneyland and
Knott's Berry Farm

$ SUNSET INN
1000 S Euclid Ave
(714) 871-7200 or
(800) 225-7343
Near Anaheim Stadium

Gardena

$$$ PREMIER RESIDENTIAL
SUITES
1390 W 186th St
(310) 532-8200
3-story hotel off I-405

Grass Valley

$ HOLIDAY LODGE
1221 E Main St
(916) 273-4406
Motel, some rooms feature
Gold Rush motifs

Hawthorne

$$$ RAMADA LAX SOUTH
5250 W El Segundo Blvd
(310) 536-9800 or
(800) 547-2329
6-story hotel, open
courtyard has waterfall

🔟 🍸 💻 🚫 🏊 ♿ 🍴
✈️ 🚌

Hemet

$$ RAMADA INN HEMET
3885 W Florida Ave
(909) 929-8900 or
(800) 858-8584 (CA) or
(800) 858-8574
Hotel off I-215 near Lake
Perris State Recreation Area

💻 🚫 🏊 📺

Hollywood

$$$ HOLIDAY INN HOLLYWOOD
1755 N Highland Ave
(213) 462-7181
23-story hotel in downtown
near Mann's Chinese Theater,
revolving rooftop restaurant

🔟 🍸 🚫 🏊 🍴 🅿️

$$$ HOLLYWOOD METROPOLITAN HOTEL
5825 Sunset Blvd
(213) 962-5800 or
(800) 962-5800
Downtown hotel off US 101

🔟 🍸 🚫

$$$ HOLLYWOOD PALM HOTEL
2005 N Highland Ave
(213) 850-5811 or
(800) 338-PALM
Downtown hotel

🔟 🍸 🚫 🏊 ♿

$$$ RADISSON HOLLYWOOD ROOSEVELT HOTEL
7000 Hollywood Blvd
(213) 466-7000
12-story hotel opposite
Mann's Chinese Theater, host-
ed first Academy Awards
Ceremony in 1927

🔟 🍸 🚫 🏊 🍴

$$ RAMADA LIMITED HOLLYWOOD
1160 N Vermont Ave
(213) 660-1788 or
(800) 800-9733
3-story hotel near
Dodger Stadium

🔟 🚫 🏊 ♿ 🚌

$$ THE OBAN HOTEL
6364 Yucca St
(213) 466-0524
Downtown motel

💻 🚫 📺

Huntington Beach

$$$ REGENCY INN
19360 Beach Blvd
(714) 962-4244
3-story hotel off I-405
(max 5-night stay)

💻 🚫 🏊 ♿ 🅱️

Indian Wells

$$$ HOTEL INDIAN WELLS
76-661 Hwy 111
(619) 345-6466 or
(800) 248-3220
3-story hotel overlooking
Indian Wells Country Club

🔟 🍸 💻 🚫 🏊 ♿
🚶 🎾

Indio

$$$ BEST WESTERN DATE TREE HOTEL
81-909 Indio Blvd
(619) 347-3421
Motel off I-10 in citrus grove area

Inglewood

$$$ BEST WESTERN AIRPARK HOTEL
640 W Manchester Blvd
(310) 677-7378
4-story motel off I-405

Irvine

$$$ AIRPORTER GARDEN HOTEL
18700 MacArthur Blvd
(714) 833-2770
3-story hotel off I-405 opposite John Wayne Airport

$$$$ EMBASSY SUITES HOTEL
2120 Main St
(714) 553-8332
10-story hotel off I-405 with outdoor sundeck

$$$ HOLIDAY INN IRVINE
17941 Von Karman Ave
(714) 863-1999
13-story hotel off I-405 in business district

$$$ RADISSON PLAZA HOTEL
18800 MacArthur Blvd
(714) 833-9999
10-story hotel off I-405 opposite John Wayne Airport

La Jolla

$$$ BEST WESTERN INN BY THE SEA
7830 Fay Ave
(619) 459-4461 or
(800) 462-9732
5-story downtown hotel, some rooms have ocean views

$$$ TORREY PINES INN
11480 N Torrey Pines Rd
(619) 453-4420 or
(800) 777-1700
Japanese-style hotel overlooking Torrey Pines golf course, some rooms have ocean views

La Mirada

$$$ HOLIDAY INN GATEWAY PLAZA
14299 Firestone Blvd
(714) 739-8500 or
(800) 35-MOUSE
8-story hotel off I-5 next to 5-screen movie theater, free shuttle service to Disneyland and Knott's Berry Farm

Lawndale

$$ BEST WESTERN SOUTH BAY HOTEL
15000 Hawthorne Blvd
(310) 973-0998
3-story motel off I-405

🔳 🍸 💻 🚭 🏊 🛗 🚌

Lompoc

$$ INN OF LOMPOC
1122 North H Street
(805) 735-7744 or
(800) 548-8231
Downtown motel

🍸 💻 🚭 🏊 🍴 ✈

$$$ QUALITY INN AND EXECUTIVE SUITES
1621 North H St
(805) 735-8555
3-story downtown motel

💻 🚭 🏊 🛗 ✈ 🐕

Long Beach

$ ECONO LODGE
150 Alomitos Ave
(310) 435-7621 or
(800) 446-6900
Motel near Convention Center and beach

💻 🚭 🏊 🐕

$$$ HOLIDAY INN - LONG BEACH AIRPORT
2640 Lakewood Blvd
(310) 597-4401 or
(800) 235-9556
13-story circular hotel off I-405

🔳 🍸 💻 🚭 🏊 🍴 🚌
🐕 🅿

$$$ HOLIDAY INN- CONVENTION CENTER
500 E 1st St
(310) 435-8511
9-story hotel near Convention Center

🔳 🍸 🚭 🍴 🚌

$$ HOWARD JOHNSON PLAZA
1133 Atlantic Ave
(310) 590-8858 or
(800) 442-1688
4-story hotel in business district

🔳 🍸 💻 🚭 🏊 🏊 🛗
🚌 🐕

$$$$ LONG BEACH MARRIOTT
4700 Airport Plaza Dr
(310) 425-5210 or
(800) 321-5642
8-story hotel off I-405 near Long Beach Airport

🔳 🍸 🚭 🏊 🏊 🍴
✈ 🚌

$$$ LONG BEACH HILTON
2 World Trade Center
(310) 983-3400
15-story hotel off I-710 in World Trade Center complex

🔳 🍸 🚭 🏊 🛗 🍴
🚌 🐕

$$ RAMADA INN
5325 E Pacific Coast Hwy
(310) 597-1341
Hotel opposite recreation park and near beach (excluding Apr 8-12, no resv more than 14 days in advance)

💻 🚭 🏊 ✈ 🚌 🐕

$$$ LONG BEACH RENAISSANCE HOTEL
111 E Ocean Blvd
(310) 437-5900 or
(800) 228-9898
12-story hotel opposite Convention Center, many rooms have ocean views

🔳 🍸 🚭 🏊 🛗 🍴 🚌

$$$ TRAVELODGE HOTEL RESORT AND MARINA
700 Queensway Dr
(310) 435-7676
5-story motel off I-710
near Queen Mary

Los Angeles

$$$ AIRPORT MARINA RESORT HOTEL
8601 Lincoln Blvd
(310) 670-8111 or
(800) 225-8126
12-story hotel near
Marina del Rey Yacht Harbor

$$$ BEST WESTERN MAYFAIR HOTEL
1256 W 7th St
(213) 484-9789 or
(800) 821-8682
15-story downtown hotel
near Garment District

$$$$ BEVERLY PLAZA HOTEL
8384 W 3rd St
(213) 658-6600 or
(800) 62-HOTEL
6-story hotel near
Pacific Design Center and
Farmers Market

$$$$ CARLYLE INN
1119 S Robertson Blvd
(310) 275-4445
4-story hotel with sun deck

$$$ CONTINENTAL PLAZA HOTEL
9750 Airport Blvd
(310) 645-4600 or
(800) 529-4683
9-story hotel near airport

$$$ COURTYARD BY MARRIOTT HOTEL
10320 W Olympic Blvd
(310) 556-2777 or
(800) 321-2211
4-story hotel near
Century City and Beverly Hills
shopping districts

$$$$ HOLIDAY INN CROWNE PLAZA-LAX AIRORT
5985 W Century Blvd
(310) 642-7500 or
(800) 255-7606
15-story hotel

$$$$ EMBASSY SUITES HOTEL
9801 Airport Blvd
(310) 215-1000
8-story hotel near airport
(excluding Dec 30-Jan 1,
no reservations more than
14 days before arrival)

$$$ HOLIDAY INN AIRPORT
9901 La Cienega Blvd
(310) 649-5151
12-story hotel

$$$ HOLIDAY INN BRENTWOOD
170 Church Ln
(310) 476-6411
Hotel off I-405, free
shuttle service to UCLA and
Westwood Village

$$$ HOLIDAY INN CITY CENTER
1020 S Figueroa St
(213) 748-1291
9-story downtown hotel
opposite Convention Center

$$$ HOLIDAY INN CROWNE PLAZA
3540 S Figueroa St
(213) 748-4141 or
(800) 872-1104
11-story downtown hotel
near University of
Southern California

$$$ HOLIDAY INN DOWNTOWN
750 Garland Ave
(213) 628-5242
6-story downtown hotel near
Convention Center

$$ HOWARD JOHNSON CENTRAL
1640 Marengo St
(213) 223-3841
7-story hotel opposite LA
County Hospital, free shuttle
service to nearby Union Station

$$$ HOWARD JOHNSON HOTEL INTERNATIONAL
8620 Airport Blvd
(310) 645-7700
6-story hotel near airport

$$$ LOS ANGELES AIRPORT HILTON AND TOWERS
5711 W Century Blvd
(310) 410-4000
17-story hotel with
concierge rooms

$$$$ LOS ANGELES HILTON AND TOWERS
930 Wilshire Blvd
(213) 629-4321
16-story downtown hotel

$$$ OXFORD PALACE HOTEL
745 S Oxford Ave
(213) 389-8000 or
(800) 532-7887
Downtown hotel in
business district

$$ PARK PLAZA HOTEL
607 S Park View St
(213) 384-5281
Hotel near downtown
named a cultural and
historic landmark in 1983

$$$ QUALITY HOTEL-LAX AIRPORT
5249 W Century Blvd
(310) 645-2200 or
(800) 266-2200
10-story hotel near
Marina del Rey

$$$ RAMADA HOTEL
1150 S Beverly Dr
(310) 553-6561
12-story hotel near
Century City and Beverly Hills
shopping districts

$$$ REGENCY HOTEL
7940 Hollywood Blvd
(213) 656-4555
All-suite hotel near Hollywood

$$$$ THE NEW OTANI HOTEL AND GARDEN
120 S Los Angeles St
(213) 629-1200 or
(800) 421-8795 or
(800) 273-2294 (CA)
21-story downtown
Japanese-style hotel in
Little Tokyo area,
Japanese roof garden

Marina Del Rey

$$$ BEST WESTERN JAMAICA BAY INN
4175 Admiralty Way
(310) 823-5333
Motel near Venice Beach,
some rooms overlook marina
harbor (excluding Dec 31)

$$$$ DOUBLETREE HOTEL
4100 Admiralty Way
(310) 301-3000
10-story hotel opposite
the beach, some rooms
overlook marina harbor
(max 5-night stay)

$$$$ MARINA DEL REY HOTEL
13534 Bali Way
(310) 301-1000
3-story hotel, some rooms
overlook marina harbor
(max 5-night stay)

$$$$ MARINA DEL REY MARRIOTT
13480 Maxella Ave
(310) 822-8555 or
(800) 228-9290
5-story hotel next to Villa
Marina Shopping Center

$$$ MARINA INTERNATIONAL HOTEL AND BUNGALOWS
4200 Admiralty Way
(310) 301-2000
3-story hotel with individually
decorated rooms and
European-style bugalows
(max 5-night stay)

Millbrae

$$$$ THE WESTIN HOTEL-SAN FRANCISCO AIRPORT
1 Old Bayshore Hwy
(415) 692-3500
7-story hotel on landscaped
grounds, many rooms have
bay views

Milpitas

$$$ HOLIDAY INN SAN JOSE NORTH
777 Bellew Dr
(408) 321-9500 or
(800) 524-2929
12-story hotel off I-880

Monrovia

$$ HOLIDAY INN MONROVIA
924 W Huntington Dr
(818) 357-1900
10-story hotel off I-210

$$$ WYNDHAM GARDEN HOTEL
700 W Huntington Dr
(818) 357-5211
9-story hotel off I-210

Monterey

HOLIDAY INN RESORT $$$$
1000 Aguajito Rd
(408) 373-6141
4-story hotel near
Pebble Beach, Carmel,
and 17-Mile Drive

HOTEL PACIFIC $$$$
300 Pacific St
(408) 373-5700 or
(800) 554-5542
4-story all-suite motel
near waterfront and
Convention Center

MONTEREY BAY INN $$$$
242 Cannery Row
(408) 373-6242 or
(800) 424-6242
4-story motel near water-
front and Convention Center,
some rooms have bay views

MONTEREY HOTEL $$$
406 Alvarado St
(408) 375-3184 or
(800) 727-0960
Restored 1904 hotel near
waterfront and Convention
Center featuring antique
furnishings

SPINDRIFT INN $$$$
652 Cannery Row
(408) 646-8900 or
(800) 841-1879
4-story motel near water-
front and Convention Center,
all rooms have fireplaces and
many have ocean views

VICTORIAN INN $$$$
487 Foam St
(408) 373-8000 or
(800) 232-4141
Near waterfront and
Convention Center, many
rooms have fireplaces and
some have vaulted ceilings

Moreno Valley

BEST WESTERN IMAGE SUITES $
24840 Elder Ave
(909) 924-4546 or
(800) 544-7756
3-story hotel

ECONO LODGE $
24810 Sunnymead Blvd
(909) 247-8582
Motel near March Air
Force Base

ROADSIDE INN $$
23330 Sunnymead Blvd
(909) 242-0699
3-story motel

Mountain View

COUNTY INN $$
850 Leong Dr
(415) 961-1131 or
(800) 828-1131
Motel off US 101

$$$$ RESIDENCE INN BY MARRIOTT
1854 El Camino Real W
(415) 940-1300 or
(800) 331-3131
All-suite motel off US 101,
some rooms have fireplaces

Newark

$$ PARK INN
5977 Mowry Ave
(510) 795-7995 or
(800) 624-0085
Spanish-style hotel
opposite Newpark Mall

Newport Beach

$$$$ FOUR SEASONS HOTEL
690 Newport Center Dr
(714) 759-0808 or
(800) 332-3442
19-story hotel opposite
Fashion Island complex
with several acres of
landscaped grounds

$$$$ NEWPORT BEACH MARRIOTT HOTEL
900 Newport Center Dr
(714) 640-4000
Hotel with 16-story tower
and two 3-story wings oppo-
site Fashion Island complex,
some rooms have ocean views

$$$$ SHERATON NEWPORT BEACH HOTEL
4545 MacArthur Blvd
(714) 833-0570
10-story hotel in business
district near John Wayne
Airport, has basketball court

North Hollywood

$$$ BEVERLY GARLAND HOLIDAY INN
4222 Vineland Ave
(818) 980-8000
7-story hotel off US 101
near Universal Studios
(excluding Dec 30-31)

Norwalk

$$$ SHERATON NORWALK HOTEL
13111 Sycamore Dr
(310) 863-6666 or
(800) 553-1666
8-story hotel off I-5, free
shuttle service to Disneyland
and Knott's Berry Farm

Oakland

$$$ DAYS INN OAKLAND AIRPORT
8350 Edes Ave
(510) 568-1880
Hotel near Oakland Stadium
and Coliseum

HOLIDAY INN OAKLAND AIRPORT
$$$
500 Hegenberger Rd
(510) 562-5311
Multistory hotel off I-880
next to Oakland Stadium
and Coliseum

🛏 🍸 🚭 🏊 🍴 ✈ 🚌

JACK LONDON INN
$$
444 Embarcadero
(510) 444-2032
Hotel at Jack London Square
near Convention Center

🛏 🍸 🏊 🅿

Ontario

COUNTRY SIDE SUITES
$$$
204 N Vineyard Ave
(909) 986-8550
All-suite hotel off I-10, rooms
feature country French decor

🛏 💻 🚭 🏊 🍴 ✈ 🚌

DOUBLETREE CLUB HOTEL
$$$$
429 N Vineyard Ave
(909) 391-6411
6-story hotel off I-10

🛏 🍸 💻 🚭 🏊 🍴 🍴 ✈ 🚌

HOLIDAY INN EXPRESS
$$
1818 E Holt Blvd
(909) 988-8466
4-story motel off I-10

💻 🚭 🏊 🍴 🍴 ✈ 🚌

MARRIOTT HOTEL ONTARIO
$$$
2200 E Holt Blvd
(909) 986-8811 or
(800) 284-8811
3-story hotel off I-10
(max 5-night stay)

🛏 🍸 🚭 🏊 🍴 🍴 🚶 ✈ 🚌

ONTARIO AIRPORT HILTON
$$$
700 N Haven Ave
(909) 980-0400 or
(800) 654-1379
10-story hotel off I-10 next
to Discount Shopping outlet,
has concierge level

🛏 🍸 🚭 🏊 🍴 🍴 ✈ 🚌

Orange

DOUBLETREE HOTEL
$$$
100 The City Dr
(714) 634-4500
20-story hotel off I-5 with
concierge level

🛏 🍸 🚭 🏊 🍴 🍴 🚶

WASHINGTON SUITES HOTEL
$$$
720 The City Dr S
(714) 740-2700 or
(800) 278-4837
3-story all-suite motel in business park, free shuttle service
to Disneyland (no reservations
more than 7 days before week-
day arrival)

💻 🚭 🏊 🍴

Oxnard

CASA SIRENA MARINA RESORT
$$$
3605 Peninsula Rd
(805) 985-6311 or
(800) 228-6026
3-story hotel in Channel
Islands Harbor, many rooms
overlook marina

🛏 🍸 🚭 🏊 🍴 🍴 🚶
🍴 ✈ 🚌

$$$ OXNARD HILTON INN
600 Esplanade Dr
(805) 485-9666
6-story hotel off US 101 in
Financial Plaza complex near
downtown (max 3-night stay)

Pacifica

$$$ COLONY LIGHTHOUSE
105 Rockaway Beach Ave
(415) 355-6300
4-story hotel with beach access

Palm Springs

**$$$ PALM SPRINGS
HILTON RESORT**
400 E Tahquitz Canyon Way
(619) 320-6868 or
(800) 522-6900
3-story hotel set on 13 acres
near Convention Center and
luxury shopping district

**$$$$ PALM SPRINGS
RIVIERA RESORT**
1600 N Indian Canyon Dr
(619) 327-8311 or
(800) 444-8311
25-acre resort hotel

**$$$ SPA HOTEL RESORT AND
MINERAL SPRINGS**
100 N Indian Canyon Dr
(619) 325-1461 or
(800) 854-1279
5-story hotel near downtown

Palmdale

$ PALMDALE INN
217 E Palmdale Blvd
(805) 273-5106
Motel off Highway 14

Palo Alto

$$$$ HYATT RICKEYS
4219 El Camino Real
(415) 493-8000
22-acre hotel in garden setting,
some rooms have fireplaces

Pasadena

**$$$ DOUBLETREE HOTEL AT
PLAZA LAS FUENTES**
191 N Los Robles Ave
(818) 792-2727
12-story hotel in Old Pasadena
area with concierge floor

$$$$ PASADENA HILTON
150 S Los Robles Ave
(818) 577-1000
12-story downtown hotel

Pine Mountain Club

$$$ PINE MOUNTAIN INN
16231 Askin Dr
(805) 242-0144
Resort hotel at private
community in Los Padres
National Forest

Pleasanton

$$$ DOUBLETREE CLUB HOTEL
5990 Stoneridge Mall Rd
(510) 463-3330
6-story hotel off I-580 and
I-680 opposite Stoneridge Mall

🛏 Ⓨ ▣ 🚫 ≈ 💪
🍽 🏠

$$$ HOLIDAY INN
11950 Dublin Canyon Rd
(510) 847-6000
6-story hotel off I-580

🛏 Ⓨ 🚫 ≈ 💪 🍽 🏠

Port Hueneme

$$$ COUNTRY INN AT PORT HUENEME
350 E Hueneme Rd
(805) 986-5353
3-story motel near beach
(max 3-night stay)

Ⓨ ▣ 🚫 ≈ 💪

Rancho Bernardo

$$$ DOUBLETREE CLUB HOTEL RANCHO BERNARDO
11611 Bernardo Plaza Ct
(619) 485-9250 or
(800) 528-0444
4-story hotel off I-15

🛏 Ⓨ ▣ 🚫 ≈ 💪 🍽

$$$ HOLIDAY INN RANCHO BERNARDO
17065 W Bernardo Dr
(619) 485-6530 or
(800) 777-0020
3-story motel off I-15

🛏 🚫 ≈ 💪 🍽 🚌 🏠

$$$ RADISSON SUITE HOTEL
11520 W Bernardo Ct
(619) 451-6600
3-story all-suite hotel off I-15

🛏 Ⓨ ▣ 🚫 ≈ 💪
🍽 🏠

$$$ RESIDENCE INN BY MARRIOTT RANCHO BERNARDO
11002 Rancho Carmel Dr
(619) 673-1900 or
(800) 331-3131
3-story all-suite motel off I-15

▣ 🚫 ≈ 💪 🍽 🚌 🏠

Rancho Cordova

$$ COMFORT INN
3240 Mather Field Rd
(916) 363-3344
4-story motel off US 50
(max 5-night stay)

▣ 🚫 ≈ 💪 🚌 🏠

Rancho Cucamonga

$$$$ BEST WESTERN HERITAGE INN
8179 Spruce Ave
(909) 466-1111 or
(800) 682-STAY
6-story motel off I-15 and I-10
near Ontario International
Airport (excluding Dec 31)

▣ 🚫 ≈ 💪 ✈

Redondo Beach

$$$ BEST WESTERN SUNRISE
400 N Harbor Dr
(310) 376-0746 or
(800) 334-7384
3-story hotel opposite the
beach and King Harbor Marina,
some rooms have ocean views

🛏 🚫 ≈ 💪 🍽 ⚓

Reseda

$$$ HOWARD JOHNSON LODGE
7432 Reseda Blvd
(818) 344-0324 or
(800) 523-4825
Between US 101 and Hwy 118

🍸 🖥 🚭 🏊 💪 🍽

Richmond

DAYS HOTEL HILLTOP
$$$ 3150 Garrity Way
(510) 262-0700
5-story hotel off I-80

📺 🍸 🚭 🏊 💪 🍽

Rosemead

SHERATON ROSEMEAD
$$$ 888 Montebello Blvd
(213) 722-8800 or
(800) 635-6713
5-story hotel opposite
Montebello Towne Center
complex (max 5-night stay)

📺 🍸 🚭 🏊 💪 🍽

Rowland Heights

BEST WESTERN
$$ EXECUTIVE INN
18880 E Gale Ave
(818) 810-1818
3-story motel in
business district

🖥 🚭 🏊 💪 🍽

Sacramento

$$ CANTERBURY INN
1900 Canterbury Rd
(916) 927-0927 or
(800) 932-3492
Downtown hotel near State
Capitol and Old Sacramento

📺 🍸 🖥 🚭 🏊 💪
🚌 🎯

$$$ CLARION HOTEL
SACRAMENTO
700 16th St
(916) 444-8000
Downtown hotel near State
Capitol and Old Sacramento,
executive level rooms
(excluding May 26-28)

📺 🍸 🚭 🏊 🚌 🎯 🅿

$$$ SACRAMENTO HILTON
2200 Harvard St
(916) 922-4700 or
(800) 344-4321
12-story hotel with sand
volleyball court

📺 🍸 🚭 🏊 💪 🍽
🚌 🎯

$$ SIERRA INN
2600 Auburn Ave
(916) 487-7600
Hotel near Old Sacramento

📺 🏊

San Bernardino

$$ BEST WESTERN SANDS
MOTEL
606 North H St
(909) 889-8391 or
(800) 331-4409
Downtown hotel off I-215

📺 🚭 🏊 💪 🎯

$$ **RAMADA INN**
2000 Ostrems Way
(909) 887-3001
4-story hotel off I-215

San Diego

$$$ **BAY CLUB HOTEL AND MARINA**
2131 Shelter Island Dr
(619) 224-8888 or
(800) 672-0800
Hotel on Shelter Island
near airport, many rooms
have bay views

$$$ **BEST WESTERN POSADA INN**
5005 N Harbor Dr
(619) 224-3254 or
(800) 231-3811
6-story motel at Point Loma
near airport, many rooms
have harbor views

$$ **BEST WESTERN SEVEN SEAS**
411 Hotel Cir S
(619) 291-1300
Hotel off I-8 with
children's playground

$$$ **BRISTOL COURT**
1055 1st Ave
(619) 232-6141 or
(800) 662-4477
Multistory hotel in
financial district near
Convention Center

$$$ **CABRILLO MOTOR LODGE**
1150 Rosecrans St
(619) 223-5544
Motel near the bay

$$$ **CARMEL HIGHLAND DOUBLETREE RESORT**
14455 Penasquitos Dr
(619) 672-9100 or
(800) 622-9223
130-acre resort hotel

$$$ **CLARION HOTEL BAY VIEW**
660 K St
(619) 696-0234 or
(800) 766-0234
21-story downtown hotel
near Convention Center,
some rooms have bay views

$$$ **COMFORT INN DOWNTOWN**
719 Ash St
(619) 232-2525
3-story downtown motel
near Balboa Park

$$ **DAYS INN AND SUITES/GOLDEN TRIANGLE**
5550 Clairemont Mesa Blvd
(619) 560-4551
Hotel off I-805

$$$$ **DOUBLETREE HOTEL AT HORTON PLAZA**
910 Broadway Cir
(619) 239-2200
16-story downtown hotel
next to Horton Plaza shopping complex and near
Convention Center

$$$ ECONO LODGE AT POINT LOMA
3880 Greenwood St
(619) 543-9944 ext 103 or
(800) 841-0909 ext 103
Hotel off I-5 near Old Town

$$$$ GASLAMP PLAZA SUITES
520 E Street
(619) 232-9500 or
(800) 443-8012
All-suite downtown hotel,
building listed in National
Register of Historic Places
(limited availability in Sep)

$$$ GROSVENOR INN
3145 Sports Arena Blvd
(619) 225-9999 or
(800) 232-1212
Hotel off I-5 and I-8 near
Old Town and Sea World

$$$ HANDLERY HOTEL AND COUNTRY CLUB
950 Hotel Circle N
(619) 298-0511 or
(800) 676-6567
Resort hotel off I-8 near
Sea World and San Diego
Zoo, has paddle tennis court

$$$ HOLIDAY INN EXPRESS-ZOO
9550 Murray Dr
(619) 466-0200
4-story hotel
convenient to beaches

$$$ HOLIDAY INN MISSION VALLEY NORTH
3805 Murphy Canyon Rd
(619) 277-1199 or
(800) 666-6996
Hotel near San Diego Zoo
(max 5-night stay)

$$$ HOLIDAY INN NORTH MIRAMAR
9335 Kearny Mesa Rd
(619) 695-2300
6-story hotel off I-15

$$$ HORTON GRAND HOTEL
311 Island Ave
(619) 544-1886 or
(800) 542-1886
Restored historic 1886
hotel in downtown,
all rooms have fireplaces,
English courtyard garden

$$$$ HOWARD JOHNSON HARBORVIEW
1430 7th Ave
(619) 696-0911
3-story downtown hotel

$$$ HOWARD JOHNSON HOTEL CIRCLE
1631 Hotel Circle S
(619) 293-7792 or
(800) 876-8937
4-story motel off I-8

$$ LEXINGTON HOTEL AND SUITES
3888 Greenwood St
(619) 299-6633 or
(800) 944-8668
3-story motel off I-5 and I-8
near Sports Arena and Sea
World (max 5-night stay)

$$$$ MARRIOTT SUITES DOWNTOWN
701 A Street
(619) 696-9800 or
(800) 962-1367
All-suite downtown hotel in
financial district

$$ OUTRIGGER MOTEL POINT LOMA
1370 Scott St
(619) 223-7105 or
(800) 232-1212
Motel near Cabrillo Point

$$$ PAN PACIFIC HOTEL
400 W Broadway
(619) 239-4500 or
(800) 626-3988
26-story downtown hotel

$$$ QUALITY INN AIRPORT
2901 Nimitz Blvd
(619) 224-3655
6-story hotel overlooking
San Diego Harbor

$$$ QUALITY INN STADIUM
5343 Adobe Falls Rd
(619) 287-1911
Hotel off I-8 near San Diego
State University

$$$ RADISSON HOTEL HARBOR VIEW
1646 Front St
(619) 239-6800
16-story downtown hotel,
some rooms have harbor views

$$ RAMADA INN SAN DIEGO NORTH
5550 Kearny Mesa Rd
(619) 278-0800 or
(800) 447-2637
Hotel north of San Diego

$$$ REGENCY PLAZA HOTEL
1515 Hotel Circle S
(619) 291-8790
8-story hotel off I-8

$$ RICHMAR INN
3330 Rosecrans St
(619) 224-8266 or
(800) RICHMAR
Motel off I-5

$$$ SAN DIEGO MARRIOTT MISSION VALLEY
8757 Rio San Diego Dr
(619) 692-3800 or
(800) 228-9290
15-story hotel off I-8 near
Jack Murphy Stadium
(excluding Dec 28-Jan 1)

⟦🌙⟧ ⟦Y⟧ ⟦🚭⟧ ⟦≈⟧ ⟦♨⟧ ⟦🍴⟧
⟦🚶⟧ ⟦🐕⟧

$$$$ SAN DIEGO MISSION VALLEY HILTON
901 Camino del Rio S
(619) 543-9000 or
(800) 733-2332
8-story hotel off I-8

⟦🌙⟧ ⟦Y⟧ ⟦🚭⟧ ⟦≈⟧ ⟦🍴⟧ ⟦🚌⟧ ⟦🐕⟧

$$$ SAN DIEGO PRINCESS RESORT
1404 W Vacation Rd
(619) 274-4630 or
(800) 344-2626
Resort hotel with bungalows
on 44-acre island complex,
opposite Sea World, many
rooms have bay views

⟦🌙⟧ ⟦Y⟧ ⟦🚭⟧ ⟦≈⟧ ⟦♨⟧ ⟦🍴⟧ ⟦🚶⟧
⟦🐕⟧ ⟦🐕⟧

$$$ SHERATON INN
8110 E Aero Dr
(619) 277-8888
Multistory hotel off I-805
and I-15 with club floors

⟦🌙⟧ ⟦Y⟧ ⟦≈⟧ ⟦♨⟧ ⟦🍴⟧ ⟦🚌⟧ ⟦P⟧

$$$ SOMMERSET SUITES HOTEL
606 Washington St
(619) 692-5200 or
(800) 962-9665
All-suite hotel near
San Diego Zoo

⟦💻⟧ ⟦🚭⟧ ⟦≈⟧ ⟦🚶⟧ ⟦🚌⟧

$$ SUPER 8 HARBORSIDE
1403 Rosecrans
(619) 225-9461 or
(800) 232-1212
3-story motel, many rooms
have harbor views

⟦Y⟧ ⟦🚭⟧ ⟦≈⟧ ⟦🚶⟧ ⟦🚌⟧

$$ SUPER 8 MISSION BAY
4540 Mission Bay Dr
(619) 274-7888 or
(800) 232-1212
3-story motel off I-5
opposite Mission Bay

⟦💻⟧ ⟦🚭⟧ ⟦≈⟧ ⟦🚌⟧ ⟦🐕⟧

$$ TRAVELODGE SPORTS ARENA
3737 Sports Arena Blvd
(619) 226-3711
3-story hotel off I-5 and
I-8 near Sea World and
Sports Arena

⟦🌙⟧ ⟦Y⟧ ⟦🚭⟧ ⟦≈⟧ ⟦🍴⟧ ⟦🍴⟧
⟦🚶⟧ ⟦🚌⟧

$$$ TRAVELODGE AT THE ZOO
2223 El Cajon Blvd
(619) 296-2101
Hotel near San Diego Zoo

⟦🌙⟧ ⟦Y⟧ ⟦💻⟧ ⟦🚭⟧ ⟦≈⟧ ⟦♨⟧
⟦🍴⟧ ⟦🚌⟧

$$$$ U.S. GRANT HOTEL
326 Broadway
(619) 232-3121 or
(800) 237-5029
11-story historic 1910
hotel in downtown,
individually furnished rooms

⟦🌙⟧ ⟦Y⟧ ⟦🚭⟧ ⟦🍴⟧ ⟦🚌⟧

$ WAYFARERS INN
3275 Rosecrans St
(619) 224-2411 or
(800) 266-2411
Motel near Sea World

$$$ WILLIAM PENN
SUITES HOTEL
511 F St
(619) 531-0833
All-suite downtown hotel

$$$ WYNDHAM GARDEN
HOTEL
5975 Lusk Blvd
(619) 558-1818
7-story hotel off I-805

San Dimas

$$ HOLIDAY INN EXPRESS
204 N Village Ct
(909) 599-2362
Hotel off 210 Frwy

San Francisco

$$$$ FAIRMONT HOTEL
950 Mason St
(415) 772-5000 or
(800) 527-4727
22-story 1907 hotel
downtown on Nob Hill
with semitropical garden

$$$$ GALLERIA PARK HOTEL
191 Sutter St
(415) 781-3060 or
(800) 792-9639
9-story 1911 hotel downtown
next to Crocker Galleria com-
plex, art nouveau lobby

$$$ GROSVENOR HOTEL
380 S Airport Blvd
(415) 873-3200 or
(800) 722-7141
8-story hotel off US 101
near airport, some rooms
have bay views

$$$ HOLIDAY INN
CIVIC CENTER
50 8th St
(415) 626-6103
14-story downtown hotel

$$$ BEDFORD HOTEL
761 Post St
(415) 673-6040 or
(800) 227-5642
17-story downtown hotel

$$$$ HOTEL RICHELIEU
1050 Van Ness Ave
(415) 673-4711 or
(800) 295-7424
5-story 1908
downtown hotel

$$$$ HOTEL TRITON
342 Grant Ave
(415) 394-0500
Downtown hotel with displays
of local artists in public areas

$$$ KING GEORGE HOTEL
334 Mason St
(415) 781-5050 or
(800) 288-6005
9-story 1914
downtown hotel

$$$$ MAJESTIC HOTEL
1500 Sutter St
(415) 441-1100 or
(800) 869-8966
Restored 1902 downtown
hotel with individually decorated rooms and antiques,
some rooms have four-poster
beds and fireplaces
(excluding Dec 31)

$$$$ MONTICELLO INN
127 Ellis St
(415) 392-8800 or
(800) 669-7777
5-story 1906 downtown
hotel with Colonial-style decor

$$$$ PARC FIFTY FIVE HOTEL
55 Cyril Magnin St
(415) 392-8000 or
(800) 338-1338
32-story downtown hotel
with concierge level

$$$ RAMADA HOTEL
1231 Market St
(415) 626-8000 or
(800) 227-4747
8-story 1911
downtown hotel

$$$ RAMADA INN NORTH
245 S Airport Blvd
(415) 589-7200 or
(800) 452-3456
Multistory hotel near airport

$$$ RAMADA INN AT UNION SQUARE
345 Taylor St
(415) 673-2332
Downtown hotel in
business district

$$$$ SAN FRANCISCO AIRPORT HILTON
PO Box 8355
(415) 875-3029
Multistory hotel next
to airport

$$$ SAVOY HOTEL
580 Geary St
(415) 441-2700 or
(800) 227-4223
Multistory 1913 downtown
hotel (no reservations more
than 14 days before arrival)

$$$$ SIR FRANCIS DRAKE HOTEL
450 Powell St
(415) 392-7755 or
(800) 227-5480
24-story 1928
downtown hotel,
lobby with art deco murals

San Jose

$$$ AIRPORT INN INTERNATIONAL
1355 N 4th Street
(408) 453-5340 or
(800) 453-5340
Motel off US 101
near airport

$$$ GATEWAY INN
2585 Seaboard Ave
(408) 435-8800 or
(800) 437-8855
Hotel off US 101 near airport, free shuttle service to
Paramount's Great America

$$ **HOWARD JOHNSON LODGE**
1755 N 1st St
(408) 453-3133
Motel near airport

$$$$ **HYATT SAN JOSE**
1740 N 1st St
(408) 993-1234
3-story hotel near airport set
in 18 acres of grounds

$$$ **LE BARON HOTEL**
1350 N 1st St
(408) 453-6200 or
(800) 538-6818
9-story hotel off US 101
near airport

San Juan Capistrano

$$ **BEST WESTERN
CAPISTRANO INN**
27174 Ortega Hwy
(714) 493-5661 or
(800) 441-9438 (CA)
Motel off I-5

San Mateo

$$$ **BEST WESTERN
LOS PRADOS**
2940 S Norfolk St
(415) 341-3300
3-story motel off US 101
opposite Bay Meadow
Racetrack

$$$ **DUNFEY SAN MATEO
HOTEL**
1770 S Amphlett Blvd
(415) 573-7661 or
(800) THE-OMNI
Mock Tudor-style hotel
off US 101

San Pedro

$$$ **HOLIDAY INN LOS ANGELES
CRUISE CENTER**
111 Gaffey St
(310) 514-1414
4-story hotel off I-110
near cruise terminals,
some rooms have Victorian-
style decor and fireplaces

Santa Ana

$$$ **DOUBLETREE CLUB HOTEL**
7 Hutton Centre Dr
(714) 751-2400
6-story hotel in business
park overlooking lake

$$ **HOLIDAY INN**
1600 E 1st St
(714) 835-3051
10-story hotel off I-5

$$ **HOWARD JOHNSON LODGE**
939 E 17th St
(714) 558-3700
Hotel off I-5, free shuttle
service to Disneyland

QUALITY SUITES
2701 Hotel Terrace Dr
(714) 957-9200
3-story all-suite motel

🛏 🍸 💻 🚭 ≋ ⛎
✈ 🚌

RAMADA GRAND AVENUE
2726 S Grand Ave
(714) 966-1955
3-story hotel with jogging path

🛏 🍸 🚭 ≋ ⛎ 🎾
✈ 🚌

SADDLEBACK INN
1660 E 1st St
(714) 835-3311 or
(800) 854-3911
Hotel next to Santa Ana Zoo

🛏 🍸 🚭 🐾

**WINDSOR SUITES HOTEL/
ORANGE COUNTY AIRPORT**
1325 E Dyer Rd
(714) 241-3800
10-story all-suite hotel
near John Wayne Airport
(excluding Dec 31)

🛏 🍸 💻 ≋ ⛎ Ⓟ ✈

Santa Barbara

SANDMAN INN
3714 State St
(805) 687-2468 or
(800) 350-8174
Downtown motel off US 101

🛏 💻 🚭 ≋ 🎾 🚌

Santa Clara

BILTMORE HOTEL AND SUITES
2151 Laurelwood Rd
(408) 988-8411
Multistory hotel off US 101
near Great America theme park

🛏 🍸 🚭 ≋ ⛎ 🎾
✈ 🚌

DAYS INN HOTEL
4200 Great America Pkwy
(408) 980-1525 or
(800) 782-9466
4-story motel off US 101 near
Great America theme park

🛏 🍸 ≋ ⛎ 🚌

HOWARD JOHNSON LODGE
5405 Stevens Creek Blvd
(408) 257-8600
Motel off I-280

🚭 ≋

QUALITY SUITES HOTEL
3100 Lakeside Dr
(408) 748-9800 or
(800) 345-1554
7-story all-suite hotel
off US 101

🍸 💻 🚭 ≋ ⛎ 🎾
✈ 🚌

Santa Cruz

DREAM INN
175 W Cliff Dr
(408) 426-4330 or
(800) 662-3838
Multistory beachfront hotel,
all rooms overlook ocean

🛏 🍸 🚭 ≋ ⛎ 🚌

Santa Maria

$$$ BEST WESTERN BIG AMERICA
1725 N Broadway
(805) 922-5200 or
(800) 426-3213
Hotel off US 101

$$$ SANTA MARIA AIRPORT HILTON
3455 Skyway Dr
(805) 928-8000
4-story hotel off US 101
next to airport

$$$ SANTA MARIA INN
801 S Broadway
(805) 928-7777
Multistory 1917 downtown
hotel off US 101 with
English country decor
(max 3-night stay)

Santa Monica

$$$$ GUEST QUARTERS SUITE HOTEL
1707 4th St
(310) 395-3332 or
(800) 424-2900
8-story all-suite
downtown hotel off I-10

Santa Nella

$$ LA FONTAINE INN
28976 W Plaza Dr
(209) 826-8282 or
(800) 428-3687
Motel off I-5 with
French-style decor

Santa Rosa

$$$ LOS ROBLES LODGE
1985 Cleveland Ave
(707) 545-6330 or
(800) 255-6330
Motor lodge off US 101
next to Coddingtown Center
shopping area

Seal Beach

$$$ RADISSON INN
600 Marina Dr
(310) 493-7501
Motel near beach in
Old Town area

Sherman Oaks

$$$ CARRIAGE INN
5525 Sepulveda Blvd
(818) 787-2300 or
(800) 77-ATLAS
Multistory hotel off
I-405, rooms have
New England-style decor

Simi Valley

$$$ RADISSON HOTEL
999 Enchanted Way
(805) 583-2000
Multistory hotel with
nightclub

Solvang

$$$ DANISH COUNTRY INN
1455 Mission Dr
(805) 688-2018
3-story motel near downtown
(max 3-night stay)

South Lake Tahoe

$$ BEST TAHOE WEST INN
4082 Pine Blvd
(916) 544-6455
Multistory motel off US 50,
free shuttle service to casinos

$$$ TAHOE VALLEY MOTEL
2241 Lake Tahoe Blvd
(916) 541-0353 or
(800) 669-7544
Motel off US 50

Stockton

**$$ BEST WESTERN
CHARTER WAY INN**
550 W Charter Way
(209) 948-0321 or
(800) 545-8388
Motel off I-5

Sunnyvale

**$$$ RADISSON HAUS INN-
SUNNYVALE**
1085 E El Camino Real
(408) 247-0800
3-story hotel

**$$$ SHERATON INN
SUNNYVALE**
1100 N Mathilda Ave
(408) 745-6000 or
(800) 836-7676
Hotel off US 101 opposite
Lockheed commercial area

$$$ SUNDOWNER INN
504 Ross Dr
(408) 734-9900 or
(800) 223-9901
Motel off US 101

$$$$ SUNNYVALE HILTON
1250 Lakeside Dr
(408) 738-4888
3-story hotel off US 101 with
9 acres of landscaped grounds
and jogging path (discount on
deluxe rooms only)

**$$$ WYNDHAM GARDEN
HOTEL**
1300 Chesapeake Terrace
(408) 747-0999
5-story hotel off US 101

Temecula

$$ RAMADA INN
28980 Front St
(909) 676-8770
Motel off I-15

Thousand Oaks

$$ DAYS INN
1320 Newbury Rd
(805) 499-5910
3-story hotel off US 101

Union City

$$$ RADISSON HOTEL
32083 Alvarado/Niles Rd
(510) 489-2200
6-story hotel off I-880

Vallejo

$$$ RAMADA INN VALLEJO
1000 Admiral Callaghan Ln
(707) 643-2700 or
(800) 677-4466
3-story motel off I-80

Van Nuys

$$$ HOLIDAY INN
8244 Orion Ave
(818) 989-5010
Hotel off I-405 near
Van Nuys Airport

$$ TRAVELODGE SEPULVEDA
6909 Sepulveda Blvd
(818) 787-5400
3-story motel off I-405
near Van Nuys Airport

$$ VOYAGER MOTOR INN
6500 Sepulveda Blvd
(818) 997-6007
Motel off I-405 near
Van Nuys Airport

Ventura

$$$ CLOCKTOWER INN
181 E Santa Clara St
(805) 652-0141
Hotel off US 101 next to
Mission San Buenaventura
and near beach, some rooms
have fireplaces

**$$$ COLONY HARBORTOWN
MARINA RESORT**
1050 Schooner Dr
(805) 658-1212
3-story hotel off US 101 next
to Channel Islands National
Park headquarters, many
rooms have marina views

$$$ COUNTRY INN AT VENTURA
298 Chestnut St
(805) 653-1434 or
(800) 447-3529
3-story motel off US 101
near beach, some rooms
have ocean views
(max 3-night stay)

**$$$ DOUBLETREE HOTEL
AT VENTURA**
2055 Harbor Blvd
(805) 643-6000
4-story hotel off US 101
near beach

Visalia

$$$ HOLIDAY INN PLAZA PARK
9000 W Airport Dr
(209) 651-5000 or
(800) 821-1127
Multistory hotel next to
Plaza Park sports complex
(max 5-night stay)

🍸 🖥 🚭 🛏 🏊 🍴 🛎
✈ 🚌 🏨

$$$$ RADISSON HOTEL
300 S Court St
(209) 636-1111
8-story downtown hotel
next to Convention Center
(excluding Feb 12-16)

📶 🍸 🚭 🏊 🛁 🍴 🚌

Walnut

$$ HOLIDAY INN EXPRESS
1170 Fairway Dr
(909) 594-9999
Motel with Mission-style
architecture

📶 🖥 🚭 🏊 🛁 🍴 🚌

Wasco

$ WASCO INN MOTEL
PO Box 819
1126 Hwy 46
(805) 758-5317
Motel in rose growing area

🍸 🚭 🏊 🛎 ✈

West Covina

$$ BEST WESTERN WEST COVINA INN
3275 E Garvey Ave N
(818) 915-1611
4-story motel off I-10

🍸 🖥 🚭 🏊 🛁 🍴

$$$ HOLIDAY INN WEST COVINA
3223 E Garvey N
(818) 966-8311 or
(800) 638-9938
5-story hotel off I-10

📶 🍸 🚭 🏊 🍴 🚌

$$ WEST COVINA COMFORT INN
2804 E Garvey Ave S
(818) 915-6077
3-story motel off I-10

🖥 🚭 🏊 P

West Hollywood

$$$$ LE MONTROSE SUITE HOTEL DE GRAN LUXE
900 Hammond St
310-855-1115 or
(800) 776-0666
6-story all-suite hotel near
Los Angeles Design Center,
many rooms have fireplaces
(max 5-night stay)

📶 🍸 🚭 🏊 🛁 🍴
✈ 🏨

$$$$ LE PARC HOTEL
733 N West Knoll Dr
(310) 855-8888 or
(800) 578-4837
4-story all-suite hotel, all
rooms have fireplaces
(max 5-night stay)

📶 🍸 🚭 🏊 🛁 🍴 🏨

$$$$ LE REVE HOTEL
8822 Cynthia St
(310) 854-1114
4-story all-suite motel

📶 🚭 🏊

$$$ PARK SUNSET HOTEL
8462 Sunset Blvd
(213) 654-6470 or
(800) 821-3660
3-story hotel
(discount on suites only)

$$$$ SUMMERFIELD SUITE HOTEL
1000 Westmount Dr
(310) 657-7400
4-story all-suite hotel

West Sacramento

$$ BEST WESTERN HARBOR INN AND SUITES
1250 Halyard Dr
(916) 371-2100
Motel 2 miles from
Sacramento

Whittier

$$ BEST WHITTIER INN
14226 Whittier Blvd
(310) 698-0323
Motel near business district

Woodland Hills

$$$ WARNER CENTER HILTON AND TOWERS
6360 Canoga Ave
(818) 595-1000 or
(800) 922-2400
14-story hotel at the
Warner Center Business Park,
concierge level

Yorba Linda

$$$ COUNTRY SIDE SUITES
22677 Oak Crest Circle
(714) 921-8688
4-story motel with rural
French-style decor

Colorado

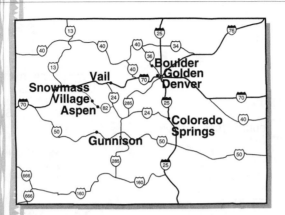

 ew states offer such a study in scenic contrasts as Colorado—from the soaring heights of the jagged Rocky Mountains to the endless expanse of the Great Plains. Splitting these distinctive geographic regions neatly in two is the Continental Divide. To the west lie more than 50 of the 80 North American peaks above 14,000 feet, while to the east the prairie stretches for hundreds of miles.

In the foothills of the Rockies nestles the bustling city of **Denver**, capital not just to Colorado but to all the states in the Mountain time zone. Eastern sophistication mixes with Western frontier charm to produce a dynamic cosmopolitan center. Sightseeing highlights include Denver Botanic Gardens, Colorado History Museum, Denver Art Museum, and the State Capitol.

When it comes to recreation, one of the best places to be is **Colorado Springs**, a popular vacation destination at the foot of famous Pikes Peak. Home of the U.S. Air Force Academy, this bracing resort city also plays host to the U.S. Olympic Training Center, the Pro Rodeo Hall of Fame, and the spectacular Garden of the Gods.

When it comes to skiing, Colorado leads the way, thanks to the stunning slopes of **Aspen** and the towering peaks of **Snowmass Village**, to name but two premier resorts.

Other notable places to visit in the Centennial State include **Boulder**, famed for its gorgeous scenery and renowned scientific institutions; **Golden**, historically the center of Colorado's mining industry and now blessed with many museums as well as the National Earthquake Information Center; and **Gunnison**, with its celebrated pioneer background still very much in evidence.

Aspen

$$$$ GRAND ASPEN HOTEL
515 S Galena St
(303) 925-1150
Downtown hotel at foot of
Aspen Mountain, some rooms
have fireplaces

Aurora

**$$$ DOUBLETREE HOTEL
DENVER**
13696 E Iliff Pl
(303) 337-2800 or
(800) 243-3112
6-story hotel off I-255

Avon

**$$$ COMFORT INN-VAIL/
BEAVER CREEK**
0161 W Beaver Creek Blvd
(303) 949-5511 or
(800) 423-4374
4-story motel off I-70
with free shuttle service to
Beaver Creek ski resort
(excluding Dec 22-31)

Colorado Springs

$$$ ALIKAR GARDENS RESORT
1123 Verde Dr, Suite D
(719) 475-2564 or
(800) 456-1123
3-story resort motel off
I-25 near airport

**$$$ ANTLERS DOUBLETREE
HOTEL**
4 S Cascade Ave
(719) 473-5600 or
(800) 528-0444
13-story downtown hotel off
I-25 with its own brewpub

**$$$ SHERATON COLORADO
SPRINGS**
2886 S Circle Dr
(719) 576-5900
Hotel on 11 acres of
ground off I-25

Denver

**$$ BEST WESTERN
LANDMARK INN**
455 S Colorado Blvd
(303) 388-5561
9-story hotel off I-25, some
rooms have mountain views

**$$$ BURNSLEY ALL-SUITE
HOTEL**
1000 Grant St
(303) 830-1000 or
(800) 231-3915
17-story all-suite hotel
downtown near State Capitol

**$$$$ DENVER MARRIOTT HOTEL
CITY CENTER**
1701 California St
(303) 297-1300 or
(800) 228-9290
20-story downtown hotel
in financial district

$$$ EXECUTIVE TOWER INN
1405 Curtis St
(303) 571-0300 or
(800) 525-6651
16-story downtown hotel
next to Convention Center

$$$$ OXFORD HOTEL
1600 17th St
(303) 628-5400
Restored 1891 hotel
downtown near Coors Field,
antiques in rooms
(excluding Dec 31)

$$ RAMADA DENVER MIDTOWN
1475 S Colorado Blvd
(303) 757-8797
11-story hotel off I-25

$$ REGENCY HOTEL
3900 Elati St
(303) 458-0808
Multistory hotel off I-25
and I-70

$$$ SHERATON INN DENVER AIRPORT
3535 Quebec St
(303) 333-7711 or
(800) 328-2268
8-story hotel off I-70

$$$ STAPLETON PLAZA HOTEL AND FITNESS CENTER
3333 Quebec St
(303) 321-3500 or
(800) 950-0670
11-story hotel off I-70

$$$$ WARWICK HOTEL
1776 Grant St
(303) 861-2000 or
(800) 525-2888
Downtown hotel in
financial district

Englewood

$$$ HOLIDAY INN DENVER SOUTH
7770 S Peoria St
(303) 790-7770
5-story hotel off I-25
near airport

$$$ HOLTZE-TECH CENTER SOUTH
6380 S Boston St
(303) 290-1100 or
(800) 422-2092
Hotel off I-25 near Denver
Technological Center

$$$$ RADISSON HOTEL DENVER SOUTH
7007 S Clinton St
(303) 799-6200
10-story hotel off I-25
near Denver Technological
Center, some rooms have
mountain views

$$$ RESIDENCE INN BY MARRIOTT-DENVER SOUTH
6565 S Yosemite St
(303) 740-7177 or
(800) 331-3131
All-suite hotel off I-25,
many suites have fireplaces

$$$ SCANTICON-DENVER
200 Inverness Dr W
(303) 799-5800 or
(800) 346-4891
5-story resort hotel off I-25
with Scandinavian-style
decor, some rooms have
mountain views

Golden

$$$ DENVER MARRIOTT WEST HOTEL
1717 Denver W Blvd
(303) 279-9100 or
(800) 228-9290
6-story hotel off I-70

Granby

$$$ INN AT SILVER CREEK
62927 US Hwy 40
PO Box 4222
(303) 887-2131
Resort hotel near Silver Creek
ski area, all rooms have
mountain views and some
have fireplaces

Gunnison

$ MONARCH VALLEY RESORT
67366 Hwy 5 E
(303) 641-0626
Ranch resort at Rock
Mountain 11 miles west of
the Continental Divide

Lakewood

$$$ BEST WESTERN DENVER WEST
11595 W 6th Ave
(303) 238-7751
Hotel off US 6 near
Denver Federal Center

Snowmass Village

$$$$ CRESTWOOD LODGE
400 Wood Rd
PO Box 5460
(303) 923-2450 or
(800) 356-5949
Condo complex at
Snowmass ski area,
all rooms have fireplaces

$$$ STONEBRIDGE INN
300 Carriage Way
(303) 923-2420 or
(800) 525-4200
Hotel at Snowmass
ski area

Thornton

$$ RADISSON GRAYSTONE CASTLE
83 E 120th Ave
(303) 451-1002
5-story hotel off I-25
resembling medieval castle

Connecticut

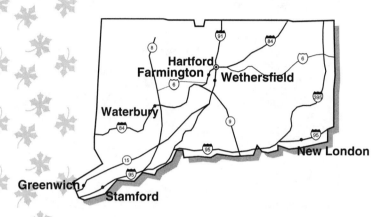

*C*onnecticut, with its rolling green hills and picture-perfect little villages, recalls much of the splendor of America's Colonial past. Even in the state's major industrial centers, plenty of historical reminders of bygone times are still on display for all to enjoy.

There is no better example of this pervasive sense of history amid modern urban development than **Hartford**, the state capital and unofficial "insurance capital of the world." At the Mark Twain House and Harriet Beecher Stowe House, you can tour the 19th-century homes of two of Hartford's most famous citizens, while the Wadsworth Atheneum is reputed to be the country's oldest public art gallery, having been founded in 1842.

Much of the past has also been beautifully preserved in **Waterbury**, once America's biggest brass center and now the site of many historic buildings that have been restored to their former glory.

If it's nautical history you're interested in, proceed to **New London**, an important port during the American Revolution and later a major whaling center. Today, you can visit the U.S. Coast Guard Academy, explore one of America's oldest lighthouses, or take a cruise on a replica of a Victorian clipper ship.

Also well worth investigating are **Stamford**, a corporate center and virtual suburb of New York City, with a lively arts scene and many pretty outdoor hideaways; **Wethersfield**, which is said to be the oldest English settlement in the state and still boasts many fine 18th-century houses; and **Farmington**, a charming old town with a lovely main street and several wonderful museums.

Cromwell

$$$ HOLIDAY INN
4 Sebethe Dr
(203) 635-1001
4-story hotel off I-91
with luxury level rooms

$ SUPER 8 MOTEL
1 Industrial Park Rd
(203) 632-8888
3-story mock Tudor-style
motel off I-91

Danbury

$$$ RAMADA INN
Jct I-84 Exit 8
(203) 792-3800
Multistory hotel off I-84

Darien

$$ COMFORT INN OF DARIEN
50 Ledge Rd
(203) 655-8211
3-story hotel off I-95
near Stamford

East Hartford

$$$ RAMADA HOTEL
100 E River Dr
(203) 528-9703
8-story hotel off I-84
near downtown Hartford
with club level rooms

$$ WELLESLEY INN
333 Roberts St
(203) 289-4950 or
(800) 444-8888
4-story motel off I-84

Farmington

$$$$ FARMINGTON INN
827 Farmington Ave
(203) 677-2821 or
(800) 648-9804
Motel off I-84 with
country-style decor

Greenwich

$$$ GREENWICH HARBOR INN
500 Steamboat Rd
(203) 661-9800 or
(800) 243-8511
4-story hotel off I-95 near
business district with its own
boat dock, many rooms have
harbor views

Hartford

$ DAYS INN
207 Brainard Rd
(203) 247-3297
Hotel off I-91
near downtown

Meriden

$$ DAYS INN HOTEL
900 E Main St
(203) 238-1211
Hotel off I-91

$$$ RAMADA INN
275 Research Pkwy
(203) 238-2380
6-story hotel off I-91
near Yale University

Middletown

$ MIDDLETOWN MOTOR INN
988 Washington St
(203) 346-9251
Hotel off I-95

New Britain

$$ RAMADA INN
65 Columbus Blvd
(203) 224-9161 or
(800) 826-2002
6-story hotel off I-84

New London

$$$ LIGHTHOUSE INN
6 Guthrie Place
(203) 443-8411
Restored 1928 inn with private beach, all rooms have period furniture and many overlook Long Island Sound

$$$ RADISSON HOTEL NEW LONDON
35 Governor Winthrop Blvd
(203) 443-7000
5-story downtown hotel off I-95 with luxury level rooms

Newington

$ CARRIER MOTOR LODGE
2660 Berlin Turnpike
(203) 666-1421
Hotel off I-95

Norwalk

$$$ HOLIDAY INN
789 Connecticut Ave
(203) 853-3477
8-story hotel off I-95

Rocky Hill

$ HOWARD JOHNSON LODGE
1499 Silas Deane Hwy
(203) 529-7446 or
(800) 446-4656
Hotel off I-91

Shelton

$$$$ RAMADA INN
780 Bridgeport Ave
(203) 929-1500
7-story hotel with
art deco lobby

Stamford

$$$ BUDGET HOST HOSPITALITY INN
19 Clark's Hill Ave
(203) 327-4300
6-story motel
downtown off I-95

Stratford

$$ **HO JO INN**
360 Honeyspot Rd
(203) 375-5666
Hotel off I-95 near airport

🍸 💻 🚫 🏊 ✈️

Waterbury

$$$ **HOLIDAY INN**
63 Grand St
(203) 596-1000
11-story hotel off I-84
with luxury level rooms

📶 🍸 🚫 🏊 🛗 🍴 🐾

$$ **QUALITY INN**
88 Union St
(203) 575-1500
8-story hotel off I-84 near
University of Connecticut
(discount on deluxe
rooms only)

📶 🍸 🚫 🏊

$$ **RAMADA INN**
1 Schraffts Dr
(203) 597-8000
Hotel off I-84 with scenic
hilltop setting

📶 🍸 💻 🚫 🏊 🍴 🐾

Wethersfield

$$ **RAMADA INN**
1330 Silas Deane Hwy
(203) 563-2311
4-story motel off I-91

💻 🚫 🐾

Windsor

$$$ **RESIDENCE INN BY
MARRIOTT**
100 Dunfey Ln
(203) 688-7474 or
(800) 331-3131
All-suite hotel off I-91,
most suites have fireplaces

💻 🚫 🏊 🛗 🍴 🏃
🚌 🐾

Windsor Locks

$$$ **HOLIDAY INN BRADLEY
INT'L AIRPORT**
16 Ella T Grasso Tpk
(203) 627-5171
5-story hotel off I-91 near
airport with art deco exterior
and luxury level rooms

📶 🍸 🚫 🏊 🛗 ✈️ 🚌

Delaware

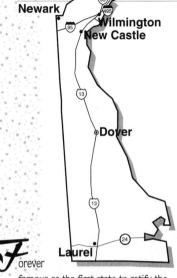

Newark

Wilmington

New Castle

Dover

Laurel

*F*orever famous as the first state to ratify the U.S. Constitution in 1787, Delaware has more recently developed a heavily industrialized economy, based largely on the Du Pont chemical company. Nevertheless, despite its tiny size, the state still offers much rural diversity, including some beautiful natural beaches.

Far and away the biggest city in Delaware, **Wilmington** owes its preeminence as an industrial, financial, and shipping center to the arrival in the early 19th century of the Du Pont family, who still dominate the place to this day. At the Hagley Museum, which occupies the site of the original Du Pont mills, you can relive American economic history, while at the Nemours Mansion and Gardens, you can see the extravagant French-style estate of Alfred du Pont. Also close at hand is Winterthur, famous for its magnificent collection of American fine arts and lovely landscaped grounds, as well as the Delaware Art Museum, notable for its 19th-century American paintings, and the ornate Old Swedes Church, reputed to be the oldest active Protestant church in the United States.

Equally historic and interesting is **New Castle**, where William Penn first stepped on American soil. Much of the city's Colonial and Federal architecture may still be admired, especially on The Strand, a beautifully preserved 18th-century brick street near the Delaware River. New Castle's Court House, constructed in 1732 and occupied by the Colonial Assembly until 1776, has now been authentically restored to its 1804 appearance.

Also worth a visit is **Newark**, site of the University of Delaware in addition to a natural history museum housed in a one-room schoolhouse built by one of the du Ponts in 1923.

Laurel

$$	**LAUREL'S LITTLE INN** 206 E 6th St (302) 875-0127 1875 inn on Rt 13 near antiques area

🍸 🖳 🎿 🚌

New Castle

$$	**RAMADA INN** I-295 and Rte 13 (302) 658-8511 Hotel near Delaware Memorial Bridge

📶 🍸 🚭 🏊 🎿 🛗

Newark

$$	**BEST WESTERN** 260 Chapman Rd (302) 738-3400 Hotel off I-95

📶 🖳 🚭 🏊 🎿 🛗

$$$	**HOWARD JOHNSON LODGE** 1119 S College Ave (302) 368-8521 3-story motel off I-95 near University of Delaware

🍸 🖳 🚭 🏊 🍽 🛗

Wilmington

$$$	**RADISSON HOTEL** 4727 Concord Pike (302) 478-6000 7-story hotel off I-95 decorated with English hunt country motif

📶 🍸 🚭 🏊 🍽 🛗

$$$	**WILMINGTON HILTON** 630 Naamans Rd at I-95 (302) 792-2700 Hotel off I-95

📶 🍸 🚭 🏊 🍽 🎿 🚌 🛗

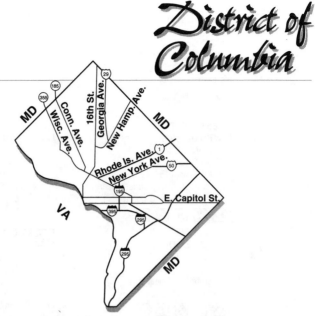

What began life as a mosquito-infested swamp is now one of the world's classic capitals. Thanks to the masterful work of Pierre L'Enfant at the turn of the 18th century, Washington, D.C., is graced today with wide boulevards, sweeping circles, handsome monuments, and imposing buildings. The place is a curious mix of government bureaucracy, national associations, and tourism attractions, but nevertheless Washington is both lively and interesting.

Like all great cities, **Washington** is made up of many diverse neighborhoods. One of the oldest is Capitol Hill, where both the judicial (the Supreme Court) and the legislative (the U.S. Capitol) branches of government are located, as well as the Library of Congress.

Linking Capitol Hill with the magnificent Lincoln Memorial is the Mall, a wide swath of parkland liberally sprinkled with government offices, monuments, and the many museums of the Smithsonian Institution—truly one of Washington's crown jewels—including most notably the National Air and Space Museum, the Hirshhorn Museum and Sculpture Garden, the National Museum of American History, and the National Museum of Natural History. Other prime Mall sights are the National Gallery of Art, the U.S. Botanic Garden, the Washington Monument, and the National Archives.

Situated on the points of a cross bisecting the Mall are two more Washington landmarks, the White House and the Jefferson Memorial.

If at all possible, also seek out the National Zoo, the Kennedy Center (offering music, opera, drama, dance, and film), the National Cathedral (a Gothic marvel), the U.S. Holocaust Memorial Museum, and the Vietnam Veterans Memorial.

$$$ **BELVUE HOTEL**
15 E St, NW
(202) 638-0900
Hotel near Capitol Hill
and Union Station with
art deco interior

$$$ **BEST WESTERN
CAPITOL HILL**
724 3rd St, NW
(202) 842-4466 or
(800) 242-4831
Hotel in Judiciary Square near
Union Station and Capitol Hill

$$$ **CARLYLE SUITES**
1731 New Hampshire Ave, NW
(202) 234-3200
All-suite hotel near
Dupont Circle

$$$ **CENTER CITY HOTEL**
1201 13th St, NW
(202) 682-5300
9-story hotel near White House

$$$ **COMFORT INN DOWNTOWN**
500 H St, NW
(202) 289-5959
10-story hotel off I-395
in Chinatown

$$$$ **DOUBLETREE PARK
TERRACE**
1515 Rhode Island Ave, NW
(202) 233-7000
8-story hotel near White House

$$$$ **DUPONT PLAZA HOTEL**
1500 New Hampshire Ave
(202) 483-6000 or
(800) 421-6662
Hotel at Dupont Circle near
White House

$$$ **EMBASSY INN**
1627 16th St, NW
(202) 234-7800 or
(800) 423-9111
B&B inn near Dupont Circle
with Federalist-style decor

$$$$ **EMBASSY ROW HOTEL**
2015 Massachusetts Ave, NW
(202) 265-1600 or
(800) 424-2400
9-story hotel near
Dupont Circle

$$$$ **EMBASSY SQUARE SUITES**
2000 N St, NW
(202) 659-9000 or
(800) 424-2999
10-story all-suite hotel
near Dupont Circle and
White House

$$$$ **GEORGETOWN DUTCH INN**
1075 Thomas Jefferson St, NW
(202) 337-0900
All-suite hotel next to C&O
Canal in Georgetown

$$$$ **GUEST QUARTERS SUITE
HOTEL-NEW HAMPSHIRE
AVENUE**
801 New Hampshire Ave, NW
(202) 785-2000
10-story all-suite hotel near
Kennedy Center

$$$$ **GUEST QUARTERS SUITE
HOTEL-PENNSYLVANIA
AVENUE**
2500 Pennsylvania Ave
(202) 333-8060
10-story all-suite hotel near
Georgetown

$$$$ HAMPSHIRE HOTEL
1310 New Hampshire Ave, NW
(202) 296-7600 or
(800) 368-5691
10-story all-suite hotel
near Dupont Circle

$$$$ HENLEY PARK HOTEL
926 Massachusetts Ave, NW
(202) 638-5200 or
(800) 222-8474
9-story hotel in restored
1918 building near
Convention Center
and White House

**$$$ HOLIDAY INN
FRANKLIN SQUARE**
1155 14th St, NW
(202) 737-1200
13-story hotel near White
House and Convention Center

**$$$ HOLIDAY INN
GEORGETOWN**
2101 Wisconsin Ave, NW
(202) 338-4600
7-story hotel in Georgetown
near National Cathedral

$$$ HOTEL ANTHONY
1823 L St, NW
(202) 223-4320 or
(800) 424-2970
All-suite hotel near
White House

**$$$ HOWARD JOHNSON HOTEL
AND SUITES**
1430 Rhode Island Ave, NW
(202) 462-7777 or
(800) 368-5690
10-story hotel near
White House

**$$$$ JW MARRIOTT HOTEL AT
NATIONAL PLACE**
1331 Pennsylvania Ave, NW
(202) 393-2000 or
(800) 228-9290
18-story hotel near White
House with luxury level rooms
and its own shopping center

**$$$$ LATHAM HOTEL
GEORGETOWN**
3000 M St, NW
(202) 726-5000 or
(800) 368-5922
10-story hotel in Georgetown
near Kennedy Center

**$$$$ LOEWS L'ENFANT PLAZA
HOTEL**
480 L'Enfant Plaza, SW
(202) 484-1000
Hotel near the Mall with
club level rooms

$$$$ LOMBARDY HOTEL
2019 I St, NW
(202) 828-2600 or
(800) 424-5486
Hotel near White House

$$$$ MORRISON-CLARK INN
1015 L St, NW
(202) 898-1200 or
(800) 332-7898
6-story historic 1864 hotel
near Convention Center with
individually decorated rooms

$$$ QUALITY HOTEL
415 New Jersey Ave, NW
(202) 638-1616 or
(800) 638-1116
10-story hotel on Capitol Hill
near Union Station

$$$$ RADISSON BARCELO
2121 P St, NW
(202) 293-3100
10-story hotel near
Dupont Circle

$$$$ SAVOY SUITES HOTEL
2505 Wisconsin Ave, NW
(202) 337-9700 or
(800) 944-5377
8-story hotel in Georgetown

$$$ STATE PLAZA HOTEL
2117 E St, NW
(202) 861-8200 or
(800) 424-2859
8-story all-suite hotel
near Lincoln Memorial
and White House

$$ SWISS INN
1204 Massachusetts Ave, NW
(202) 371-1816 or
(800) 955-7947
Small hotel near White House

$$$ WINDSOR INN
1842 16th St, NW
(202) 667-0300 or
(800) 423-9111
Art deco-style B&B inn
near Dupont Circle

Florida

Florida's immensely long coastline, its string of golden sandy beaches, its myriad of family oriented theme parks, and, above all, its warm, sun-drenched climate have all combined to make the state a haven for visitors.

For the ultimate in warmth, travel to **Miami**, Florida's most populous city, which has a gloriously Latin American flavor, as reflected in both the buildings and the people. Be sure to experience Miami's rich diversity—from the colorful Art Deco district to lively Little Havana, from the bustling boardwalk of Miami Beach to the bohemian charm of Coconut Grove. Miami is also the gateway to spectacular Everglades National Park and the 150-mile chain of tropical islands known as the **Florida Keys**.

Up the coast in the other direction lies **Fort Lauderdale**, with its fashionable homes and idyllic beaches, and **Cape Canaveral**, where American rockets blast off from the Kennedy Space Center.

Florida's biggest tourist destination of all is **Orlando**—along with satellite suburbs **Kissimmee** and **Lake Buena Vista**—where the main draw is ever-popular Walt Disney World and Epcot Center, although Sea World and Universal Studios have plenty of fans, too.

Over on the Gulf Coast, visitors flock to **Tampa**—not just for the fun of Busch Gardens but also to browse through quaint Ybor City—and its sister city of **St. Petersburg**, where recreation is usually the order of the day given an average of 360 sunny days a year.

The sun also shines a lot in **Daytona Beach**, host of the world famous stock car race; **Palm Beach**, noted for its polo and luxury shopping; and **Jacksonville**, home of the Gator Bowl and a thriving riverfront area.

Altamonte Springs

$$$ **HILTON HOTEL ORLANDO NORTH**
350 S North Lake Blvd
(407) 830-1985 or
(800) 247-1985
8-story hotel off I-4
with luxury level rooms

Boca Raton

$$$ **RADISSON BRIDGE RESORT OF BOCA RATON**
999 E Camino Real
(407) 368-9500
11-story hotel near beach,
many rooms overlook
Intracoastal Waterway

Clearwater

$$$$ **BELLEVIEW MIDO RESORT HOTEL**
25 Belleview Blvd
(813) 442-6171 or
(800) 237-8947
4-story historic 1896 resort
hotel off US 60, has luxury level
rooms and its own boat dock

$$ **HOLIDAY INN EXPRESS**
13625 Icot Blvd
(813) 536-7275
3-story motel within
Icot Center off US 19

Cocoa Beach

$$ **CARAVELLE MOTEL AND LOUNGE**
375 W Cocoa Beach Causeway
(407) 799-1600
Motel near beach with
its own boat access

$$$ **COCOA BEACH OCEANSIDE INN**
1 Hendry Ave
(407) 784-3126 or
(800) 874-7958
6-story motel, some
rooms have ocean views

$$$ **HOLIDAY INN COCOA BEACH**
1300 N Atlantic Ave
(407) 783-2271 or
(800) 226-6587
3-story hotel near downtown
with activity programs for
kids (discount on standard
rooms only)

$$$ **MARYSVILLE SPORTS RESORT**
415-A Sunrise Dr
(407) 784-8439 or
Resort hotel near beach

Cross City

$$ **CARRIAGE INN**
PO Box 1360
(904) 498-3910 or
(800) 682-4816
Motel off US 19 and 98

Cypress Gardens

$$$ ADMIRALS INN
5651 Cypress Gardens Blvd
(813) 324-5950 or
(800) 282-9159 (FL)
On Hwy 540 opposite
Cypress Gardens

Dania

$$$ SHERATON DESIGN CENTER HOTEL
1825 Griffin Rd
(305) 920-3500
12-story hotel off I-95 next to
Design Center of the Americas
and near Fort Lauderdale
Airport, has luxury level rooms

Davenport

$$ RED CARPET INN
US 27 N
(813) 424-2450
Hotel near Baseball City

Daytona Beach

$$$ BEACH RESORT
2700 N Atlantic Ave
(904) 672-3770 or
(800) 874-7426
Hotel opposite Bellair
Plaza shopping center
and near beach

$$$ BEST WESTERN MAYAN INN
103 S Ocean Ave
(904) 252-0584 or
(800) 443-5323
8-story hotel off
US 92 near beach

$$$ COMFORT INN OCEANFRONT
3135 S Atlantic Ave
(904) 767-8533 or
(800) 822-7707
Beachfront 8-story hotel

$$$ DAYS INN OCEANSIDE
800 N Atlantic Ave
(904) 252-6494
Beachfront hotel near
Convention Center

$$$ DAYS INN SPEEDWAY
2900 W International
Speedway Blvd
(904) 255-0541
Motel off I-95 near Daytona
International Speedway

$$$ HOLIDAY INN OCEANSIDE
905 S Atlantic Ave
(904) 255-5432 or
(800) 334-4484
5-story beachfront hotel

$$$ HOLIDAY INN SPEEDWAY
1798 W International
Speedway Blvd
(904) 255-2422 or
(800) 352-2722
Hotel off I-95 next to Volusia
Mall and near Daytona
International Speedway

$$ **HOWARD JOHNSON HOTEL**
600 N Atlantic Ave
(904) 255-4471 or
(800) 767-4471
Beachfront 14-story hotel
near Convention Center

$$$ **INDIGO LAKES HOLIDAY INN CROWNE PLAZA RESORT**
2620 W International
Speedway Blvd
(904) 258-6333
640-acre resort hotel off US 92

$$$ **OCEAN SANDS HOTEL**
1024 N Atlantic Ave
(904) 255-1131 or
(800) 543-2923
Beachfront 8-story hotel
off US 92

$$$ **QUALITY INN OCEANSIDE**
251 S Atlantic Ave
(904) 672-8510 or
(800) 227-7220
Beachfront 7-story hotel

$$ **THE REEF**
935 S Atlantic Ave
(904) 252-2581 or
(800) 874-0136
Beachfront hotel

$$ **SCOTTISH INN**
1515 S Ridgewood Ave
(904) 258-5742 or
(800) 331-4647
Motel off I-95 near beach

Daytona Beach Shores

$$$ **ACAPULCO INN**
2505 S Atlantic Ave
(904) 761-2210 or
(800) 245-3580
8-story beachfront hotel
off US 92

$$$ **BAHAMA HOUSE**
2001 S Atlantic Ave
(904) 248-2001 or
(800) 571-2001
10-story beachfront hotel
off US 92

Delray Beach

$$$ **SPANISH RIVER RESORT**
1111 E Atlantic Ave
(407) 243-SWIM or
(800) 543-SWIM
Resort hotel near beach
(reservations accepted up
to 60 days in advance)

Dundee

$$$ **HOLIDAY INN CYPRESS GARDENS**
339 US Hwy 27 N
(813) 439-1591
Hotel off US 27

Ft. Lauderdale

$$ BAHIA CABANA BEACH RESORT
3001 Harbor Dr
(305) 524-1555 or
(800) 922-3008 (FL)
Multistory waterfront hotel
with its own dock

🔳 🍸 🚫 🏊 🛁

$$$$ BAHIA MAR RESORT AND YACHTING CENTER
801 Seabreeze Blvd
(305) 764-2233 or
(800) 327-8154
16-story waterfront hotel

🔳 🍸 🚫 🏊 🎿

$$$ BEST WESTERN OCEANSIDE INN
1180 Seabreeze Blvd
(305) 525-8115 or
(800) 367-1007
5-story beachfront hotel

🔳 🍸 🖥 🏊 🚌

$$ DAYS INN OCEANSIDE
435 N Atlantic Blvd
(305) 462-0444 or
(800) 243-3550
Multistory beachfront hotel

🔳 🍸 🚫 🏊

$$$ HOLIDAY INN FT. LAUDERDALE BEACH
999 N Atlantic Blvd
(305) 563-5961
12-story beachfront hotel

🔳 🍸 🚫 🏊 🛁

$$ HOLIDAY INN NORTH
4900 Powerline Rd
(305) 776-4880
Hotel near Lockhart Stadium
(reservations no more than
14 days in advance)

🔳 🍸 🚫 🏊 ✈

$$$ INVERRARY PLAZA GOLF RESORT AND CONFERENCE CENTER
3501 Inverrary Blvd
(305) 485-0500
206-room hotel,
Hotel off I-95

🔳 🍸 🎿

$$$ PELICAN BEACH RESORT
2000 N Atlantic Blvd
(305) 568-9431 or
(800) 525-6232
Art deco motel on beachfront

🖥 🏊

$$$ PLAZA BEACH RESORT
4060 Galt Ocean Dr
(305) 565-6611 or
(800) 678-9022
Beachfront hotel off I-95

🔳 🍸 🚫 🏊 🎿 🚌

$$ POLYNESIAN VILLAGE
3711 N Ocean Blvd
(305) 566-3394 or
(800) 451-8937
4-story hotel near beach

🍸 🚫 🏊

$$$ RAMADA BEACH RESORT
4060 Galt Ocean Dr
(305) 565-6611 or
(800) 678-9022
9-story oceanfront hotel
with its own private beach

🔳 🍸 🚫 🏊 🎿

$$$ RIVERSIDE HOTEL
620 E Las Olas Blvd
(305) 467-0671 or
(800) 325-3280
6-story 1936 hotel with
attractive gardens on banks
of New River

**$$$$ WESTIN HOTEL
CYPRESS CREEK**
400 Corporate Dr
(305) 772-1331
14-story lakeside hotel off
I-95 with luxury level rooms

Ft. Myers

$$ DAYS INN CAPE CORAL
13353 N Cleveland Ave
(813) 995-0535
Motel on US 41

Gainesville

**$$ HOLIDAY INN
UNIVERSITY CENTER**
1250 W University Ave
(904) 376-1661
Hotel off I-75 near
University of Florida with
executive level rooms

Hialeah

$$$ HOLIDAY INN HIALEAH
6650 W 20th Ave
(305) 362-7777
5-story hotel near
Hialeah racetrack

$$$ PARK PLAZA HOTEL
7707 NW 103rd St
(305) 825-1000
10-story hotel next to
Westland shopping center
and near Hialeah racetrack
(excluding Dec 26-31)

$$$ RAMADA INN HIALEAH
1950 W 49th St
(305) 823-2000
4-story hotel in
business district

Hollywood

**$$$ COMFORT INN
FT. LAUDERDALE/
HOLLYWOOD AIRPORT**
2520 Stirling Rd
(305) 922-1600 or
(800) 333-1492
4-story motel off I-95

Hollywood
Beach

$$$ HOLIDAY BEACH INN
4111 S Ocean Dr
(305) 457-8000 or
(800) 544-7887
Beachfront hotel

**$$$ HOLLYWOOD BEACH
HILTON**
4000 S Ocean Dr
(305) 458-1900
9-story hotel opposite beach
on Intracoastal Waterway
with executive level rooms

HOLLYWOOD BEACH RESORT HOTEL
$$$
101 N Ocean Dr
(305) 921-0990 or
(800) 331-6103
All-suite 1925 art deco
hotel on beachfront
(extra charge for ocean view)

HOWARD JOHNSON HOLLYWOOD BEACH RESORT INN
$$$$
2501 N Ocean Dr
(305) 925-1411 or
(800) 423-9867
11-story beachfront hotel
near downtown (discount
only on luxury rate)

Jacksonville

COMFORT SUITES
$$
8333 Dix Ellis Trail
(904) 739-1155
3-story all-suite motel off
I-95 (excluding Dec 27-Jan 1)

DOUBLETREE CLUB HOTEL
$$$
4700 Salisbury Rd
(904) 281-9700
6-story motel off I-95 near
Southpoint Business Park

HOSPITALITY INN
$$
901 N Main St
(904) 355-3744
5-story downtown hotel
off I-95 in financial
district near Gator Bowl

HOSPITALITY INN BED AND BREAKFAST
$$
7071 103rd St
(904) 777-5700
All-suite hotel off I-295

JACKSONVILLE MARRIOTT
$$$
4670 Salisbury Rd
(904) 296-2222 or
(800) 228-9290
9-story hotel off I-95

MARINA HOTEL AND CONFERENCE CENTER AT ST. JOHNS PLACE
$$$
1515 Prudential Dr
(904) 396-5100
5-story hotel on banks of St.
Johns River near downtown

Jensen Beach

VISTANA'S BEACH CLUB
$$$$
10740 S Ocean Dr
(407) 229-9200
Beachfront resort hotel on
Hutchinson Island with
2-bedroom condos

Key Largo

COLONY'S PORT LARGO RESORT AND MARINA
$$$$
99751 Overseas Hwy
(305) 451-3939
3-story oceanside hotel on
US 1 near John Pennekamp
Underwater Park

$$$ HOWARD JOHNSON RESORT
Mile Marker 102
PO Box 1024
(305) 451-1400 or
(800) 947-1320
Bayside hotel on US 1 near
John Pennekamp Underwater
Park (reservations up to 12
months in advance)

Key West

$$$ COLONY'S BAYSIDE KEY WEST RESORT
3444 N Roosevelt Blvd
(305) 296-7593
5-story resort hotel on
US 1 opposite the Gulf

$$$$ PELICAN LANDING RESORT AND MARINA
915 Eisenhower Dr
(305) 296-7583
Resort hotel off US 1

Kissimmee

$$ BEST WESTERN EASTGATE
5565 W Irlo Bronson Hwy
(407) 396-0707 or
(800) 223-5361
5-story hotel on US 192

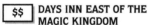

$$ DAYS INN EAST OF THE MAGIC KINGDOM
5840 W Irlo Bronson Hwy
(407) 396-7969 or
(800) 327-9126
3-story hotel on US 192
next to Old Town shopping
complex (excluding Dec 20-
Jan 1)

$$ DAYS INN MAINGATE WEST
7980 W Irlo Bronson Hwy
(407) 396-1000 or
(800) 327-9173
3-story hotel on US 192 next
to Splendid China theme park

$$$ DAYS SUITES EAST OF THE MAGIC KINGDOM
5820 W Irlo Bronson Hwy
(407) 396-7900 or
(800) 327-9126
All-suite motel on
US 192 next to Old Town
shopping complex
(excluding Dec 20-Jan 1)

$$$$ DELUXE FLORIDA RENTALS
2777 Poinciana Blvd
(407) 396-2744 or
(800) 949-2744
2- and 3-bedroom villas
off US 192 near Old Town
shopping complex

$$ ECONO LODGE MAINGATE HAWAIIAN RESORT
7514 W Irlo Bronson Hwy
(407) 396-2000
Hotel on US 192
near Disney World

$$ ECONO LODGE MAINGATE EAST
4311 W Irlo Bronson Hwy
(407) 396-7100 or
(800) 365-6935
3-story motel on US 192

$$$$ FLORIDA VACATION VILLAS
2770 Poinciana Blvd
(407) 396-6010 or
(800) 881-9070
Off Hwy 192

$$ GALA VISTA MOTOR INN
5995 W Irlo Bronson Hwy
(407) 396-4300 or
(800) 223-1584
Motel on US 192

$$$ GATEWAY HILTON INN
7470 Hwy 192 W
(407) 396-4400 or
(800) 327-9170
8-story hotel on US 192
near Disney World

$$$ HOLIDAY INN MAINGATE WEST
7601 Black Lake Rd
(407) 396-1100
6-story hotel on US 192
with free shuttle service to
Disney World

$$ HOWARD JOHNSON KISSIMMEE LODGE
2323 E Irlo Bronson Hwy
(407) 846-4900
Hotel on US 192

$$ HOWARD JOHNSON MAINGATE WEST
7600 W Irlo Bronson Hwy
(407) 396-2500
Hotel on US 192

$$$ LAGUNA BAY VILLAS
2928 Vineland Rd
(407) 397-0700 or
(800) 344-3959
2- and 3-bedroom villas

$$ QUALITY INN AND SUITES
2039 E Irlo Bronson Hwy
(407) 846-7814
Hotel on US 192

$$ QUALITY INN LAKE CECILE
4944 W Irlo Bronson Hwy
(407) 396-4455 or
(800) 864-4855
5-story lakeside hotel
on US 192

$$ QUALITY SUITES MAINGATE EAST
5876 W Irlo Bronson Hwy
(407) 396-8040 or
(800) 848-4148
5-story all-suite hotel
on US 192

$$ RAMADA INN ORLANDO WESTGATE
9200 Hwy 192
(813) 424-2621
Hotel at intersection of
US 192 and US 27

$$$ RAMADA RESORT MAINGATE AT THE PARKWAY
2900 Parkway Blvd
(407) 396-7000 or
(800) 634-4774
8-story hotel off I-4
(discount on deluxe rooms only)

RAMADA RESORT MAINGATE
$$$

2950 Reedy Creek Blvd
(407) 396-4466
Hotel on US 192 near
Disney World

SHERATON INN LAKESIDE
$$$

7769 W Irlo Bronson Hwy
(407) 396-2222 or
(800) 848-0801
Lakefront hotel on US 192
opposite Splendid China theme
park free shuttle service to
Disney World

SLEEP INN MAINGATE
$$

8536 W Irlo Bronson Hwy
(407) 396-1600 or
(800) 225-0086
3-story motel on US 192
(excluding Dec 23-Jan 1)

TRAVELODGE MAIN GATE EAST
$$$

5711 W Irlo Bronson Hwy
(407) 396-4222 or
(800) 327-1128
8-story hotel on US 192

TRAVELODGE MAIN GATE WEST
$$

7785 W Irlo Bronson Hwy
(407) 396-1828 or
(800) 634-5525
3-story hotel on US 192

VILLAS OF SOMERSET
$$$

2928 Vineland Rd
(407) 397-0700 or
(800) 344-3959
2- and 3-bedroom villas
off US 192

WYNFIELD INN MAINGATE
$$

5335 W Irlo Bronson Hwy
(407) 396-2121 or
(800) 346-1551
3-story motel on US 192

Lake Buena Vista

DAYS INN LAKE BUENA VISTA VILLAGE
$$$

12490 Apopka-Vineland Rd
(407) 239-4646 or
(800) 521-3297
7-story hotel off I-4 with free
shuttle service to Disney World

DOUBLETREE CLUB HOTEL
$$$

8688 Palm Pkwy
PO Box 22783
(407) 239-8500 or
(800) 228-2846
6-story hotel with free shut-
tle service to Disney World

HOLIDAY INN SUNSPREE RESORT
$$$

13351 State Rt 535
(407) 239-4500 or
(800) FON-MAXX
6-story hotel off I-4 with free
shuttle service to Disney World

HOTEL ROYAL PLAZA
$$$$

1905 Hotel Plaza Blvd
(407) 828-2828 or
(800) 248-7890
Newly built multistory
hotel off I-4

RESIDENCE INN BY MARRIOTT
8800 Meadow Creek Dr
(407) 239-7700
All-suite hotel off I-4

 WYNDHAM GARDEN HOTEL
8688 Palm Pkwy
(407) 239-8500
6-story hotel off I-4 with free shuttle service to Disney World (excluding Apr 13-23)

Lakeland

 HOLIDAY INN LAKELAND SOUTH
3405 S Florida Ave
(813) 646-5731 or
(800) 833-4902
Hotel off I-4

Lehigh

 ADMIRAL LEHIGH GOLF RESORT
225 E Joel Blvd
(813) 369-2121 or
(800) 843-0971
Resort hotel with supervised children's programs

Marathon

 HOWARD JOHNSON
13351 Overseas Hwy
(305) 743-8550
Oceanfront hotel on US 1

Marianna

 HILLTOP INN
4655 Hwy 90E
(904) 526-3251
Hotel off I-10 near Florida Caverns State Park

Melbourne

 MELBOURNE HILTON AT RIALTO PLACE
200 Rialto Pl
(407) 768-0200 or
(800) 437-8010
8-story hotel off I-95 in business district near airport, has luxury level rooms

 RADISSON SUITE OCEANFRONT
3101 N Hwy A1A
(407) 773-9260
15-story all-suite hotel on beach with club level rooms

Merritt Island

 HOLIDAY INN MERRITT ISLAND
260 E Merritt Island Cswy
(407) 452-7711
Hotel on island between Cocoa and Cocoa Beach

Miami

 AIRPORT REGENCY HOTEL
1000 NW 42nd Ave
(305) 441-1600
6-story hotel with penthouse level

$$$ BEST WESTERN MIAMI AIRPORT INN
1550 NW Le Jeune Rd
(305) 871-2345
6-story hotel with luxury
level rooms

$$$ COMFORT INN AND SUITES
5301 NW 36th St
(305) 871-6000
11-story hotel near
airport (excluding Jan 26-30
and Feb 16-22)

$$ CROSSWAY AIRPORT INN
1850 NW Le Jeune Rd
(305) 871-4350 or
(800) 338-3816
Hotel near airport

$$$ CROWNE PLAZA HOTEL
1601 Biscayne Blvd
(305) 374-0000
20-story downtown hotel
on US 1 in shopping/
entertainment complex

$$ DAYS INN CIVIC CENTER
1050 NW 14th St
(305) 324-0200
5-story hotel near downtown
and next to major hospitals

$$$$ DAYS INN MIAMI AIRPORT
3401 NW LeJeune Rd
(305) 871-4221
5-story hotel with
executive level rooms

$$$ DUPONT PLAZA HOTEL
300 Biscayne Blvd Way
(305) 358-2541 or
(800) 327-3480
Downtown hotel with pent-
house suites in business district
next to Convention Center

$$ HOLIDAY INN CONVENTION CENTER
200 SE 2nd Ave
(305) 374-3000
13-story downtown hotel
next to Convention Center

$$ HOWARD JOHNSON GOLDEN GLADES
16500 NW 2nd Ave
(305) 945-2621 or
(800) 477-5429
4-story hotel off I-95

$$$$ MIAMI MARRIOTT DADELAND
9090 S Dadeland Blvd
(305) 670-1035 or
(800) 228-9290
South Miami hotel in
Datran Center complex
with concierge level rooms

$$$ PLAZA VENETIA
555 NE 15th St
(305) 374-2900
35-story hotel
on Biscayne Bay

Miami Beach

$$$ DORCHESTER DECO BEACH HOTEL
1850 Collins Ave
(305) 672-2676 or
(800) 829-3003
1940 hotel in Art Deco
district opposite beach and
near Convention Center

🔲 🍸 ≈

$$ HOWARD JOHNSON OCEANSIDE
6261 Collins Ave
(305) 868-1200
9-story beachfront hotel

🔲 🍸 🚭

$$$ INDIAN CREEK HOTEL
2727 Indian Creek Dr
(305) 531-2727
Hotel near beach and
Convention Center
(excluding Jan 26-30)

🔲 🍸 🚭 ≈ 🍽

$$$ MARSEILLES DECO BEACH HOTEL
1741 Collins Ave
(305) 672-2676 or
(800) 829-3003
Art deco hotel near
Convention Center with
its own private beach

🔲 🍸 🚭 ≈

$$$ QUALITY SHAWNEE BEACH RESORT
4343 Collins Ave
(305) 532-3311 or
(800) 832-8332
Beachfront hotel near
Art Deco district

🔲 🍸 🚭 ≈ 🍽 🏃

$$ SHORE CLUB HOTEL
1901 Collins Ave
(305) 538-7811 or
(800) 327-8330
Hotel in Art Deco district
near Convention Center
with its own private beach

🔲 🚭 ≈ 🍽

Naples

$$$ WORLD TENNIS CENTER AND RESORT
4800 Airport Rd
(813) 263-1900
On Hwy 896 and
Hwy 31

🔲 🍸 🚭 ≈ 🍽 🏃

Ocala

$$$ SILVER SPRINGS HILTON
3600 SW 36th Ave
(904) 854-1400
9-story hotel off I-75
with VIP floor

🔲 🍸 🚭 ≈ 🍽 🏃

Ocoee

$$$ COLONY PLAZA HOTEL - ORLANDO WEST
11100 W Colonial Dr
(407) 656-3333 or
(800) 821-0136
Hotel in West Orlando

🔲 🍸 🚭 ≈ 🏃

Orange Park

$$ HOLIDAY INN
150 Park Ave
(904) 264-9513
Hotel at I-295 and US 17 near
Orange Park shopping mall

🔲 🍸 🚭 🍽 🎮

Orlando

$ CHOICE INN-WINTER PARK
650 Lee Rd
(800) 352-3297
Off I-4

$$$ CLARION PLAZA HOTEL-ORLANDO
9700 International Dr
(407) 352-9700 or
(800) 627-VALU
14-story hotel next to
Convention Center and near
Sea World

$$$ COMFORT INN
830 Lee Rd
(407) 629-4000 or
(800) 227-5393
5-story motel

$$ COMFORT INN-ORLANDO
8421 S Orange Blossom Trail
(407) 855-6060 or
(800) 327-9742
Motel on US 17/92/441 next
to Florida Mall shopping center,
free shuttle service to Disney
World (excluding Feb 13-20
and Dec 25-31)

$$ DAYS INN
2500 W 33rd St
(407) 841-3731
4-story hotel off I-4

$$ DAYS INN EAST
5827 Caravan Ct
(407) 351-3800
Hotel off I-4 near
Universal Studios

$$ DAYS INN FLORIDA MALL
1851 W Landstreet Rd
(407) 859-7700 or
(800) 231-5514
3-story hotel off I-4 near
Florida Mall shopping center

$$ DAYS INN LAKESIDE
7335 Sand Lake Rd
(407) 351-1900
3-story lakeside hotel off I-4
near Universal Studios

$$ DELTA ORLANDO RESORT
5715 Major Blvd
(407) 351-3340
4-story hotel off I-4 opposite
Universal Studios

$$ GATEWAY INN
7050 Kirkman Rd
(407) 351-2000 or
(800) 327-3808
Hotel off I-4 with free shuttle
service to Disney World (discount on luxury rooms only)

$$$ HOLIDAY INN EXPRESS
6323 International Dr
(407) 351-4430
Motel off I-4 opposite
Wet 'n Wild

$$ **HOWARD JOHNSON
SOUTH AIRPORT**
8700 S Orange Blossom Trail
(407) 851-2330 or
(800) 327-7460
Hotel on US 17/92/441

$$ **INTERNATIONAL
GATEWAY INN**
5859 American Way
(407) 345-8880
4-story motel off I-4

$$ **LAS PALMAS HOTEL**
6233 International Dr
(407) 351-3900 or
(800) 327-2114
Hotel off I-4

$$$ **ORLANDO HERITAGE INN**
9861 International Dr
(407) 352-0008 or
(800) 447-1890
Hotel off I-4 opposite
Convention Center

$$$ **ORLANDO MARRIOTT**
8001 International Dr
(407) 351-2420 or
(800) 228-9290
Resort hotel off I-4

$$ **QUALITY HOTEL
ORLANDO AIRPORT**
3835 McCoy Rd
(407) 859-2711 or
(800) 824-2213
4-story hotel with free shuttle service to Disney World,
has executive level rooms

$$$ **RADISSON PLAZA HOTEL**
60 S Ivanhoe Blvd
(407) 425-4455
Multistory hotel off I-4 in
business district with club
level rooms

$$$ **RAMADA HOTEL RESORT**
7400 International Dr
(407) 351-4600 or
(800) 327-1363
5-story hotel off I-4 at Florida
Center shopping/entertainment
complex, has free shuttle
service to Disney World

$$$ **RAMADA LIMITED**
8296 S Orange Blossom Trail
(407) 240-0570
Motel on US 17/92/441 next
to Florida Mall shopping center

$$ **RAMADA ORLANDO
CENTRAL**
3200 W Colonial Dr
(407) 295-5270 or
(800) 828-5270
Hotel off I-4 near downtown

$$ **REGENCY INN**
4049 S Orange Blossom Trail
(407) 843-1350
At I-4 and US 441

$$$ RENAISSANCE HOTEL ORLANDO AIRPORT
5445 Forbes Pl
(407) 240-1000
9-story hotel with
luxury level rooms

$$$ SHERATON ORLANDO NORTH HOTEL
I-4 and Maitland Blvd,
(407) 660-9000
6-story hotel in Maitland
Center Office Park

$$$$ SUMMERFIELD SUITES HOTEL
8480 International Dr
(407) 352-2400 or
(800) 833-4353
5-story all-suite hotel off I-4

$$$ TRAVELODGE CENTRAL PARK
7101 S Orange Blossom Trail
(407) 851-4300
Hotel on US 17/92/441 near
Florida Mall shopping center

$$$$ TWIN TOWERS HOTEL
5780 Major Blvd
(407) 351-1000 or
(800) 327-2110
18-story hotel off I-4
opposite Universal Studios

$$ WYNFIELD INN WESTWOOD
6263 Westwood Blvd
(407) 345-8000 or
(800) 346-1551
3-story motel off I-4
next to Sea World

Ormond Beach

$$$ CASA DEL MAR BEACH RESORT
621 S Atlantic Ave
(904) 672-4550 or
(800) 245-1590
7-story oceanfront hotel

$$ HOLIDAY INN I-95 NORTH
1614 N US Hwy 1
(904) 672-1060
Hotel off I-95

Palm Beach

$$$ COLONY HOTEL
155 Hammon Ave
(407) 655-5430 or
(800) 521-5525
Downtown hotel near beach
with rooftop penthouses

$$$ HEART OF PALM BEACH HOTEL
160 Royal Palm Way
(407) 655-5600 or
(800) 523-5377
3-story hotel near ocean

Palm Beach Gardens

$$$$ PALM BEACH GARDENS MARRIOTT
4000 RCA Blvd
(407) 622-8888
11-story hotel off I-95
with luxury level rooms

Panama City Beach

$$ INN AT ST. THOMAS SQUARE
8600 Thomas Dr
(904) 234-0349 or
(800) 874-8600
Off Hwy 98 and
Hwy 231

Pensacola

$$ HOSPITALITY INN
6900 Pensacola Blvd
(904) 477-2333
All-suite motel on
US 29 off I-10

$$ HOSPITALITY INN II
4910 W Mobile Hwy
(904) 453-3333
All-suite motel on US 90

$$ SEVILLE INN
223 E Garden St
(904) 433-8331 or
(800) 277-7275
Hotel near Civic Center
and historical district

Perry

$ BEST BUDGET INN
2220 US 19 S
(904) 584-6231 or
(800) 458-7215
Motel on US 19 and 98

Pinellas Park

$$ DAYS INN GATEWAY
9359 US Hwy 19 N
(813) 577-3838
Off Hwy 275 on beach

$$ LA MARK CHARLES MOTEL
6200 34th St N
(813) 527-7334 or
(800) 448-6781
Motel off I-275 near
Pinellas Park Mall (discount
on standard rooms only)

Plantation

$ PLANTATION INN
375 N State Rd 7
(305) 584-7220
Hotel located off I-95

Pompano Beach

$$$ HOLIDAY INN
1350 S Ocean Blvd
(305) 941-7300 or
(800) 332-2735
3-story oceanfront hotel
overlooking Spanish River
with its own private beach

$$$ HOWARD JOHNSON POMPANO BEACH RESORT
9 N Pompano Beach Blvd
(305) 781-1300 or
(800) 223-5844
8-story oceanfront hotel
opposite beach (discount
on luxury rooms only)

Port Richey

$$ **COMFORT INN**
11810 US Hwy 19
(813) 863-3336 or
(800) 553-1157
Motel on US 19

St. Augustine

$$$ **PONCE DE LEON GOLF AND CONFERENCE RESORT**
4000 US Hwy 1
(904) 824-2821
4-story 350-acre hotel on US 1

St. Augustine Beach

$$$ **HOLIDAY INN ST. AUGUSTINE BEACH**
860 A1A Beach Blvd S
(904) 471-2555
5-story oceanfront hotel

St. Petersburg

$$$ **HOWARD JOHNSON HOTEL**
3600 34th St S
(813) 867-6070
4-story hotel on
US 19 off I-275

St. Petersburg Beach

$$ **COLONIAL GATEWAY RESORT INN**
6300 Gulf Blvd
(813) 367-2711 or
(800) 237-8918
Hotel with its own private beach

Sarasota

$ **RED CARPET INN**
8110 N Tamiami Trail
(813) 355-8861
Hotel off I-75

Sebring

$$ **HOLIDAY INN SEBRING**
6525 US 27 N
(813) 385-4500 or
(800) 654-7235
Hotel on US 27 and US 98

Starke

$$$ **DAYS INN**
1101 N Temple Ave
(904) 964-7600
Hotel on US 301

Tampa

$ **DAYS INN BUSCH GARDENS NORTH**
701 E Fletcher Ave
(813) 977-1550
3-story hotel off I-275

$$ DAYS INN BUSCH GARDENS MAINGATE
2901 E Busch Blvd
(813) 933-6471
Hotel near Busch Gardens
(excluding Jul 3-5 and
Nov 22-26)

$$$ GUEST QUARTERS SUITE HOTEL ON TAMPA BAY
3050 N Rocky Point Dr W
(813) 888-8800
7-story all-suite hotel off
I-275 near airport

$$$ HOLIDAY INN CROWNE PLAZA WESTSHORE BLVD
700 N Westshore Blvd
(813) 289-8200
11-story hotel off I-275

$$$ HOLIDAY INN CROWNE PLAZA
10221 Princess Palm Ave
(813) 623-6363 or
(800) 866-ROOM
5-story hotel off I-275 in
Sabal Business Park (excluding Feb 8-12 and Oct 13-14)

$$ HOLIDAY INN EXPRESS TAMPA STADIUM
4732 N Dale Mabry
(813) 877-6061
Hotel off I-275 near Tampa
Stadium and Tampa Bay Mall
shopping center

$$ HOLIDAY INN STATE FAIR
2708 N 50th St
(813) 621-2081 or
(800) 423-3749
Hotel near State Fairgrounds
(excluding Feb 5-16)

$$$ HOLIDAY INN TAMPA AIRPORT
4500 W Cypress St
(813) 879-4800
10-story hotel near airport

$$$ QUALITY HOTEL RIVERSIDE
200 N Ashley Dr
(813) 223-2222 or
(800) 288-2672
6-story downtown hotel off
I-275 on Hillsborough River
opposite University of Tampa,
has its own boat dock

$$ QUALITY INN
210 E Fowler Ave
(813) 933-7275
3-story hotel off I-275

$$$ RADISSON BAY HARBOR INN
7700 Courtney Campbell
Causeway
(813) 281-8900
6-story beachfront hotel off
I-275 with luxury level rooms

$$$ **TAMPA RESORT BUSCH GARDENS**
820 E Busch Blvd
(813) 933-4011 or
(800) 288-4011
4-story hotel off I-275
opposite University of
South Florida and near
Busch Gardens

Titusville

$$$ **HOLIDAY INN KENNEDY SPACE CENTER**
4951 S Washington Ave
(407) 269-2121
Riverside hotel on US 1

$$ **HOWARD JOHNSON LODGE**
1829 Riverside Dr
(407) 267-7900
Riverside motel on US 1

Venice

$$$ **BEST WESTERN VENICE RESORT**
455 N US 41 Bypass
(813) 485-5411 or
(800) 237-3712
Hotel off I-275 near downtown and beaches with its
own dinner theater

West Palm Beach

$$$ **COMFORT INN ON PALM BEACH LAKES**
1901 Palm Beach Lakes Blvd
(407) 689-6100
6-story motel off I-95

$$ **DAYS INN AIRPORT NORTH**
2300 45th St
(407) 689-0450 or
(800) 543-1613
Hotel off I-95

$$$ **OMNI WEST PALM BEACH HOTEL**
1601 Belvedere Rd
(407) 689-6400
15-story hotel off
I-95 next to airport

$$$ **RADISSON SUITE INN**
1808 Australian Ave S
(407) 689-6888
6-story all-suite hotel off
I-95 in Commerce Point
Executive Center near
downtown and airport

$$$ **RAMADA HOTEL AND RESORT**
630 Clearwater Park Rd
(407) 833-1234 or
(800) 444-PALM
10-story hotel off I-95
near airport with
executive level rooms

Georgia

The largest state east of the Mississippi, Georgia offers surprising diversity—from the Appalachian Mountains in the north to the low-lying coastal plains in the south. In between is a fertile land of lazily flowing rivers and gently rolling hills.

The dynamic growth of Georgia's capital, **Atlanta**, has established this booming city as the commercial, industrial, and financial center of the entire Southeast. Amid all the towering skyscrapers and sleek buildings, however, the city has retained its gracious Southern hospitality and down-home roots. There's much to appreciate. The World of Coca-Cola celebrates Atlanta as the birthplace of the popular soft drink, the Martin Luther King, Jr. National Historic Site celebrates the great civil rights leader, and Underground Atlanta celebrates the joy of shopping. Just outside the city is 3,200-acre Stone Mountain Park,

with its colossal equestrian carving of Jefferson Davis, Stonewall Jackson, and Robert E. Lee, and Six Flags Over Georgia, one of the country's most thrilling theme parks.

For a complete change of pace, go to **Savannah**, which boasts the largest urban historic district in the country. With its handsome mansions and lush green vegetation, there's a wonderful 18th-century air about the place. Of particular interest is Riverfront Plaza, a nine-block stretch overlooking the Savannah River that is awash with shops, pubs, and other attractions.

A little way down the coast is **Brunswick**, famous for its fine plantation homes, and Georgia's fabled Golden Isles, including **Jekyll Island**, a lovely resort area with 10 miles of broad sandy beaches.

And there's also **Macon**, full of exquisite antebellum homes as well as a magnificently restored opera house.

Albany

$ **DAYS INN DOWNTOWN**
422 W Oglethorpe Blvd
(912) 888-2632
Downtown hotel
near Civic Center

Americus

$$$ **WINDSOR HOTEL**
125 W Lamar St
(912) 924-1555
1892 hotel on US 280 in
downtown historic district
with many period features

Atlanta

$$$ **ATLANTA DOWNTOWN TRAVELODGE**
311 Courtland St NE
(404) 659-4545
3-story downtown motel
off I-75 and I-85

$$$ **ATLANTA MARRIOTT NORTHWEST**
200 Interstate N Pkwy
(404) 952-7900 or
(800) 228-9290
16-story hotel off I-75
with luxury level rooms

$$$$ **BILTMORE SUITES HOTEL**
30 5th St NE
(404) 874-0824
10-story 1924 all-suite
hotel near downtown,
listed on National Register
of Historic Places

$$$ **CLARION HOTEL DOWNTOWN**
70 John Wesley Dobbs Ave NE
(404) 659-2660
Downtown hotel off I-75
and I-85 near State Capitol

$$$ **COMFORT INN**
101 International Blvd
(404) 524-5555 or
(800) 535-0707
11-story downtown hotel
off I-75 and I-85 next to
Merchandise Mart and
State Capitol

$$$ **DAYS INN DOWNTOWN**
300 Spring St
(404) 523-1144
10-story downtown hotel
off I-75 and I-85 next to
Merchandise Mart and World
Congress Center

$$ **DAYS INN NORTHLAKE**
2158 Ranchwood Dr
(404) 934-6000
5-story motel off I-285

$$$ **GUEST QUARTERS SUITE HOTEL**
6120 Peachtree Dunwoody Rd
(404) 668-0808 or
(800) 424-2900
6-story all-suite hotel off
I-285 near Perimeter Mall
shopping center

$$$ **HOLIDAY INN ATLANTA CENTRAL**
418 Armour Dr
(404) 873-4661 or
(800) 282-8222
5-story hotel off I-85, some
rooms have fireplaces

$$$ HOWARD JOHNSON ATLANTA AIRPORT
1377 Virginia Ave
(404) 762-5111
Hotel off I-85 near airport

$$$ MARQUE OF ATLANTA
111 Perimeter Center W
(404) 396-6800 or
(800) 683-6100
12-story hotel off I-285
opposite Perimeter Mall
shopping center

$$ RAMADA ATLANTA AIRPORT NORTH
1419 Virginia Ave
(404) 768-7800 or
(800) 476-1120
6-story hotel off I-85
near airport

$$$ RAMADA ATLANTA AIRPORT SOUTH
1551 Phoenix Blvd
(404) 996-4321
6-story hotel off I-285
near airport

$$$ RAMADA HOTEL DOWNTOWN
175 Piedmont Ave NE
(404) 659-2727
7-story downtown hotel
in financial district

$$ RAMADA INN DUNWOODY
1850 Cotillion Dr
(404) 394-5000
4-story hotel off I-285

$$$ REGENCY SUITES HOTEL
975 W Peachtree St
(404) 876-5003 or
(800) 642-3629
9-story all-suite hotel
off I-75 and I-85

$$$ RESIDENCE INN BY MARRIOTT-MIDTOWN
1041 W Peachtree St
(404) 872-8885 or
(800) 331-3131
7-story all-suite hotel off
I-75 and I-85 near Woodruff
Arts Center

$$$ SHERATON CENTURY CENTER HOTEL
2000 Century Pkwy NE
(404) 325-0000
Hotel off I-85 with
jogging trail

$$$$ WESTIN PEACHTREE PLAZA
210 Peachtree St
(404) 659-1400
72-story downtown hotel
(the tallest in America) off
I-75 and I-85 with luxury
level rooms

$$$ WYNDHAM GARDEN HOTEL-BUCKHEAD
3340 Peachtree Rd NE
(404) 231-1234
Hotel off I-85 in
Tower Place complex

$$$$ WYNDHAM GARDEN HOTEL-VININGS
2857 Paces Ferry Rd
(404) 432-5555
4-story hotel off I-285 in
turn-of-the-century building
near historic Vinings area

$$$ WYNDHAM GARDEN PERIMETER CIRCLE
800 Hammond Dr NE
(404) 252-3344
4-story hotel off I-285 in
Perimeter Corporate Center

$$$$ WYNDHAM MIDTOWN
125 10th St
(404) 873-4800
11-story hotel off I-75
and I-85

Augusta

$$ COMFORT INN
629 Frontage Rd NW
(706) 855-6060
Hotel at I-20 and I-520

Brunswick

$$ COMFORT INN I-95
5308 New Jessup Hwy
(912) 264-6540
5-story hotel off I-95

$$ HOLIDAY INN BRUNSWICK
5252 New Jessup Hwy
(912) 264-4033
Hotel off I-95

College Park

$$$$ ATLANTA AIRPORT EMBASSY SUITES
4700 Southport Rd
(404) 767-1988
All-suite hotel at I-285 and
I-85 near airport

$$ DAYS INN ATLANTA AIRPORT
4601 Best Rd
(404) 761-6500
Hotel off I-85 near airport

Doraville

$$ BEST WESTERN PERIMETER NORTH INN
2001 Clearview Ave
(404) 455-1811
Hotel off I-85 and I-285

$ HOLIDAY INN ATLANTA NORTHEAST
4422 NE Expressway
(404) 448-7220
4-story hotel off I-85
and I-285

Duluth

$$	**DAYS INN GWINNETT PLACE**

1948 Day Dr
(404) 476-1211
5-story motel off I-85
opposite Gwinnett Mall
shopping center

East Point

$$	**HOLIDAY INN AIRPORT NORTH**

1380 Virginia Ave
(404) 762-8411
5-story hotel off I-85
near airport

Jekyll Island

$$	**CLARION RESORT BUCCANEER**

85 S Beachview Dr
(912) 635-2261
4-story oceanfront hotel off
US 17 with luxury level rooms

$	**COMFORT INN ISLAND SUITES**

711 N Beachview Dr
(912) 635-2211
Oceanfront all-suite hotel

$$$	**HOLIDAY INN BEACH RESORT**

200 S Beachview Dr
(912) 635-3311
Beachfront hotel

Kingsland

$$	**COMFORT INN KINGSLAND**

I-95 and SR 40 E
(912) 729-6979
Hotel off I-95

Macon

$$	**RADISSON HOTEL**

108 1st St
(912) 746-1461
16-story downtown hotel
overlooking Ocmulgee River
(discount on king rooms only)

Norcross

$	**HERITAGE INN**

5990 Western Hills Dr
(404) 368-0218
Motel off I-85
(excluding Jun 30-Jul 4
and Sept 1-3)

$$$	**MARRIOTT NORCROSS**

475 Technology Pkwy
(404) 263-8558 or
(800) 228-9290
Hotel off I-85 next to
Technology Park

$$$	**NORTHEAST ATLANTA HILTON**

5993 Peachtree Industrial Blvd
(404) 447-4747
10-story hotel off I-285 with
luxury level rooms

Savannah

$$ **DAYS INN AND DAYS SUITES-HISTORIC SAVANNAH**
201 W Bay St
(912) 236-4440
7-story downtown hotel
opposite Riverfront Plaza
(excluding Mar 15-31)

$$$ **SHERATON SAVANNAH RESORT AND COUNTRY CLUB**
612 Wilmington Island Rd
(912) 897-1612 or
(800) 533-6706
8-story 200-acre resort hotel
on Wilmington Island

Smyrna

$$ **HOWARD JOHNSON CUMBERLAND**
2700 Curtis Dr
(404) 435-4990
6-story motel off I-285
near Cumberland Mall
shopping center

Suwanee

$ **BEST WESTERN FALCON INN**
Suwanee Rd at I-85
(404) 945-6751
Hotel off I-85, training camp
of NFL's Atlanta Falcons

Sycamore

$ **BUDGET LAKEVIEW INN**
Rt 1, Box 77
(912) 567-3357
Motel off I-75

Hawaii

Kauai

Oahu
Honolulu

Molokai
Lahaina Kahului
Kihei Maui
Wailea

Kailua-Kona Hawaii Hilo

When it comes to sand, surf, and sun, Hawaii stands head and shoulders above every other state. This huge chain of volcanic islands, ringed with coral reef, in the Pacific Ocean about 2,400 miles southwest of California is a tropical paradise—although increasing development threatens the state's fragile ecosystem.

The most visited island is **Oahu**, the industrial and commercial center of the state, where almost 80% of Hawaii's residents live. The primary destination is the capital city, **Honolulu**, which enjoys a truly beautiful natural setting. Most visitors go to Waikiki, famous for its glistening skyscrapers, frenetic night life, and sizzling beach, although few fail to make the pilgrimage to Pearl Harbor to see the USS Arizona Memorial.

To avoid confusion, the island of **Hawaii** is also known as the Big Island, although the epithet is appro-

priate since it's almost twice as large as all the other major islands combined. The state's high point, Mauna Kea, at nearly 14,000 feet, is an extinct volcano, although its counterparts Kilauea and Mauna Loa are still active. **Hilo**, with its gorgeous gardens, and the resort community of **Kailua-Kona** are the two biggest draws on the Big Island.

On **Maui**, the major attraction is Haleakala, a dormant volcano with one of the world's largest craters, although the old whaling port of **Lahaina** and the beaches of **Kihei**, **Kahului**, and **Wailea** have become equally popular.

Island hoppers will also want to investigate **Kauai**, one of the wettest spots in the world, which explains its gloriously verdant vegetation, and **Molokai**, a land of rugged mountains and incredibly steep sea cliffs that remains still largely unspoiled.

Hawaii
Hilo

$$$ HAWAII NANILOA HOTEL
93 Banyan Dr
(808) 969-3333 or
(800) 367-5360
Multistory hotel overlooking
Hilo Bay (excluding Apr 15-18)

$$$ HILO HAWAIIAN HOTEL
71 Banyon Dr
(808) 935-9361 or
(800) 367-5004
8-story hotel
overlooking Hilo Bay

$$$ HILO SEASIDE HOTEL
126 Banyan Dr
(808) 935-0821 or
(800) 367-7000
Hotel overlooking Hilo Bay

Kailua-Kona

$$$ ASTON KONA ISLANDER INN
75-5776 Kuakini Hwy
(808) 329-3181 or
(800) 922-7866
Plantation-style hotel

$$$ KONA REEF HOTEL
75-5888 Alii Dr
(808) 329-4780 or
(800) 367-5004
Beachfront condominium
hotel near downtown
(excluding Dec 17-Jan 1)

$$$ KONA SEASIDE HOTEL
75-5646 Palani Rd
(808) 329-2455 or
(800) 367-7000
Downtown hotel

$$$ KONA SURF RESORT AND COUNTRY CLUB
78-128 Ehukai St
(808) 322-3411 or
(800) 367-8011
Oceanfront hotel on 14-acre
peninsula (discount unavail-
able on studios and suites)

$$$$ ROYAL KONA RESORT
75-5852 Alii Dr
(808) 329-3111 or
(800) 774-5662
Multistory oceanfront hotel
near downtown

Waikoloa

$$$ ELIMA LANI
Lua Kula St
(800) 367-5004
Oceanfront all-suite hotel

$$$ MARC WAIKOLOA VILLAS
Lua Kula St,
(808) 883-9144 or
(800) 535-0085
Oceanfront condominium
hotel (excluding Dec 23-31)

Kauai
Hanalei

$$$$ HANALEI BAY RESORT AND SUITES
5380 Honoiki Rd
(808) 826-6522 or
(800) 367-5004
4-story 22-acre hotel in
Princeville resort area

Kapaa

$$$ ASTON KAUAI BEACHBOY HOTEL
484 Kuhio Hwy #100
(808) 822-3441 or
(800) 922-7866
Beachfront hotel in Coconut
Plantation Market Place (discount unavailable on oceanfront rooms)

$$$ KAUAI COCONUT BEACH RESORT
PO Box 830, Coconut
Plantation
(808) 822-3455 or
(800) 22-ALOHA
4-story beachfront hotel
near Coconut Plantation
Market Place

$$$ KAUAI RESORT HOTEL
3-5920 Kuhio Hwy
(808) 245-3931 or
(800) 367-5004
Beachfront hotel next to
Wailua River

$$$ KAUAI SANDS HOTEL
420 Papaloa Rd
(808) 822-4951 or
(800) 367-7000
Beachfront hotel at Coconut
Plantation Market Place

Koloa

$$$$ POIPU SHORES
1775 Pe'e Rd
(808) 742-7700 or
(800) 367-5004
Oceanfront condominium
hotel at Poipu Beach

Maui
Kahului

$$$ MAUI BEACH HOTEL
170 Kaahumanu Ave
(808) 877-0051 or
(800) 367-5004
Polynesian-style hotel

$ MAUI PALMS
150 Kaahumanu Ave
(808) 877-0071 or
(800) 367-5004
Beachfront hotel

$$$ MAUI SEASIDE HOTEL
100 W Kaahumanu Ave
(808) 877-3311 or
(800) 367-7000
Beachfront hotel opposite
Kahului shopping center

Kihei

$$$ ASTON MAUI LU RESORT
575 S Kihei Rd
(808) 879-5881 or
(800) 922-7866
28-acre oceanfront hotel

⬚ 🍸 🚭 🏊 🚶

$$ ASTON MAUI VISTA
2191 S Kihei Rd
(808) 879-7966 or
(800) 922-7866
10-acre condominium hotel
opposite Kamaole Beach

🏊 🚶

$$$$ KAMAOLE SANDS
2695 S Kihei Rd
(808) 874-8700 or
(800) 367-5004
4-story 15-acre condominium
hotel near Kamaole Beach

⬚ 🍸 🏊 🛁 🚶 🚌

$$$ WAILEA OCEANFRONT HOTEL
2980 S Kihei Rd
(808) 879-7744 or
(800) 367-5004
Oceanfront hotel

⬚ 🍸 🖥 P

Lahaina

$$ ASTON MAUI PARK
3626 Lower Honoapiilani Hwy
(808) 669-6622 or
(800) 922-7866
Condominium hotel
near beach

🏊 🛁

$$$ KAHANA BEACH CONDOMINIUM
4221 Lower Honoapiilani Rd
(808) 669-8611
Condominium hotel on
Kahana Beach

🏊 🚶

$$$ KAHANA VILLA
4242 Lower Honoapiilani Rd
(808) 669-5613 or
(800) 535-0085
Condominium hotel
opposite Kahana Beach

⬚ 🍸 🏊 🚶 🚶

$$$ MARC PAKI MAUI
3615 Lower Honoapiilaoi Hwy
(808) 669-8235 or
(800) 535-0085
4-story 11-acre beachfront
all-suite hotel
(excluding Dec 23-31)

🏊 🛁 🚶

$$$$ MAUI MARRIOTT
100 Nohea Kai Dr
(808) 667-1200
9-story oceanfront hotel on
Kaanapali Beach (excluding
Christmas week)

⬚ 🍸 🚭 🏊 🍴 🚶

$$$ ROYAL KAHANA RESORT-A MARC SUITE
4365 Lower Honoapiilani Rd
(808) 922-9700 or
(800) 535-0085
Beachfront condominium
hotel (excluding Dec 23-31)

🖥 🚭 🏊 🛁 🍴 🚶 P

$$$$ ROYAL LAHAINA RESORT
2780 Kekaa Dr
(808) 661-3611 or
(800) 447-6925
12-story 27-acre beachfront
hotel

⬚ 🍸 🚭 🏊 🚶

Wailea

$$$$ STOUFFER WAILEA BEACH RESORT
3550 Wailea Alanui Dr
(808) 879-4900 or
(800) 9-WAILEA
7-story 15-acre oceanfront
hotel with luxury level rooms
(discount unavailable on suites
or Mokapu Beach Club rooms)

Molokai
Maunaloa

$$$ KALUAKOI VILLAS
1131 Kaluakoi Rd
(808) 552-2721 or
(800) 367-5004
Beachfront
condominium hotel
(excluding Dec 24-Jan 1)

Oahu
Honolulu

$$$ ASTON CORAL REEF HOTEL
2299 Kuhio Ave
(800) 922-7866
Waikiki hotel next to
International Marketplace

$$$ ASTON HONOLULU PRINCE
415 Nahua St
(808) 922-1616 or
(800) 922-7866
Multistory Waikiki hotel
near beach

$$$ ASTON INN ON THE PARK
1920 Ala Moana Blvd
(808) 946-8355 or
(800) 922-7866
Multistory Waikiki hotel near
Fort DeRussy and Ala Moana
shopping center

$$$$ ASTON WAIKIKI BEACHSIDE
2452 Kalakaua Ave
(808) 931-2100 or
(800) 922-7866
Waikiki hotel opposite beach

$$$ ASTON WAIKIKIAN ON THE BEACH
1811 Ala Moana Blvd
(808) 949-5331 or
(800) 922-7866
Waikiki hotel near
Ala Moana shopping center

$$$ COLONY'S HAWAII POLO INN
1696 Ala Moana Blvd
(808) 949-0061
Waikiki hotel near
Ala Moana shopping center

$$$$ DIAMOND HEAD BEACH HOTEL
2947 Kalakaua Ave
(808) 922-1928 or US
(800) 367-2317
Beachfront Waikiki hotel
opposite Kapiolani Park

$$$$ ILIKAI HOTEL NIKKO WAIKIKI
1777 Ala Moana Blvd
(808) 949-3811 or
(800) 367-8434
25-story Waikiki hotel near beach, nightly Polynesian torch lighting ceremony (discount on tower rooms only)

$$$ ILIMA HOTEL
445 Nohonani St
(808) 923-1877
17-story Waikiki hotel near beach and International Marketplace (max 5-night stay)

$$$ KUHIO VILLAGE RESORT
2463 Kuhio Ave
(808) 926-0641 or
(800) 367-5004
Twin-tower Waikiki hotel near beach

$$$ MARC HAWAIIAN MONARCH
444 Niu St
(808) 949-3911 or
(800) 535-0085
Waikiki hotel in 44-story building
(excluding Dec 23-31)

$$$ OCEAN RESORT HOTEL WAIKIKI
175 Paoakalani Ave
(808) 922-3861 or
(800) 367-2317
Twin-tower Waikiki hotel near beach and Kapiolani Park

$$$ OUTRIGGER ALA WAI TOWER
1700 Ala Moana Blvd
(808) 942-7722 or
(800) 462-6262
Waikiki hotel near beach and Ala Moana shopping center with executive floor (excluding Dec 19-Jan 3; max 5-night stay)

$$$ OUTRIGGER EAST
150 Kaiulani Ave
(808) 922-5353 or
(800) 462-6262
19-story Waikiki hotel near beach (excluding Dec 19-Jan 3; max 5-night stay)

$$$ OUTRIGGER HOBRON
343 Hobron Ln
(808) 942-7777 or
(800) 462-6262
Waikiki hotel near Ala Moana shopping center (excluding Dec 19-Jan 3; max 5-night stay)

$$$ OUTRIGGER MAILE SKY COURT
2058 Kuhio Ave
(808) 947-2828 or
(800) 462-6262
Waikiki hotel near beach and International Marketplace (excluding Dec 19-Jan 3; max 5-night stay)

$$$ OUTRIGGER REEF TOWERS
227 Lewers St
(808) 924-8844 or
(800) 462-6262
Waikiki hotel near beach
(excluding Dec 19-Jan 3;
max 5-night stay)

**$$$ OUTRIGGER REEF
ON THE BEACH-A ROYAL
OUTRIGGER**
2169 Kalia Rd
(808) 923-3111 or
(800) 462-6262
Waikiki beachfront hotel
(excluding Dec 19-Jan 3;
max 5-night stay)

$$$ OUTRIGGER SURF
2280 Kuhio Ave
(808) 922-5777 or
(800) 462-6262
Waikiki hotel near beach
(excluding Dec 19-Jan 3;
max 5-night stay)

$$$ OUTRIGGER VILLAGE
240 Lewers St
(808) 923-3881 or
(800) 462-6262
Waikiki hotel near beach
(excluding Dec 19-Jan 3;
max 5-night stay)

$$$ OUTRIGGER WAIKIKI SURF
2200 Kuhio Ave
(808) 923-7671 or
(800) 462-6262
Waikiki hotel near beach
(excluding Dec 19-Jan 3;
max 5-night stay)

**$$$ OUTRIGGER WAIKIKI
SURF EAST**
422 Royal Hawaiian Ave
(808) 923-7671 or
(800) 462-6262
Multistory Waikiki hotel near
beach (excluding Dec 19-Jan
3; max 5-night stay)

**$$$ OUTRIGGER WAIKIKI
SURF WEST**
412 Lewers St
(808) 923-7671 or
(800) 462-6262
9-story Waikiki hotel near
beach (excluding Dec 19-Jan
3; max 5-night stay)

**$$$ OUTRIGGER WAIKIKI
TOWER**
200 Lewers St
(808) 922-6424 or
(800) 462-6262
Waikiki hotel near beach
(excluding Dec 19-Jan 3;
max 5-night stay)

$$$ OUTRIGGER WEST
2330 Kuhio Ave
(808) 922-5022 or
(800) 462-6262
Waikiki hotel near beach
(excluding Dec 19-Jan 3;
max 5-night stay)

$$ PLEASANT HOLIDAY ISLE
270 Lewers St
(808) 923-0777
Waikiki hotel near beach
and Royal Hawaiian
shopping center

QUEEN KAPIOLANI HOTEL $$$
150 Kapahulu Ave
(808) 922-1941 or
(800) 367-5004
19-story Waikiki hotel near
beach and Kapiolani Park

WAIKIKI GRAND HOTEL $$$
134 Kapahulu Ave
(808) 922-9700 or
(800) 535-0085
Waikiki hotel near beach
and Kapiolani Park
(excluding Dec 23-31)

WAIKIKI HANA HOTEL $$$$
2424 Koa Ave
(808) 926-8841 or
(800) 367-5004
Waikiki hotel near beach and
International Marketplace

WAIKIKI LANAIS $$$
2452 Tusitala St
(808) 923-1511 or
(800) 535-0085
Waikiki condominium hotel
(excluding Dec 23-31)

WAIKIKI PARKSIDE HOTEL $$$
1850 Ala Moana Blvd
(808) 955-1567 or
(800) 237-9666
12-story Waikiki hotel near
Ala Moana shopping center
(excluding Dec 26-Jan 10)

WAIKIKI ROYAL SUITES $$$
255 Beachwalk
(808) 926-5641 or
(800) 535-0085
8-story Waikiki hotel near
beach and Fort DeRussy
(excluding Dec 23-31)

Makaha

**SHERATON MAKAHA
RESORT AND COUNTRY
CLUB** $$$
84-626 Makaha Valley Rd
(808) 695-9511
Resort hotel near beach

Idaho

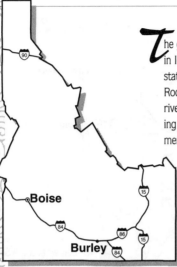

*T*he great outdoors is the big attraction in Idaho. Dominating this beautiful state are range upon range of the great Rocky Mountains. Several powerful rivers cut through the mountains, creating sweeping valleys and gorges. Most memorable of all is the tumultuous Snake River, responsible for forming Hell's Canyon, the deepest gorge in North America.

To appreciate the Snake's raw power, plan to be in **Burley** for the annual speedboat championships in June.

The capital city of **Boise** has much to offer, too, including the Discovery Center of Idaho, a fine hands-on science museum, and an impressive State Capitol.

Boise

$$$	**RESIDENCE INN BY MARRIOTT**

1401 Lusk
(208) 344-1200 or
(800) 331-3131
All-suite hotel near downtown and Boise State University

Burley

$$	**BEST WESTERN BURLEY INN**

800 N Overland Ave
(208) 678-3501
Hotel off I-84 near boat docks on Snake River

$	**BUDGET MOTEL**

900 N Overland Ave
(208) 678-2200
Motel off I-84

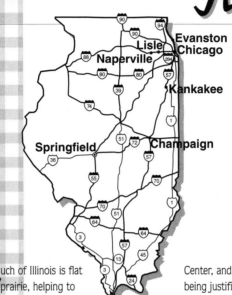

Illinois

*M*uch of Illinois is flat prairie, helping to maintain the state's position as the largest producer of soybeans and second biggest producer of corn, but "the land of Lincoln" (as the license plates proclaim) is also the location of America's second biggest city, a huge cultural and commercial force that spreads its influence far and wide.

In fact, **Chicago** dominates not just the state but the entire mid-portion of the country. As a transportation center, it reigns supreme—O'Hare is the world's busiest airport, all of America's major railroads converge on the city, and Chicago is a major Great Lakes port. Culturally, it boasts the Art Institute, the Field Museum (of natural history), and the world class Chicago Symphony Orchestra. And it's also home to some of America's most distinctive structures, including the Wrigley Building, the John Hancock Center, and the Sears Tower, as well as being justifiably famous for its imposing public sculpture.

Chicago's suburbs are as lively as its downtown neighborhoods. If possible, explore **Naperville**, where costumed guides re-create a 19th-century rural settlement; **Evanston**, the charming home of Northwestern University; and **Lisle**, which plays host to the acclaimed Morton Arboretum.

At the other end of the state is the capital, **Springfield**, where Abraham Lincoln lived for most of his adult life. You can see the only home he ever owned as well as the office in which he practiced law and the tomb in which he and his family are buried.

Other places worth seeking out include **Kankakee**, a lively prairie community with some early Frank Lloyd Wright homes, and **Champaign**, which with its twin city of Urbana is the site of the University of Illinois.

Arlington Heights

$$$ RADISSON HOTEL
75 W Algonquin Rd
(708) 364-7600
6-story hotel off I-90
with executive club floor
and jogging track

Bradley

$$ HOWARD JOHNSON LODGE
800 N Kinzie Ave
(815) 939-3501
5-story hotel off I-57

Champaign

$$$ HOLIDAY INN
1505 N Neil St
(217) 359-1601
3-story hotel off I-74

Chicago

$$$ THE AMBASSADOR WEST
1300 N State Pkwy
(312) 787-3700 or
(800) 300-WEST
12-story hotel
near downtown

$$$$ BARCLAY CHICAGO HOTEL
166 E Superior St
(312) 787-6000
28-story all-suite
downtown hotel

$$$ BEST WESTERN GRANT PARK HOTEL
1100 S Michigan Ave
(312) 922-2900 or
(800) GRANT-PK
Downtown hotel near Grant
Park and Convention Center

$$$ BEST WESTERN INN
162 E Ohio at N Michigan Ave
(312) 787-3100
22-story downtown hotel

$$$ BLACKSTONE HOTEL
636 S Michigan Blvd
(312) 427-4300 or
(800) 622-6330
1910 downtown hotel near
Grant Park with jazz club,
listed on National Register
of Historic Places

$$ CITY SUITES HOTEL
933 W Belmont Ave
(312) 404-3400
Hotel near Wrigley Field

$$$$ EXECUTIVE PLAZA HOTEL
71 E Wacker Dr
(312) 346-7100 or
(800) 621-4005
39-story downtown hotel
overlooking Chicago River

$$$ INN AT UNIVERSITY VILLAGE
625 S Ashland Ave
(312) 243-7200 or
(800) 662-5233
4-story hotel off I-290 near
University of Illinois-Chicago

$$$ OXFORD HOUSE
225 N Wabash
(312) 346-6585 or
(800) 344-4111
14-story downtown hotel

$$ PARK BROMPTON HOTEL
528 W Brompton Place
(312) 404-3499
Hotel near Wrigley Field

$$$ SURF HOTEL
555 W Surf St
(312) 528-8400
Hotel near Wrigley Field
and Lincoln Park Zoo

**$$$$ WYNDHAM GARDEN
HOTEL**
5615 N Cumberland Ave
(312) 693-5800
Multistory hotel off I-90
near O'Hare Airport

Danville

$$ DAYS INN
77 N Gilbert
(217) 443-6600 or
(800) 344-5861
6-story downtown hotel off
I-74 near Civic Center

Deerfield

$$$$ EMBASSY SUITES HOTEL
1445 Lake Cook Rd
(708) 945-4500
7-story all-suite hotel off I-94
in Arbor Lake Centre complex

Downers Grove

$$ HOLIDAY INN EXPRESS
3031 Finley Rd
(708) 810-9500
3-story motel off I-355

$$$ RADISSON SUITE HOTEL
2111 Butterfield Rd
(708) 971-2000
7-story all-suite hotel
off I-355

Elk Grove Village

$$ HAMPTON INN
100 Busse Rd
(708) 593-8600
4-story motel

Evanston

$$$ OMNI ORRINGTON HOTEL
1710 Orrington Ave
(708) 866-8700 or
(800) THE-OMNI
9-story 1928 hotel next to
Northwestern University (discount on double room rate only)

Glenview

$$$ RADISSON SUITE HOTEL
1400 Milwaukee Ave
(708) 803-9800
7-story all-suite hotel off I-294

Kankakee

$$ **DAYS INN**
1975 E Court St
(815) 939-7171
4-story motel off I-57

Lisle

$$$ **HYATT LISLE**
1400 Corporetum Dr
(708) 852-1234
13-story hotel off I-88
in Illinois Research and
Development Corridor
next to Morton Arboretum

$$$ **RADISSON HOTEL**
3000 Warrenville Rd
(708) 505-1000
8-story 17-acre hotel off I-88
next to Lisle Executive Center
with luxury level rooms
(excluding Dec 31)

Lombard

$$$ **RESIDENCE INN BY
MARRIOTT**
2001 S Highland Ave
(708) 629-7800 or
(800) 331-3131
All-suite hotel off I-88, some
rooms have fireplaces

Mattoon

$$ **RAMADA INN AND
CONFERENCE CENTER**
300 Broadway Ave
(217) 235-0313
Hotel off I-57 near downtown

Mount Prospect

$$$ **HOLIDAY INN MOUNT
PROSPECT**
200 E Rand Rd
(708) 255-8800
Hotel opposite Randhurst
Mall shopping center

Murphysboro

$ **APPLE TREE INN**
100 N 2nd St
(618) 687-2345 or
(800) 626-4356
Motel near Lake Kindaid and
Lake Murphysboro

Naperville

$$$ **HOLIDAY INN NAPERVILLE**
1801 N Naper Blvd
(708) 505-4900 or
(800) 536-4136
7-story hotel off I-88

$$$ **WYNDHAM GARDEN
HOTEL**
1837 Centre Point Cir
(708) 505-3353
4-story hotel off I-88

Northbrook

$$$ SHERATON NORTH SHORE INN
933 Skokie Blvd
(708) 498-6500 or
(800) 535-9131
10-story hotel off I-94
near Chicago Botanic Garden
with luxury level rooms

Oak Brook

$$$ DRAKE OAK BROOK HOTEL
2301 York Rd
(708) 574-5700
4-story hotel off I-88
opposite Butler National golf
course (excluding Dec 31)

Oak Brook Terrace

$$$ WYNDHAM GARDEN HOTEL
17 W 350 22nd St
(708) 833-3600
7-story hotel off I-294

🔌 🍸 🚭 🏊

Palatine

$$ RAMADA HOTEL
920 E Northwest Hwy
(708) 359-6900
5-story hotel next to Arlington
racetrack (excluding Arlington
Million and New Year's Eve)

Paxton

$$ PAXTON INN MOTEL
980 W Ottawa St
(217) 379-2316
Motel off I-57

🔌 🚭 🅿

Rosemont

$$ BEST WESTERN O'HARE
10300 W Higgins Rd
(708) 296-4471
3-story motel off US 12
and US 45 near airport and
Rosemont Horizon stadium

$$$ HOLIDAY INN O'HARE
5440 N River Rd
(708) 671-6350
14-story hotel off I-190
opposite Expo Center

🔌 🍸 🚭 🏊 🏊 ⚕ 🍽
✈ 🚌 🎰

$$$$ WESTIN HOTEL O'HARE
6100 N River Rd
(708) 698-6000
12-story hotel off I-190 near
Expo Center with luxury level
rooms (excluding Dec 31)

🔌 🍸 🚭 🏊 🍽 ✈
🚌 🎰

Schaumburg

$$$ HOMEWOOD SUITES
815 E American Ln
(708) 605-0400 or
(800) CALL-HOME
3-story all-suite hotel off
I-290, some suites have
fireplaces

🍸 🖥 🚭 🏊 ⚕ 🍽 🎰

$$$ WYNDHAM GARDEN HOTEL
800 National Pkwy
(708) 605-9222
6-story hotel off I-290
with executive rooms

Schiller Park

$$$$ RESIDENCE INN BY MARRIOTT-O'HARE
9450 W Lawrence Ave
(708) 678-2210 or
(800) 331-3131
6-story all-suite hotel off
US 12 and US 45

Skokie

$$ HOWARD JOHNSON HOTEL
9333 Skokie Blvd
(708) 679-4200
5-story hotel off I-94 on
US 41 with executive section
(excluding Oct 25-26 and
Jun 19-20)

Springfield

$$$ BEST WESTERN LINCOLN PLAZA
101 E Adams St
(217) 523-5661
8-story downtown
hotel opposite Capitol
and near Lincoln Home

$$$ SPRINGFIELD HILTON
700 E Adams St
(217) 789-1530 or
(800) 445-8667
30-story downtown hotel
near Capitol and Lincoln
Home with luxury level rooms

Wood Dale

$$$ WYNDHAM GARDEN HOTEL
1200 N Mittel Blvd
(708) 860-2900
3-story hotel off I-290 in
Chancellory Business Park

Indiana

*I*ndiana is classic Middle America. From its geography of rolling farmland and well kept small towns to its sustaining economy of heavy manufacturing allied with agriculture, the state is a microcosm of much of the nation's midsection.

Located right in the middle of the state, **Indianapolis** is both capital and big city. Midwestern pride has helped to establish Indianapolis as a city of commerce, culture, and class. This is the home not just of the Indianapolis Museum of Art, renowned for its magnificent collections, but also of the Children's Museum of Indianapolis, acclaimed as one of the finest and largest museums of its type in the world. You can also tour the Benjamin Harrison Home, the residence of America's 23rd president, and see the Indianapolis Motor Speedway, built in 1909, which annually hosts an American institution, the Indy 500.

Indiana's second biggest city, **Fort Wayne**, boasts one of the country's largest rose gardens as well as an outstanding museum devoted to the life of Abraham Lincoln.

Indiana is justifiably proud of the many major educational institutions that make their home in the state. **South Bend** is synonymous with Notre Dame, one of America's greatest schools of higher learning, while Indiana University has been a vital part of **Bloomington** since its founding in 1820. Not to be outdone, **Muncie** plays host to Ball State University, another classic institution.

Other notable Indiana landmarks include the resort community of **La Porte**, the historic city of **Lafayette** (site of Tippecanoe Battlefield), and the geologically significant town of **Clarksville**, famous for its prehistoric fossil beds and coral formations in the Ohio River.

Bloomington

$ COMFORT INN
1722 N Walnut St
(812) 339-1919
4-story motel near
Indiana University

[icons]

$$$ HOLIDAY INN
1710 Kinser Pike
(812) 334-3252
4-story hotel next to
Indiana University and
near downtown

[icons]

$ RAMADA HOTEL
2601 N Walnut St
(812) 332-9453
Hotel near Indiana University

[icons]

Clarksville

$ HOWARD JOHNSON HOTEL
342 Eastern Blvd
(812) 282-7511 or
(800) 858-8937
Hotel off I-65 2 miles
north of Louisville with
luxury level rooms

[icons]

Fort Wayne

$ DAYS INN EAST
3730 E Washington Blvd
(219) 424-1980
Motel on US 24
(excluding Labor Day
weekend and Dec 31)

[icons]

$$$ FORT WAYNE MARRIOTT
305 E Washington Center Rd
(219) 484-0411
6-story hotel off I-69

[icons]

Indianapolis

$$$ ADAM'S MARK HOTEL
2544 Executive Dr
(317) 248-2481
6-story hotel off I-465
near airport

[icons]

$$ BEST WESTERN INDIANAPOLIS EAST
2141 N Post Rd
(317) 897-2000
Hotel off I-465

[icons]

$ ECONO LODGE EAST
4326 Sellers St
(317) 542-1031
Motel off I-465 (discount
on double rooms only)

[icons]

$$ HO JO INN SPEEDWAY
2602 N High School Rd
(317) 291-8800
Motel off I-74 and I-465

[icons]

$$$ INDIANAPOLIS MARRIOTT
7202 E 21st St
(317) 352-1231 or
(800) 228-9290
5-story hotel off I-70 and
I-465 with luxury level rooms
(excluding Indy 500 and
Brickyard 400 events)

[icons]

$$ NORTH MERIDIAN INN
1530 N Meridian
(317) 634-6100
Motel off I-65
(excluding Indy 500 weekend)

$$$ OMNI NORTH HOTEL
8181 N Shadeland Ave
(317) 849-6668 or
(800) THE-OMNI
6-story hotel off I-69
(excluding Mar 29-Apr 2 and
May 24-27 and Dec 31)

$$ QUALITY INN EAST
3525 N Shadeland Ave
(317) 549-2222
Hotel off I-465
(excluding Indy 500 weekend)

$$$ RADISSON PLAZA AND
SUITE HOTEL
8787 Keystone Crossing
(317) 846-2700
12-story hotel off I-465 next
to Fashion Mall shopping center (excluding May 22-24)

$$$ RAMADA INDIANAPOLIS
AIRPORT
2500 S High School Rd
(317) 244-3361 or
(800) 272-6232
6-story hotel off I-465
near airport

$$$ RAMADA INN SOUTH
4514 S Emerson Ave
(317) 787-3344
Hotel off I-465, some
rooms have fireplaces
(excluding Indy 500 and
Brickyard 400 events)

$$$ WYNDHAM GARDEN
HOTEL
251 E Pennsylvania Pkwy
(317) 574-4600
6-story hotel off I-465

Lafayette

$$ DAYS INN
400 Sagamore Pkwy S
(317) 447-4131
Hotel off I-65

La Porte

$$$ HOLIDAY INN
444 Pine Lake Ave
(219) 362-4585
4-story hotel near downtown
on US 35 (excluding Dec 31)

$$ MIDWAY MOTOR LODGE
1838 W US 20
(219) 362-7321
Off I-80 and I-90

Muncie

$$ HOTEL ROBERTS
420 S High St
(317) 741-7777 or
(800) 447-1921
7-story 1921 hotel down-
town opposite Convention
Center with period furnish-
ings and luxury level rooms,
listed on National Register of
Historic Places

$ | **PITTENGER STUDENT CENTER HOTEL**
2000 University Ave
(317) 285-1555
Hotel on Ball State
University campus

New Albany

$$ | **HOLIDAY INN NORTHWEST**
411 W Spring St
(812) 945-2771 or
(800) 465-4329
5-story hotel off I-64
5 miles north of Louisville

Portage

$$ | **HOLIDAY INN**
6200 Melton Rd
(219) 762-5546
4-story hotel off I-94

South Bend

$$$ | **HOLIDAY INN DOWNTOWN**
213 W Washington St
(219) 232-3941
16-story downtown hotel
near Century Centre with
luxury level rooms

West Lafayette

$$$ | **HOLIDAY INN**
5600 State Rd 43N
(317) 567-2131
4-story hotel off I-65 near
Tippecanoe Battlefield

Iowa

*C*ontrary to popular opinion, there's a lot more to Iowa than mile upon mile of corn and soybean fields. Unquestionably, this is a heavily agricultural state, providing more than 20% of all America's corn production, but manufacturing actually brings in more income and Iowa's urban population is steadily increasing.

Nowhere is this dynamic commercial growth more evident than **Des Moines**, the state capital, which is now the world's third largest insurance center. The city is culturally rich, too, with well-regarded symphony and ballet companies as well as an excellent Art Center. But if agriculture is what interests you, be sure to visit Living History Farms, a fascinating 600-acre open-air farming museum.

Cedar Falls

$ **MARQUIS INN**
4711 University Ave
(319) 277-1412
Motel off US 63
near University of
Northern Iowa

Des Moines

$$ **BUDGET HOST INN**
7625 Hickman Rd
(515) 276-5401
Motel off I-35 and I-80

$$ **HOWARD JOHNSON**
4800 Merle Hay Rd
(515) 278-4755
5-story hotel off I-35
and I-80

Kansas

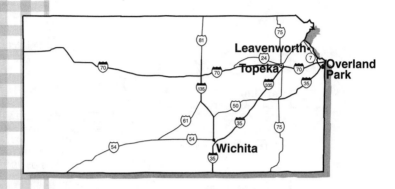

Kansas literally marks the midpoint of the contiguous United States. This central location is perfectly in keeping with the state's Middle American values and pioneering spirit. From the fertile prairieland in the east to the semi-arid high plains in the west, much of Kansas depends upon agriculture for its survival. The state leads the nation in wheat production and is the second largest producer of sorghum.

By far the biggest city in the state is **Wichita**, which has come a long way since its days as a rowdy cow town in the second half of the 19th century. Now the city relies on its huge aircraft industry, in addition to meat packing and oil refining. Wichita has also made great cultural strides, thanks in part to its magnificent Center for the Arts, which houses several galleries, a theater stage, and much outdoor sculpture. Other sightseeing attractions include Sedgwick County Zoo, with

some 1,000 animals roaming more than 200 acres (don't miss the North American Prairie elevated boardwalk section), and the Old Cow Town Museum, which recalls Wichita's colorful past.

The capital city of **Topeka**, noted for its broad, tree-lined boulevards and abundance of lakes and public parks, has much to offer, including a handsome State House, a fascinating Museum of History, and a neuropsychiatric clinic and research facility, the Menninger Foundation, acclaimed as the finest in the country.

A Kansas trip should also feature visits to **Leavenworth**, where the story of the famous Fort is recounted at the Frontier Army Museum, and **Overland Park**, headquarters of the National Collegiate Athletic Association—you can see multimedia exhibits about all 21 NCAA sports at the Visitors Center.

Colby

$ | **BUDGET HOST INN**
1745 W 4th St
(913) 462-3338
Motel off US 24

🚫 ⛵ ✈ 🏠

Junction City

$ | **DAYS INN**
1024 S Washington St
(913) 762-2727
Motel off I-70

🍸 💻 🚫 ⛵ ⛵ 🏠

$$ | **LIBERTY INN**
1133 S Washington
(913) 238-1141
Motel off I-70

💻 🏠

Leavenworth

$ | **RAMADA INN**
101 S 3rd St
(913) 651-5500
Downtown hotel near
Convention Center

📶 🍸 🚫 ⛵ 🚌 🏠

Manhattan

$ | **DAYS INN**
1501 Tuttle Creek Blvd
(913) 539-5391
Motel off US 24 near
Kansas State University

💻 🚫 ⛵ 🏠

Overland Park

$$$ | **RESIDENCE INN BY MARRIOTT-KANSAS CITY**
6300 W 110th St
(913) 491-3333 or
(800) 331-3131
All-suite hotel off I-435

💻 🚫 ⛵ 🏋 🍴 🏠

Topeka

$$ | **TOPEKA PLAZA INN**
3802 S Topeka Blvd
(913) 266-8880 or
(800) 833-8033
Hotel off US 70

📶 🍸 🚫 ⛵ 🏠

Wichita

$$$ | **INN AT TALLGRASS**
2280 N Tara
(316) 684-3466
All-suite hotel off I-35,
most rooms have fireplaces

💻 ⛵ 🏋

$$$ | **RAMADA HOTEL AT BROADVIEW PLACE**
400 W Douglas
(316) 262-5000
Downtown 1922 hotel on
banks of Arkansas River next
to Convention Center with
concierge floor

📶 🍸 🚫 ⛵ 🚌 🏠

$$$ | **RESIDENCE INN BY MARRIOTT DOWNTOWN**
120 W Orme
(316) 263-1061 or
(800) 331-3131
All-suite downtown hotel near
Convention Center, most
rooms have fireplaces

💻 🚫 ⛵ 🏋 🍴 🚶 🏠

Kentucky

The pretty state of Kentucky is neatly divided into two distinctly different sections. The Appalachian Mountains dominate the eastern portion, cut through with deep gorges, such as the famed Cumberland Gap, that form narrow scenic valleys; coal mining serves as the principal economic activity. To the west lie the fertile low plains, known the world over as the bluegrass region, which support Kentucky's renowned thoroughbred industry. The southern part of these lowlands are riddled by an amazing collection of caves, including the world's longest, Mammoth Cave, which has now become a national park.

At the forefront of Kentucky's thoroughbred scene is **Louisville**, annual host to the most glittering event in America's horse racing calendar, the Derby. At Churchill Downs racetrack, the Kentucky Derby Museum presents exhibits and audio visual displays recounting the entire history and tradition of this classic race. The city has a lot more to offer than just horse racing, however. Not only does Louisville produce more than half of all the bourbon consumed around the world, but also it has a wonderful zoo and a magnificent science center.

Kentucky's other big city, **Lexington**, depends upon tobacco and horses for its livelihood. Of particular interest are the American Saddle Horse Museum and the Kentucky Horse Park, which both showcase the state's equine heritage.

The capital city of **Frankfort** is noted for its profusion of historically and architecturally interesting buildings, while the southern Kentucky town of **Bowling Green** features a unique museum devoted to one of America's favorite cars, the Corvette.

Bowling Green

$$ **HOWARD JOHNSON HOTEL**
523 US 31 W Bypass
(502) 842-9453
Hotel off I-65 near
downtown and Western
Kentucky University

Corbin

$$ **HOLIDAY INN**
2615 Cumberland Falls Hwy
(606) 528-6301
Hotel off I-75 on hilltop

Florence

$$$ **COMMONWEALTH HILTON**
7373 Turfway Rd
(606) 371-4400
5-story hotel off I-75 and I-71
with concierge section of rooms

Frankfort

$$ **HOLIDAY INN CAPITAL PLAZA**
405 Wilkinson Blvd
(502) 227-5100
10-story downtown hotel
in Capital Plaza complex
next to Convention Center
and near Capitol

Lexington

$$$ **HILTON SUITES OF LEXINGTON GREEN**
3195 Nicholasville Rd
(606) 271-4000 or
(800) 367-4754
6-story all-suite hotel on US 27
next to the Mall at Lexington
Green shopping center

$$$ **RADISSON PLAZA LEXINGTON**
369 W Vine St
(606) 231-9000
22-story downtown hotel
in Vine Center complex

Louisville

$$$ **BRECKINRIDGE INN HOTEL**
2800 Breckinridge Ln
(502) 456-5050
Hotel off I-264
(excluding Derby Week)

$$ **HOLIDAY INN SOUTHWEST**
4110 Dixie Hwy
(502) 448-2020
6-story hotel off I-264
(excluding Dec 31)

Madisonville

$$ **DAYS INN**
1900 Lantaff Blvd
(502) 821-8620
Hotel off US 41

Louisiana

A wonderful amalgam of many different cultures make Louisiana one of America's most colorful states. Its most celebrated inhabitants are the Cajuns, descendants of French-speaking Acadians who migrated to the area from Nova Scotia, but a dynamic impact has also been made by the Creoles, descended from French and Spanish settlers.

Several major rivers, including the mighty Mississippi, make their way south through the lowlands that cover most of the state to a mass of bayous, marshes, and swamps, eventually draining into the Gulf. Louisiana summers are hot and steamy, just like the gumbo for which the state is famous.

New Orleans, one of America's truly unique cities, is a natural melting pot for Louisiana's polyglot cultures. The best place to experience this glorious diversity is the French Quarter, the 70 beautifully preserved downtown blocks that made up the original settlement. Although Mardi Gras is *the* time to visit, this teeming throng of restaurants, antique shops, nightclubs, and bars is vibrant and colorful every day of the year. New Orleans also has a lovely Garden District, a fine Museum of Art, and a first-rate zoo, as well as being the home of the huge Superdome.

Be sure to make a trip to the state capital of **Baton Rouge**, too. One of the country's most important ports, it is much celebrated for its fine antebellum mansions and plantations and old and new capitol buildings.

Two other essential Louisiana destinations are **Lafayette**, a major Acadian community and center of the Gulf oil and gas industry, and **New Iberia**, a city with a strong French and Spanish flavor that is famous for its magnificent Live Oak Gardens.

Baton Rouge

$$ COMFORT INN UNIVERSITY CENTER
2445 S Acadian Thruway
(504) 927-5790
4-story motel off I-10
(excluding Aug 9-14)

$$ HOWARD JOHNSON PLAZA SUITES
2045 N 3rd St
(504) 344-6000 or
(800) 487-8157
4-story all-suite downtown
hotel near Convention
Center and Capitol

Kenner

$$$ QUALITY INN AIRPORT
1021 Airline Hwy
(504) 464-1644 or
(800) 333-8278
4-story hotel off I-10
opposite New Orleans airport

Lafayette

$$ QUALITY INN
1605 N University Ave
(318) 232-6131 or
(800) 752-2682
Motel off I-10

$ RODEWAY INN
1801 NW Evangeline Thrwy
(318) 233-5500 or
(800) 535-5344
Hotel off I-10 next to
Northgate Mall shopping center

Metairie

$$ BEST WESTERN LANDMARK HOTEL
2601 Severn Ave
(504) 888-9500 or
(800) 277-7575
16-story hotel off I-10
with luxury level rooms

$$ HOWARD JOHNSON HOTEL AND CONFERENCE CENTER
2261 N Causeway Blvd
(504) 833-8211
10-story hotel off I-10

$$$$ SHERATON NEW ORLEANS NORTH
3838 N Causeway Blvd
(504) 836-5253
6-story hotel off I-10 on
Lake Pontchartrain with
luxury level rooms

New Iberia

$$ HOLIDAY INN NEW IBERIA
2915 Hwy 14
(318) 367-1201
Hotel off US 90 near
downtown (excluding May 6)

New Orleans

$$$ CLARION HOTEL
1500 Canal St
(504) 522-4500 or
(800) 824-3359
15-story 1925 downtown
hotel near French Quarter,
listed on National Register of
Historic Places

$$$$ DOUBLETREE HOTEL
300 Canal St
(504) 581-1300
17-story downtown hotel
near French Quarter with
penthouse suite, some
rooms have views of
Mississippi River

$$$ FAIRMONT HOTEL
123 Baronne St at University Pl
(504) 529-7111
Downtown hotel
near French Quarter
(excluding Mardi Gras
and Dec 31)

$$$$ NEW ORLEANS MARRIOTT
555 Canal St
(504) 581-1000 or
(800) 228-9290
41-story downtown hotel
near French Quarter and
Convention Center with
luxury level rooms

$$ QUALITY INN MIDTOWN
3900 Tulane Ave
(504) 486-5541
4-story hotel off I-10

St. Francisville

$$$ RAMADA ST. FRANCIS
US 61 and State Hwy 10,
(504) 635-3821
Lakeside hotel next to
Rosedown Plantation and
Gardens

Maine

For many, Maine is the perfect place to escape to, be it during the cold months, when snow blankets the state, producing an outdoor winter sports bonanza, or during the warm months, when cooling breezes moderate the heat, allowing all of its beauty and grandeur to be appreciated in the most relaxing of conditions.

An overwhelmingly rural state, Maine does not have any big cities, although **Portland** is both a busy port and a lively arts center with many tourist attractions. The capital, **Augusta**, is noted for its government buildings and museums, while **Bangor** functions as the cultural and commercial center for the northern portion of the state.

Bangor

Augusta

Portland

Augusta

| $$$ | **HOLIDAY INN CIVIC CENTER** |

110 Community Dr
(207) 622-4751 or
(800) 694-6404
Hotel off I-95
next to Civic Center

Bangor

| $$ | **PHENIX INN** |

20 Broad St
W Market Sq
(207) 947-3850
4-story 1873 B&B inn

South Portland

| $$$$ | **PORTLAND MARRIOTT AT SABLE OAKS** |

200 Sable Oaks Dr
(207) 871-8000 or
(800) 228-9290
6-story hotel off I-95

| $$$$ | **SHERATON TARA HOTEL** |

363 Maine Mall Rd
(207) 775-6161
9-story hotel
(excluding Dec 31)

Maryland

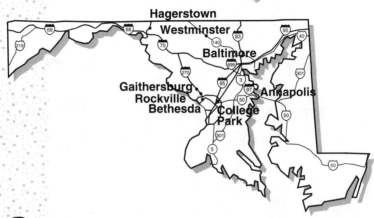

Often referred to as "America in miniature," Maryland is surprisingly varied for a state so small. Long and thin, it extends from the Allegheny Mountains in the west through the rolling piedmont of the center to the coastal plains in the east. Maryland also boasts an amazingly long coastline, courtesy of the Chesapeake Bay, which isolates the sublimely rural Eastern Shore from the more cosmopolitan remainder of the state.

Holding sway over Maryland's commercial and cultural destiny is the state's biggest city, **Baltimore**. The place has undergone something of a Renaissance in recent years, with the development of the stunning new Inner Harbor, which numbers the National Aquarium, the Maryland Science Center, and the World Trade Center among its many attractions. An old-line city with a proud past, Baltimore also offers two exceptionally fine art galleries (Walters and Baltimore Museum of Art), the country's most comprehensive railroad museum (B&O), and a much acclaimed new baseball stadium (Oriole Park at Camden Yards).

Boating enthusiasts will want to head to **Annapolis**, Maryland's capital, gateway to the Eastern Shore, and home of the U.S. Naval Academy since 1845. Historic houses abound in a city that traces its origins back to 1694.

The past is also much celebrated in two other vintage Maryland communities: **Hagerstown**, the chief town in the rural western portion of the state, and **Westminster**, an agricultural center with a fine farming museum.

Many of Washington's most attractive northern suburbs are located in Maryland, namely **Bethesda** (home to the National Institutes of Health), **Rockville**, **Gaithersburg**, and **College Park** (site of the University of Maryland).

Aberdeen

SHERATON INN
$$$
980 Beards Hill Rd
(410) 273-6300
Hotel off I-95

Annapolis

HOLIDAY INN ANNAPOLIS
$$$
210 Holiday Ct
(410) 224-3150
6-story hotel off
US 50 and US 301

WYNDHAM GARDEN HOTEL
$$$
173 Jennifer Rd
(410) 266-3131
6-story hotel opposite
Annapolis Mall shopping center

Baltimore

BALTIMORE MARRIOTT INNER HARBOR
$$$$
Pratt and Eutaw Sts
(410) 962-0202 or
(800) 228-9290
10-story downtown
hotel opposite Oriole Park
at Camden Yards and
near Inner Harbor

BROOKSHIRE INNER HARBOR SUITE HOTEL
$$$$
120 E Lombard St
(410) 625-1300 or
(800) 647-0013
14-story all-suite downtown
hotel near Inner Harbor
(excluding Dec 31)

CROSS KEYS INN
$$$
5100 Falls Rd
(410) 532-6900 or
(800) 532-KEYS
4-story hotel off I-83 in
Village of Cross Keys complex

HOLIDAY INN EXPRESS
$$
1401 Bloomfield Ave
(410) 646-1700
4-story hotel off I-95
(excluding Dec 31)

LATHAM HOTEL
$$$$
612 Cathedral St
(410) 727-7101
13-story downtown hotel in
19th-century building on historic Mount Vernon Square
(excluding Dec 31)

RADISSON PLAZA LORD BALTIMORE HOTEL
$$$
20 W Baltimore St
(410) 539-8400
23-story 1928 downtown
hotel in Charles Center
complex near Inner Harbor
and Convention Center,
has luxury level rooms

Bethesda

HOLIDAY INN BETHESDA
$$$
8120 Wisconsin Ave
(301) 652-2000
15-story hotel off
I-270 and I-495

$$$$ **RESIDENCE INN BY MARRIOTT**
7335 Wisconsin Ave
(301) 718-0200 or
(800) 331-3131
13-story all-suite downtown
hotel off I-270 and I-495,
most suites have fireplaces

Camp Springs

$$ **HOLIDAY INN**
4783 Allentown Rd
(301) 420-2800
3-story hotel off I-95/
I-495 opposite
Andrews Air Force Base

Cheverly

$$ **HOWARD JOHNSON HOTEL**
5811 Annapolis Rd
(301) 779-7700
5-story hotel off
Baltimore-Washington Pkwy

Clinton

$ **ECONO LODGE**
7851 Malcolm Rd
(301) 856-2800
Motel off I-95/I-495

College Park

$$ **DAYS INN**
9137 Baltimore Ave
(301) 345-5000 or
(800) 329-7466
Hotel off I-95/I-495 near
University of Maryland

$$ **HOLIDAY INN**
10000 Baltimore Blvd
(301) 345-6700 or
(800) 872-5564
4-story hotel off I-95/I-495
near University of Maryland

$$ **PARK VIEW INN**
9020 Baltimore Blvd
(301) 441-8110
Hotel off I-95/I-495 near
University of Maryland

$$$ **QUALITY INN**
7200 Baltimore Blvd
(301) 864-5820
4-story motel off I-95/I-495
near University of Maryland

$$ **ROYAL PINE INN**
9113 Baltimore Blvd
(301) 345-4900 or
(800) 660-5162
Motel off I-95/I-495 near
University of Maryland

Columbia

$$$ **COLUMBIA HILTON**
5485 Twin Knolls Rd
(410) 997-1060
4-story hotel off US 29

Gaithersburg

$$$ **HOLIDAY INN GAITHERSBURG**
2 Montgomery Village Ave
(301) 948-8900
8-story hotel off I-270

Germantown

$$$ RAMADA INN AND SUITES
20260 Goldenrod Ln
(301) 428-1300
Hotel off I-270 near
business district

Glen Burnie

$$$ HOLIDAY INN
6323 Ritchie Hwy
(410) 636-4300
4-story hotel off I-695

$$ HOLIDAY INN SOUTH
6600 Ritchie Hwy
(410) 761-8300
3-story hotel off I-695

Grantsville

$$ HOLIDAY INN
I-68 and US 219 N
(301) 895-5993
4-story hotel off I-68

Hagerstown

$ WELLESLEY INN
1101 Dual Hwy
(301) 733-2700
4-story hotel off I-70
near downtown

Hanover

**$$ HOLIDAY INN EXPRESS
BWI AIRPORT**
7481 New Ridge Rd
(410) 684-3388
5-story hotel off Baltimore-
Washington Pkwy

**$$ RAMADA HOTEL
BWI AIRPORT**
7253 Parkway Dr
(410) 712-4300
Hotel off Baltimore-
Washington Pkwy

Langley Park

$$ HAMPSHIRE INN
7411 New Hampshire Ave
(301) 439-3000
Hotel off I-495

Laurel

$$$ COMFORT SUITES
14402 Laurel Pl
(301) 206-2600 or
(800) 628-7760
5-story all-suite hotel off
I-95 next to Laurel Lakes Mall
shopping center

Linthicum

**$$$$ GUEST QUARTERS SUITE
HOTEL**
1300 Concourse Dr
(410) 850-0747
8-story all-suite hotel off I-295

McHenry

$$$ **WISP RESORT HOTEL**
Star Rte 2, Box 35
(301) 387-5581 or
(800) 462-9477
7-story resort hotel off
I-68 near Deep Creek Lake

Pikesville

$$$ **HOLIDAY INN PIKESVILLE**
1721 Reisterstown Rd
(410) 486-5600
Hotel off I-695 on US 140

$$$ **PIKESVILLE HILTON INN**
1726 Reisterstown Rd
(410) 653-1100 or
(800) 283-0333
Hotel off I-695 on US 140

Rockville

$$$ **POTOMAC INN**
3 Research Ct
(301) 840-0200
Hotel off I-270
with jogging track

$$$ **RAMADA INN**
1775 Rockville Pike
(301) 881-2300 or
(800) 255-1775
7-story hotel off I-495
with art deco design and
executive level rooms

Timonium

$$$ **HOLIDAY INN TIMONIUM**
2004 Green Spring Dr
(410) 252-7373
Hotel off I-83 near
Timonium Fairgrounds

Towson

$$ **HOLIDAY INN-**
TOWSON HOTEL
1100 Cromwell Bridge Rd
(410) 823-4410
6-story hotel off I-695

$$$ **SHERATON BALTIMORE**
NORTH
903 Dulaney Valley Rd
(410) 321-7400
12-story downtown hotel off
I-695 next to Towson Town
Center shopping center

Westminster

$ **DAYS INN**
25 S Cranberry Rd
(410) 857-0500
3-story motel near
Western Maryland College

Massachusetts

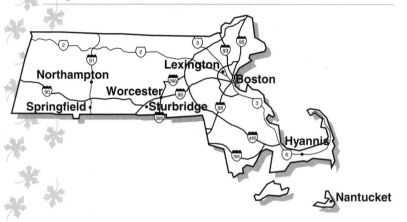

*One of the most densely populated states in the country, Massachusetts has also enjoyed more than its fair share of history. From the landing of the Pilgrims at Plymouth Rock in 1620 to the inauguration of native son John F. Kennedy as U.S. President in 1960, a rich panoply of famous events has enlivened this beautiful corner of America.

Nowhere is this glorious sense of history more evident than **Boston**, founded in 1630 and capital not just of Massachusetts but also of the entire New England region. Today the city reveres its most famous landmarks, such as Faneuil Hall ("the cradle of liberty"), the Old State House, Paul Revere's House, and Old North Church. A walk through downtown Boston is a walk back in time. Nicknamed the "Athens of America," the city abounds in cultural diversions, of which the Museum of Fine Arts, the Kennedy Library, and the Boston Symphony Orchestra (famous for its "Pops" concerts) are the most noteworthy.

Bostonians, like most visitors, seek to escape the heat and grind of big city life by flocking to Cape Cod, the state's summer playground. Among the most popular destinations are **Hyannis**, with its enormous beaches, and the island resort of **Nantucket**.

History comes alive at **Lexington**, site of the Common on which the first blood of the Revolutionary War was spilt, and **Sturbridge**, with its engaging re-creation of an 1830s' New England village.

Other recommended stops in Massachusetts include **Springfield**, where the Basketball Hall of Fame celebrates that this was where "hoops" originated; **Worcester**, famous for its fine art museum; and **Northampton**, the handsome home of Smith College.

Boston

$$$ **TREMONT HOUSE HOTEL**
275 Tremont St
(617) 426-1400 or
(800) 331-9998
15-story 1925 downtown
hotel next to Shubert Theatre
(reservations must be made
within 7 days of arrival)

Braintree

$$$$ **SHERATON TARA HOTEL**
37 Forbes Rd
(617) 848-0600
Hotel off I-93 opposite South
Shore Plaza shopping center
with luxury level rooms

Burlington

$$$ **DAYS INN**
30 Wheeler Rd
(617) 272-8800
4-story hotel off I-95 next to
Burlington Mall shopping center

Holyoke

$$$ **HOLIDAY INN HOLIDOME**
245 Whiting Farms Rd
(413) 534-3311
4-story hotel off I-91 and I-
90 near Mt Tom ski area and
Holyoke Mall shopping center,
has concierge level rooms

Hyannis

$$$ **CAPE CODDER HOTEL**
1225 Iyannough
(508) 771-3000
Hotel near beach

$$$$ **TARA HYANNIS HOTEL**
West End Cir
(508) 775-7775
Downtown resort
hotel near beach

Lawrence

$$ **HAMPTON INN**
224 Winthrop Ave
(508) 975-4050
5-story motel off I-495

Lexington

$$$ **BATTLE GREEN INN**
1720 Massachusetts Ave
(617) 862-6100 or
(800) 343-0235
Hotel off I-95 in historic area

$$$ **SHERATON TARA LEXINGTON INN**
727 Marrett Rd
(617) 862-8700
3-story hotel off I-95
near historic area

Nantucket Island

$$$ NANTUCKET BREEZE CONDOMINIUMS
133 Old South Rd
(508) 228-4889
Condominium hotel near beach (reservations must be made within 2 weeks of arrival)

Needham

$$$ SHERATON NEEDHAM HOTEL
100 Cabot St
(617) 444-1110
5-story hilltop hotel off I-95 with luxury level rooms

Newton

$$$$ SHERATON TARA HOTEL
320 Washington St
(617) 969-3010
12-story hotel off I-90 in Gateway Center (discount on double deluxe rooms only)

Randolph

$$$ HOLIDAY INN
1374 N Main St
(617) 961-1000
4-story hotel off I-93

Saugus

$$$ DAYS INN LOGAN AIRPORT
999 Broadway
(617) 233-1800
4-story motel on US 1 in Stone Hill Corporate Center

Seekonk

$$$ JOHNSON AND WALES INN
213 Taunton Ave
(508) 336-8700 or
(800) 537-8483
3-story hotel on US 44 run by Johnson and Wales University

Shrewsbury

$$ DAYS INN
889 Boston Tpk
(508) 842-8500 or
(800) 548-0058
Hotel off I-495

Springfield

$$$ HOLIDAY INN
711 Dwight St
(413) 781-0900
12-story downtown hotel off I-91 and I-291 near Civic Center

$$$ SHERATON TARA AT MONARCH PLACE
1 Monarch Pl
(413) 781-1010
12-story downtown hotel off I-91 near Basketball Hall of Fame

Sturbridge

$$ **CARRIAGE HOUSE INN**
358 Main St
(508) 347-9000
Motel off I-84 and I-90
near Old Sturbridge Village

🔲 🚫 🏊 🏠

$$$ **STURBRIDGE HOST HOTEL**
366 Main St
(508) 347-7393 or
(800) 582-3232
3-story hotel off I-84 and I-90

📺 🍽 🚫 🏊 👤 🍴
🚶 🐾

Tewksbury

$$$ **RESIDENCE INN BY MARRIOTT**
1775 Andover St
(508) 640-1003
3-story all-suite hotel off I-495,
some rooms have fireplaces

🔲 🚫 🏊 👤 🍴 🚶 🐾

Wakefield

$$$ **COLONIAL HILTON AND RESORT**
1 Audubon Rd
(617) 245-9300
11-story 220-acre
resort hotel off I-95

📺 🍽 🚫 🏊 👤 🍴 🚶
🚭 🚌

Waltham

$$$$ **GUEST QUARTERS SUITE HOTEL**
550 Winter St
(617) 890-6767 or
(800) 424-2900
8-story all-suite hotel off I-95

📺 🍽 🚫 🏊 👤 🍴

Westin Hotel

$$$$ **WESTIN HOTEL**
70 3rd Ave
(617) 290-5626
8-story hotel off I-95

📺 🍽 🚫 🏊 👤 🍴 🚌

$$$$ **WYNDHAM GARDEN HOTEL**
420 Totten Pond Rd
(617) 890-0100
Hotel off I-95

📺 🍽 🚫 🏊

West Springfield

$$$ **RAMADA HOTEL**
1080 Riverdale St
(413) 781-8750
Hotel off I-91

📺 🍽 🚫 🏊 👤 🐾 🏠

Westboro

$$ **RAMADA INN-WESTBORO**
399 Turnpike Rd
(508) 366-0202
Motel off I-495

📺 🍽 🚫 🏠

Woburn

$$$ **DAYS INN**
19 Commerce Way
(617) 935-7110
5-story hotel off I-95

📺 🍽 🔲 🚫 🏊 👤
🚌 🏠

Worcester

$$ **HAMPTON INN**
110 Summer St
(508) 757-0400
5-story downtown motel off
I-290 near Worcester Centrum

🔲 🚫 🏠

Michigan

$\mathcal{M}$uch celebrated as the home of the American automobile industry, as well as being an important center for all kinds of other heavy industry, Michigan is nevertheless a surprisingly rural state, ranking first in the nation in the production of cherries, cranberries, navy beans, and cucumbers. With four of the Great Lakes defining Michigan's shoreline, four national forests blanketing a considerable portions of the state, and a host of rivers and lakes making their serene mark on the countryside, both Michigan's Lower and Upper Peninsulas have become tourist havens.

Detroit, the state's biggest city, has come a long way since Henry Ford established it as the car capital of the world in the 1920s. The city is now a dynamic cultural center, responsible for the famous Motown sound of the 1960s, and the construction of the Renaissance Center has helped spur the revitalization of the downtown area. Among the many attractions worth sampling are the Detroit Institute of Arts, the Detroit Zoo, and the Henry Ford Museum in neighboring **Dearborn**, which along with the delightful Greenfield Village highlights more than 300 years of technological and cultural change in America.

Michigan's capital city, **Lansing**, is also dominated by the automobile industry, as a visit to the R.E. Olds Transportation Museum will show; and the same is true for **Flint**, the birthplace of General Motors (see the special exhibit at the outstanding Sloan Museum), and for friendly **Saginaw**, with its colorful parks, historic buildings, and beautiful riverfront. Also of interest is **Traverse City**, a scenic resort town famous for its cherries and wineries.

Auburn Hills

$$$ HOLIDAY INN
1500 Opdyke Rd
(810) 373-4550
8-story hotel off I-75
near Pontiac Silverdome
and Palace of Auburn Hills

🕪 🍸 🚭 🛏 🛏 🍴

Bay City

**$$$ BAY VALLEY RESORT
HOTEL**
2470 Old Bridge Rd
(517) 686-3500 or
(800) 292-5028
470-acre resort hotel off
I-75 (excluding Dec 31)

🕪 🚭 🛏 🛏 🍴 🐾 🚶
🚌 🏠

Birmingham

$$$ BARCLAY INN
145 S Hunter Blvd
(810) 646-7300 or
(800) 521-3509
5-story motel

🛏 🚭 🏠

Bloomfield Hills

**$$ HOLIDAY INN OF
BLOOMFIELD HILLS**
1801 S Telegraph Rd
(810) 334-2444
Hotel off I-75
1 mile south of Pontiac

🕪 🍸 🛏 🚭 🛏 🏠

$$$ KINGSLEY INN
1475 N Woodward Ave
(810) 644-1400 or
(800) KI-HOTEL
3-story hotel
(excluding Dec 31)

🕪 🍸 🛏 🚭 🛏 🛏
🍴 🏠

Dearborn

**$$$ DEARBORN INN AND
MARRIOTT HOTEL**
20301 Oakwood Blvd
(313) 271-2700
4-story 23-acre hotel off
US 24 near Henry Ford
Museum, includes 5
Colonial-style cottages

🕪 🍸 🛏 🚭 🛏 🌲 🍴

$$ KNIGHTS COURT
23730 Michigan Ave
(313) 565-7250 or
(800) 255-3050
Hotel on US 12 near
Henry Ford Museum

🕪 🛏 🚭 🛏 🛏 ✈ 🐾

Detroit

**$$$ DETROIT METRO
AIRPORT MARRIOTT**
Detroit Metropolitan Airport
(313) 941-9400 or
(800) 228-9290
6-story hotel between
airport terminals with
luxury level rooms

🕪 🍸 🚭 🛏 🌲 🚌 🏠

$$$ HOTEL ST. REGIS
3071 W Grand Blvd
(313) 873-3000 or
(800) 848-4810
7-story downtown
hotel off I-94

🕪 🍸 🛏 🚭 🍴 🏠

$$$ PONTCHARTRAIN HOTEL
2 Washington Blvd
(313) 965-0200
Downtown hotel on site
of Detroit's first permanent
settlement (1701)

$$$$ RIVER PLACE
1000 River Pl
(313) 259-9500 or
(800) 890-9505
5-story 1901 downtown
hotel on banks of Detroit
River near Renaissance Center
with luxury level rooms and
croquet court

**$$$$ WESTIN HOTEL
RENAISSANCE CENTER**
Renaissance Center
(313) 568-8000
70-story hotel in Renaissance
Center overlooking Detroit
River with luxury level rooms

Farmington Hills

$$$ HOLIDAY INN
38123 W Ten Mile Rd
(810) 477-4000
5-story hotel off I-96 and
I-275 with concierge level
rooms (excluding Dec 31)

$$$ RADISSON SUITE
37529 Grand River Ave
(810) 477-7800
4-story all-suite hotel off I-96
and I-275 (discount unavail-
able on upgraded suites)

Flint

$$ DAYS INN FLINT
2207 W Bristol Rd
(810) 239-4681
Hotel off I-75 near airport

Inkster

$ WHITE HOUSE INN
26121 Michigan Ave
(313) 565-6410
2-story motel near
Telegraph Road

Lansing

**$$ HOLIDAY INN LANSING
CONFERENCE CENTER**
7501 W Saginaw Hwy
(517) 627-3211
3-story hotel off I-96

$$$ HOLIDAY INN SOUTH
6820 S Cedar St
(517) 694-8144
3-story hotel off I-96 (discount on standard rooms only)

$$$ QUALITY SUITES
901 Delta Commerce Dr
(517) 886-0600 or
(800) 456-6431
4-story all-suite hotel off I-96
near Lansing Mall shopping
center (excluding Dec 31)

Livonia

$$ RAMADA INN
30375 Plymouth Rd
(313) 261-6800
Motel off I-96 near
Ladbroke Detroit racetrack
(excluding Dec 31)

🚪 🍸 🚭 🏊 🛗

Madison Heights

$$$ RESIDENCE INN BY MARRIOTT
32650 Stephenson Hwy
(810) 583-4322
All-suite motel off I-75 near
Oakland Mall shopping center
(discount on studio suites only)

🍸 🚭 🏊 🛗 🚶 🐾

Novi

$$$ NOVI HILTON
21111 Haggerty Rd
(810) 349-4000
7-story hotel
off I-96 and I-275

🚪 🍸 🚭 🏊 🛗 🍽 🐾

$$$ SHERATON INN
27000 Sheraton Dr
(810) 348-5000 or
(800) 833-OAKS
3-story hotel off I-96
opposite 12 Oaks shopping
center (excluding Dec 31)

🚪 🍸 🚭 🏊 🏊 🛗

$$$ WYNDHAM GARDEN HOTEL
42100 Crescent Blvd
(810) 344-8800
Hotel off I-96 opposite
12 Oaks shopping center

🚪 🍸 🚭 🏊 🛗 🍽

Romulus

$$$ WYNDHAM GARDEN HOTEL-DETROIT METRO AIRPORT
8600 Merriman Rd
(313) 728-7900
Hotel off I-94 near airport

🚪 🍸 🏊 🍽

Saginaw

$$ BEST WESTERN SAGINAW
3325 Davenport Ave
(517) 793-2080
2-story motel

🚪 🍸 🚭 🏊 🐾

$$ HOLIDAY INN SAGINAW
1408 S Outer Dr
(517) 755-0461
4-story hotel off I-75
near downtown

🚪 🍸 🚭 🏊 🛗 🍽 ✈
🚌 🐾

$$ PRINCESS INN
400 Johnson St
(517) 755-1161 or
(800) 669-1499
Hotel off I-675
opposite Convention Center
and Civic Center

🚪 🍸 📺 🚭 🏊 🛗 🚌

$$$ SHERATON INN-FASHION SQUARE
4960 Towne Centre Rd
(517) 790-5050
6-story hotel off I-675
near Fashion Square Mall
shopping center

🚪 🍸 🚭 🏊 🏊 🛗
🚌 🐾

Southfield

$$$ HOLIDAY INN SOUTHFIELD
26555 Telegraph Rd
(810) 353-7700
5-story hotel off I-696
on US 24 with monkey bar
gym for children

▯ ⏝ ⊘ ⛱ ⛴ ⛽ ✗ ⌂

$$$ PLAZA HOTEL
16400 JL Hudson Dr
(810) 559-6500 or
(800) 800-5112
14-story hotel in
Northland shopping center

▯ ⏝ ⊘ ⛱ ⛴ ⛽ ✗

**$$$ SOUTHFIELD HILTON
GARDEN INN**
26000 American Dr
(810) 357-1100
7-story hotel off US 10

▯ ⏝ ⊘ ⛱ ⛽ ✗ ⌂

$$ SOUTHFIELD TRAVELODGE
27650 Northwestern Hwy
(810) 353-6777
Motel off I-696

▣ ⊘ ⛽ ⌂

Sturgis

$$ HOLIDAY INN
1300 S Centerville Rd
(616) 651-7881
Hotel off US 12

▯ ⏝ ⊘ ⛱ ✈ P

Traverse City

$$$ HOLIDAY INN
615 E Front St
(616) 947-3700 or
(800) 888-8020
4-story downtown hotel off
US 31 on Grand Traverse Bay

▯ ⏝ ⊘ ⛱ ⛴ ⛽ ✗
✈ ⛌ ⌂

Troy

**$$$$ GUEST QUARTERS SUITE
HOTEL**
850 Tower Dr
(810) 879-7500
8-story all-suite hotel off I-75

▯ ⏝ ⊘ ⛱ ⛽ ✗

$$$ NORTHFIELD HILTON
5500 Crooks Rd
(810) 879-2100
3-story hotel off I-75

▯ ⏝ ▣ ⊘ ⛱ ⌂

Walloon Lake

**$$$ SPRINGBROOK HILLS
RESORT**
(616) 535-2227
Condominium hotel
off US 131, all condos
have fireplaces

⛱ ✗

Warren

**$$$ VAN DYKE PARK HOTEL
AND CONFERENCE CENTER**
31800 Van Dyke Ave
(810) 939-2860
5-story hotel off I-696
opposite GM Tech Center

▯ ⏝ ⊘ ⛱ ⛽ ✗

Minnesota

s all the state license plates proudly proclaim, Minnesota is "The Land of 10,000 Lakes." In fact, the state has more than 12,000 lakes, alone, that exceed 10 acres in size. And Minnesota is also the source of the Mississippi River, which quickly assumes mighty proportions, as well as both the Red and St. Lawrence rivers, so it's not hard to see why the state is a haven for boating, canoeing, swimming, water skiing, and fishing, not to mention ice skating and, of course, Minnesota's favorite pastime, ice fishing.

The twin cities of Minneapolis and St. Paul, sitting across from each other on opposite banks of the Mississippi, dominate the state. They are not identical twins, however. **St. Paul**, Minnesota's capital, is smaller and more rooted in the past, as the city's many stately old structures, such as the Cathedral, City Hall, and

Capitol, all testify to.

In contrast, **Minneapolis** is larger and more modern, the home of such nationally recognized institutions as the Minnesota Zoo, the Walker Art Center, and the Guthrie Theater.

Each city, however, delights in defying Minnesota's harsh winters. St. Paul actually celebrates the fact by holding its annual Winter Carnival, but both cities continue to bustle thanks to an enclosed and elevated system of walkways known as the Skyway.

Not far from the Twin Cities is **Bloomington**, where the Mall of America, the biggest retail and entertainment complex in the country, has proven to be a Mecca for shoppers and their families.

Anyone remotely interested in medicine will also want to make a pilgrimage to **Rochester**, birthplace of the internationally renowned Mayo Clinic.

Arden Hills

$$ **RAMADA NORTH HOTEL**
1201 W County Rd E
(612) 636-4123 or
(800) 777-2232
4-story hotel off I-694

Bloomington

$$$$ **WYNDHAM GARDEN HOTEL**
4460 W 78th St Cir
(612) 831-3131
8-story hotel off I-494

Brooklyn Center

$$ **PARK INN INTERNATIONAL**
1501 Freeway Blvd
(612) 566-4140
Hotel off I-94 and I-694

Brooklyn Park

$$ **BEST WESTERN NORTHWEST INN**
6900 Lakeland Blvd
(612) 566-8855
Hotel off I-94 (excl Dec 31)

Crookston

$ **NORTHLAND INN**
2200 University Ave
(218) 281-5210 or
(800) 423-7541
Motel off US 2 and US 75
near University of Minnesota

Eagan

$$$ **RESIDENCE INN BY MARRIOTT**
3040 Eagandale Pl
(612) 688-0363 or
(800) 331-3131
All-suite motel off I-35 near
Lone Oak Plaza shopping center, most suites have fireplaces

Eden Prairie

$$$ **RESIDENCE INN BY MARRIOTT-SOUTHWEST**
7780 Flying Cloud Dr
(612) 829-0033 or
(800) 331-3131
All-suite motel off I-494, most
suites have fireplaces (discount
on studio suites only)

Hill City

$$$ **QUADNA MOUNTAIN RESORT**
Hill City
(218) 697-8444
1,400-acre lakeside resort
hotel 18 miles south
of Grand Rapids

Minneapolis

$$$ **HOLIDAY INN CROWNE PLAZA NORTHSTAR**
618 2nd Ave S
(612) 338-2288 or
(800) 556-STAR
17-story downtown hotel
near Metrodome (discount
on double room rate only)

$$$$ HOLIDAY INN METRODOME
1500 Washington Ave S
(612) 333-4646 or
(800) 448-DOME (in MN)
14-story downtown hotel
overlooking Mississippi River
near Metrodome

$$$$ HOTEL LUXEFORD SUITES
1101 LaSalle Ave S
(612) 332-6800 or
(800) 662-3232
12-story all-suite
downtown hotel near
Convention Center and
Nicollet Mall shopping center

$$$ HOTEL NORMANDY
405 S 8th St
(612) 370-1400 or
(800) 372-3131
4-story downtown hotel
near Metrodome

$$$ RADISSON HOTEL METRODOME
615 Washington Ave SE
(612) 379-8888 or
(800) 822-MPLS
8-story hotel off I-94 on
University of Minnesota campus

$$$ RADISSON HOTEL SOUTH AND PLAZA TOWER
7800 Normandale Blvd
(612) 835-7800
22-story hotel off I-494

$$$ SHERATON MINNEAPOLIS METRODOME
1330 Industrial Blvd
(612) 331-1900 or
(800) 777-3277
8-story hotel off I-35

Minnetonka

$$$ RAMADA PLAZA HOTEL
12201 Ridgedale Dr
(612) 593-0000
4-story hotel off I-394 opposite Ridgedale shopping center

Monticello

$$$ RIVERWOOD HOTEL
10990 95th St NE
(612) 441-6833
40-acre hotel
off I-94 on Mississippi River
wooded bluffs

Plymouth

$$ DAYS INN WEST
2955 Empire Ln
(612) 559-2400
4-story motel off I-494

Rochester

$$$ KAHLER HOTEL
20 2nd Ave SW
(507) 282-2581 or
(800) 533-1655
12-story downtown hotel
opposite Mayo Clinic and
near Galleria shopping center,
has luxury level rooms

$$$ **RADISSON PLAZA**
150 S Broadway
(507) 281-8000
11-story downtown hotel
near Mayo Clinic and
Galleria shopping center
with luxury level rooms

Roseville

$$ **COMFORT INN**
2715 Long Lake Rd
(612) 636-5800
6-story motel off I-35
(excluding State Fair
and Dec 31)

St. Paul

$$$ **RADISSON HOTEL ST. PAUL**
11 E Kellogg Blvd
(612) 292-1900
22-story downtown hotel
near World Trade Center
and Ordway Theater

Mississippi

*N*amed after the mighty river that winds its way south to form the western boundary of this predominantly rural state, Mississippi features all the trappings of the Deep South—sprawling antebellum mansions, endless fields of cotton, and large stands of pine forest mixed in with cypress swamps.

Signs of the Civil War are everywhere. At **Tupelo**, for instance, you can tour the battlefield where Union forces repulsed Nathan Bedford Forrest's famous attack; and you can also see the house, now a museum, where "the King of Rock 'n' Roll," Elvis Presley, was born in 1935.

Columbus is noted for its more than 100 beautifully preserved antebellum homes, while **Meridian** has one of the country's oldest carousels.

Columbus

$$	**RAMADA INN** 1200 Hwy 45 N (601) 327-7077 4-story hotel on US 45

Meridian

$$	**DAYS INN** 145 Hwy 11 and 80 E (601) 483-3812 Hotel off I-20 and I-59 near downtown

Tupelo

$$	**HOLIDAY INN EXPRESS** 923 N Gloster St (601) 842-8811 or (800) 800-6891 Hotel off US 78 and US 45 near downtown

$	**TRACE INN** 3400 W Main St (601) 842-5555 3-story motel off US 78 and US 45 near down- town (excluding every 3rd week in Feb and Aug)

Missouri

*T*wo great rivers dominate the state of Missouri: the Mississippi, which defines its eastern border and sustains many of its liveliest communities, and the Missouri, which separates the plains and prairie of the north from the Ozark highlands of the south.

The point at which the Mississippi and the Missouri meet marks the site of the state's biggest city, **St. Louis**, which for many years served as the "Gateway to the West" for all those seeking to extend the American frontier—an event that is commemorated by the Gateway Arch, St. Louis' most visible landmark. Another city icon is nearby Busch Stadium, the ballpark built by America's most famous brewery. At Forest Park, visitors can explore both the St. Louis Art Museum and the St. Louis Zoo, although enough time should also be left to take in the spectacular Missouri Botanical Garden and the St. Louis Science Center.

On the other side of the state, the equally cosmopolitan **Kansas City** has its own set of charms. Here can be seen the country's first shopping center, Country Club Plaza, a stunning Italianate mix of fountains, statues, and tilework, as well as the famed Nelson-Atkins Museum of Art and two quite unusual museums, one devoted to antique dollhouses and the other to a steamboat recently unearthed and excavated from the Missouri River.

Other highlights around the state include **Branson**, the Ozark setting for an amazing collection of theaters showcasing country music; **Columbia**, home of the University of Missouri; the state capital of **Jefferson City**, renowned for its historic river landing; and **Springfield**, site of the celebrated Bass Pro Shops Outdoor World and the Fantastic Caverns, which do indeed live up to their name.

Branson

$$ **BRANSON TOWERS HOTEL**
236 Shepherd of the Hills
Expwy
(417) 336-4500
3-story hotel off US 65
next to Mel Tillis and
Shenandoah South theaters
and near Shoji Tabuchi,
Glen Campbell, Charlie Pride,
and Will Rogers theaters

$$$ **RESIDENCE INN BY MARRIOTT**
280 Wildwood Dr S
(417) 336-4077 or
(800) 331-3131
3-story all-suite hotel off US
76, most suites have fireplaces

Bridgeton

$$ **EXECUTIVE INTERNATIONAL INN**
4530 N Lindbergh Blvd
(314) 731-3800 or
(800) 325-4850
Hotel off I-70 near
St. Louis International Airport

$$ **HOLIDAY INN AIRPORT NORTH**
4545 N Lindbergh Blvd
(314) 731-2100
4-story hotel off I-70
with luxury level rooms

Holiday Inn Airport West

$$ **HOLIDAY INN AIRPORT WEST**
3551 Pennridge Dr
(314) 291-5100 or
(800) 325-1395
4-story hotel off I-270 and I-70

Chesterfield

$$$ **DOUBLETREE HOTEL AND CONFERENCE CENTER**
16625 Swingley Ridge Dr
(314) 532-5000
12-story hotel off US 40 with
luxury level rooms and basketball and volleyball courts

Clayton

$$ **HOLIDAY INN-CLAYTON PLAZA**
7730 Bonhomme Ave
(314) 863-0400
16-story hotel off US 40

Columbia

$$ **BUDGET HOST INN**
900 Vandiver Dr
(314) 449-1065
Motel off I-70

$$ **GUESTHOUSE INN**
801 Keene St
(314) 474-1408
Motel off I-70 opposite
Columbia Regional Hospital

Frontenac

$$$ FRONTENAC HILTON
1335 S Lindbergh Blvd
(314) 993-1100 or
(800) 325-7800
3-story hotel off I-64
with luxury level rooms

🛏 🍸 🚭 🏊 💆 🍽 🚌

Jefferson City

$$ DAYS HOTEL
422 Monroe St
(314) 636-5101
Multistory hotel
near State Capitol

🛏 🚭 🏊 🚌 🛗

$$$ HOTEL DE VILLE
319 W Miller St
(314) 636-5231
3-story hotel off
US 50 near State Capitol

🛏 🍸 🚭 🏊 🛗

Joplin

$$ WESTWOOD MOTEL
1700 W 30th St
(417) 782-7212
Motel off I-44 next to
St. John's Medical Center

🚭 🏊 🛗

Kansas City

$$$ DOUBLETREE HOTEL
KANSAS CITY AIRPORT
8801 NW 112th St
(816) 891-8900
11-story hotel off I-29

🛏 🍸 🚭 🏊 🏊 💆 🍽
🏃 🚌 🛗

$$$ HOLIDAY INN-KCI
11832 Plaza Cir NW
(816) 464-2345
5-story hotel off I-29
with sand volleyball court

🛏 🍸 🚭 🏊 💆 🍽
🚌 🛗

$$$ KANSAS CITY AIRPORT
MARRIOTT
775 Brasilia Ave
(816) 464-2200 or
(800) 228-9290
9-story lakefront hotel off
I-29 with luxury level rooms

🛏 🍸 🚭 🏊 💆 🍽 ✈
🚌 🛗

$$$ RADISSON SUITE HOTEL
106 W 12th St
(816) 221-7000
20-story restored 1931
downtown hotel off I-70
next to Convention Center,
has luxury level rooms

🛏 🍸 🖥 🚭 🍽 🛗

$$ RAMADA HOTEL-KCI
7301 NW Tiffany Springs Rd
(816) 741-9500 or
(800) 234-9501
11-story hotel off I-29

🛏 🍸 🚭 🏊 💆 🍽
🚌 🛗

$$$ RESIDENCE INN BY
MARRIOTT-KCI
9900 NW Prairie View Rd
(816) 891-9009
All-suite hotel off I-29, many
suites have fireplaces (discount on studio suites only)

🖥 🚭 🏊 💆 🍽 ✈
🚌 🛗

SHERATON SUITES COUNTRY CLUB PLAZA
770 W 47th St
(816) 931-4400
18-story all-suite hotel
at Country Club Plaza

Maryland Heights

$$ BEST WESTERN WESTPORT PARK
2434 Old Dorsett Rd
(314) 291-8700
4-story hotel off I-70 and
I-270 (excluding Dec 31)

Osage Beach

$$$ MARINA BAY RESORT AND LAKESIDE CONFERENCE CENTER
Lake Rd 54-30A
(314) 348-2200
Resort hotel with its own
marina on Grand Glaize
Peninsula near Osage Beach
Factory Outlet Mall, many
rooms have fireplaces

St. Louis

$$ BRIDGEPORT INN
4199 N Lindbergh Blvd
(314) 739-4600
Motel off I-70 near
St. Louis International Airport

$$$ DOUBLETREE CLUB HOTEL RIVERPORT
13735 Riverport Dr
(314) 298-3400
5-story hotel

$$$$ DOUBLETREE DOWNTOWN
806 St Charles St
(314) 421-2500 or
(800) THE-OMNI
18-story all-suite downtown
hotel near Convention Center,
Busch Stadium, and Gateway
Arch with luxury level rooms

$$$ EMBASSY SUITES
901 N 1st St
(314) 241-4200 or
(800) 241-5151
All-suite hotel on
Laclede's Landing near
Gateway Arch, Busch Stadium,
and Convention Center

$$$ HOLIDAY INN DOWNTOWN/RIVERFRONT
200 N 4th St
(314) 621-8200 or
(800) 925-1395
29-story downtown hotel
off I-70 opposite Gateway Arch
and near Busch Stadium and
Convention Center (excluding
Jul 2-6)

$$$ HOLIDAY INN-FOREST PARK
5915 Wilson Ave
(314) 645-0700
7-story hotel off I-44 near
St. Louis Art Museum and Zoo
(excluding Jul 4 and Dec 31)

QUALITY HOTEL $$$
9600 Natural Bridge Rd
(314) 427-7600
7-story hotel
off I-29 near airport

REGAL RIVERFRONT HOTEL $$$
200 S 4th St
(314) 241-9500 or
(800) 325-7353
Downtown hotel near
Gateway Arch, Busch
Stadium, and Convention
Center (excluding VP Fair
Weekend)

RESIDENCE INN BY $$$
MARRIOTT-WESTPORT
1881 Craigshire Rd
(314) 469-0060 or
(800) 331-3131
All-suite hotel off I-270

ST. LOUIS AIRPORT HILTON $$$
10330 Natural Bridge Rd
(314) 426-5500
7-story hotel off I-29
opposite airport with
luxury level rooms

STOUFFER CONCOURSE $$$
HOTEL
9801 Natural Bridge Rd
(314) 429-1100
Hotel off I-29 near airport
with luxury level rooms

Springfield

COURTYARD BY MARRIOTT $$
3370 E Battlefield Rd
(417) 883-6200
Motel off US 65 with
basketball court

Montana

With almost three-quarters of the state carpeted by the rolling grasslands of the Great Plains, it's not difficult to see how Montana received its "Big Sky" sobriquet. However, the western portion of the state presents a dramatic contrast: the towering peaks of the Bitterroot Range of the Rocky Mountains, home of Glacier National Park.

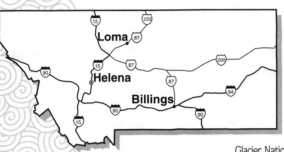

Billings, Montana's biggest city, is the gateway to Yellowstone National Park as well as the Little Bighorn Battlefield. It's a city of rodeos, livestock shows, country fairs, and museums devoted to America's western heritage.

At **Loma**, you can see where Lewis and Clark discovered the confluence of the Missouri and Marias rivers.

Billings

$$$ **RADISSON NORTHERN HOTEL**
1st Ave N and Broadway
(406) 245-5121
1904 downtown hotel

$$$ **SHERATON HOTEL**
27 N 27th St
(406) 252-7400
23-story downtown hotel

Loma

$ **ROSE RIVER INN**
101 Wood's Beach Rd
(406) 739-4242
Motel on banks of Marias River near Fort Benton

Nebraska

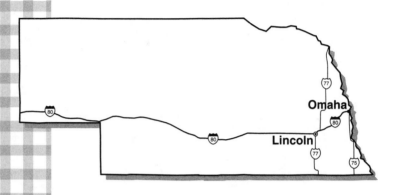

Such is the fertility of Nebraska's soil that more native grasses grow there than any other state in the country. Not surprisingly, agriculture and livestock continue to dominate Nebraska's economy, just as the state's sprawling plains, undulating sand hills, and rocky buttes still dominate the land as they did when Western pioneers blazed the Oregon and Overland Trails through what was then the territory of Nebraska in the 1840s and 1850s.

No Nebraskan city epitomizes the pioneer spirit more than **Omaha**, which owes its very existence to westward expansion, having been first settled in 1854 as a supply point for those headed toward the California gold fields. Nicknamed the "Crossroads of the Nation," Omaha remains one of the country's most important livestock markets and meat packing centers. Today, however, the city has diversified its commercial appeal to become a major insurance and banking center as well as the site of the U.S. Air Force's Strategic Command. In addition, Omaha is the home of the fashionable Joslyn Art Museum, the acclaimed Henry Doorly Zoo, and the country's largest community theatre, the Omaha Playhouse.

The state's capital, **Lincoln**, also grew out of frontier roots, but it, too, has blossomed into a lively, cosmopolitan city. Any trip to Lincoln should include visits to the Museum of Nebraska History, with a fascinating exhibit on the Plains Indians; the State Capitol, notably modern in its architectural appearance; a museum uniquely devoted to the history and practice of roller skating; and the University of Nebraska, with a museum containing one of the world's finest exhibits about elephants, both ancient and modern, as well as an outstanding performing arts center.

Lincoln

$$$ HOLIDAY INN LINCOLN AIRPORT
1101 W Bond St
(402) 475-4971
Hotel off I-80

🔲 🍸 🚭 🛏 ✈ 🚌

$$$ HOLIDAY INN NORTHEAST
5250 Cornhusker Hwy
(402) 464-3171
Hotel on US 6 and 77
near Wesleyan University

🔲 🍸 🚭 🛏 🛁 🍴

$ RAMADA INN
2301 NW 12th St
(402) 475-4400
Hotel off I-80 near airport

🔲 🍸 🚭 🛏 🍴 ✈
🚌 🛎

$$ VILLAGER MOTOR INN
5200 "O" St
(402) 464-9111
Hotel next to Cooper Theatre

🔲 🍸 🚭 🛏 🛁 🚌 🛎

Omaha

$$ DAYS INN
7101 Grover St
(402) 391-5757
Multistory hotel off I-80
near Ak-Sar-Ben racetrack

🔲 🚭 🛎 P

$$$ OMAHA MARRIOTT
10220 Regency Cir
(402) 399-9000 or
(800) 228-9290
6-story hotel off I-680 in
Regency Office Park complex
with executive level rooms

🔲 🍸 🚭 🛏 🛁 🛁
🍴 🛎

$$$ RAMADA HOTEL CENTRAL
7007 Grover St
(402) 397-7030
9-story hotel off I-80
near Ak-Sar-Ben racetrack

🍸 🚭 🛏 🛁 🍴 🚌 🛎

Nevada

Reno
80
395
50
50
Carson City
95

Las Vegas
15
95

lthough the sheer expanse of Nevada makes it one of the country's largest states, it is also one of the most sparsely populated, a testament to the fact that some 85 percent of the land is given over to animal grazing, mineral mining, national parkland, military testing, and Indian reservations.

However, while the vast majority of Nevada continues to be a virtual wilderness to the visitor, the rest of the state is undergoing booming times, stemming back to the legalization of gambling in 1931. Leading the way, not surprisingly, is **Las Vegas**, Nevada's biggest and brashest city. Once an oasis in the middle of the desert, the place is now a teeming metropolis of casinos, hotels, theaters, theme parks, and other big city attractions that operates 24 hours day and night. The major scene of all this frenetic activity is Las Vegas Boulevard,

more commonly known as the Strip. Among the glitter, many highlights abound, including a re-creation of the Emerald City from **The Wizard of Oz** at the MGM Grand Hotel, a replica of King Tut's tomb at the massive pyramid-shaped Luxor Hotel, a "staged" battle involving a British pirate ship at the Treasure Island Hotel, and a truly amazing show by famed animal illusionists Siegfried and Roy at the Mirage Hotel.

The atmosphere is a little more restrained in **Reno**, Las Vegas' counterpart to the north in the Sierra Nevada Mountains. Gamblers can take advantage of a varied array of casinos, but there are many other attractions to investigate: Pyramid Lake, the largest natural body of water in the state; the National Automobile Museum, with more than 200 vintage cars on display; and the Fleischmann Planetarium, designed by Frank Lloyd Wright.

Las Vegas

Reno

$$$$ **HOLIDAY INN CROWNE PLAZA**
4255 S Paradise Rd
(702) 369-4400
6-story all-suite hotel
off I-15 near the Strip
with luxury level rooms

$$$ **QUALITY INN HOTEL AND CASINO**
377 E Flamingo Rd
(702) 733-7777 or
(800) 634-6617
Hotel and casino
near Convention Center
and the Strip

$$$ **AIRPORT PLAZA HOTEL**
1981 Terminal Way
(702) 348-6370 or
(800) 648-3525
3-story hotel and casino off
US 395 and US 580 opposite
airport, some rooms have
fireplaces (discount on
deluxe rooms only)

$$ **HOLIDAY HOTEL CASINO**
111 Mill St
(702) 329-0411 or
(800) 648-5431
8-story downtown hotel
and casino on banks of
Truckee River, some rooms
have fireplaces

$$$ **RENO HILTON**
2500 E 2nd St
(702) 789-2000 or
(800) 648-5080
28-story hotel and
casino with theater
and comedy club off
I-80 near airport

New Hampshire

Although a mere 200 miles in length, from north to south, New Hampshire provides some of the country's most breathtakingly beautiful scenery. The White Mountains, which dominate most of the state, are broken by a series of idyllic passes and gaps, quaintly referred to as "notches" by the locals. The mountains give way to rolling foothills and valleys as the land sweeps majestically down to the Atlantic Ocean, producing the typical New England countryside of clapboard houses, village greens, and tiny farms.

The most populous portion of the state is the Merrimack Valley in the south, which has become an extension of suburban Boston. From the picturesque little community of **Bedford**, it's a short two-mile drive to Manchester, New Hampshire's principal city and cultural capital. Be sure to tour the Currier Gallery of Art, with its outstanding collection housed in an impressive Italianate building; nearby is the Zimmerman House, designed by Frank Lloyd Wright. Manchester, and its near neighbor, **Nashua**, function as the industrial heart of New Hampshire.

Moving north, you pass through the pretty village of **Jaffrey**, with its distinctive white clapboard meeting house built in 1773. Nearby Monadnock Mountain inspired Ralph Waldo Emerson to write his famous poem "Monadnoc."

For sheer grandeur, however, continue on to **North Conway**, nestled in the White Mountains, with magnificent views of mighty Mount Washington. Visitors are attracted to the Conway Scenic Railroad, offering a wonderful hour-long ride through the pristine Mount Washington Valley, as well as all the factory outlet stores on Main Street and an array of local crafts and varied artistic offerings.

Bedford

$$$$ **SHERATON TARA WAYFARER INN**
121 S River Rd
(603) 622-3766
3-story hotel of US 3
(discount on double
deluxe rooms only)

Bradford

$$ **BRADFORD INN**
11 W Main St
(603) 938-5309
Country inn off I-89,
originally an 1870s
stagecoach stop

Jaffrey

$$$ **WOODBOUND INN**
62 Woodbound Rd
(603) 532-8341 or
(800) 688-7770
3-story 200-acre 1880s'
lakeside country inn with cottages off US 202, all cottages
have fireplaces

Nashua

$$ **HOLIDAY INN**
9 Northeastern Blvd
(603) 888-1551
4-story hotel off US 3
near downtown

$$$ **SHERATON TARA HOTEL**
Tara Blvd
(603) 888-9970
7-story Tudor-style hotel
off US 3 with luxury level
rooms and racquetball court
(discount on double deluxe
rooms only)

North Conway

$$$ **EASTERN SLOPE INN RESORT**
Main St, Box 359
(603) 356-6321 or
(800) 258-4708
15-acre 1926 country inn
at base of New Hampshire's
tallest peak

$$$ **GREEN GRANITE MOTEL**
PO Box 3127
(603) 356-6901
Motel off US 302
with barbecue area

New Jersey

New Jersey is a thoroughly deceiving state. For most visitors traveling on any of its many interstates, freeways, or turnpikes, New Jersey must seem like a remorseless bastion of heavy industry, yet much of the state is actually composed of woodland, rolling green hills, and pine marshes. Not for nothing is New Jersey known as the Garden State. However, given its small size and large population, New Jersey remains the most densely populated state in the nation.

Newark, the state's biggest city, was first settled in 1666 and has grown into a major port and commercial center. By far the most impressive building in a city of many historic structures is the Catholic Cathedral, a Gothic masterpiece with more than 200 stained glass windows.

The state is rich in Revolutionary War associations. At **Morristown**, a National Historical Park celebrates the place where George Washington established his military headquarters in 1777 and again from 1779 to 1780. You can see one of his forts, the Continental Army's winter camp, and a museum and library with many exhibits on the military campaign. At nearby **Plainfield**, the house where Washington often stayed has been preserved by the local historical society.

Princeton also boasts a state battlefield park commemorating its Revolutionary War encounter, although today the town is more famous as the site of one of America's most prestigious universities. Another top caliber university, Rutgers, is located just outside **East Brunswick**.

For a complete change of pace, go to **Absecon**, close not only to the gambling resort of Atlantic City but also to the state's unique coastal pine barrens.

Absecon

$$$ COMFORT INN NORTH
405 E Absecon Blvd
(609) 646-5000
Hotel on US 30 on Absecon
Bay with free shuttle service
to Atlantic City casinos

$$$$ MARRIOTT'S SEAVIEW RESORT
401 S New York Rd
(609) 748-1990
4-story 670-acre 1912
resort hotel on US 9

Cherry Hill

$$$ RESIDENCE INN BY MARRIOTT
1821 Old Cuthbert Rd
(609) 429-6111 or
(800) 331-3131
All-suite motel off I-295,
most suites have fireplaces

$$$ SHERATON INN
1450 Rt 70 E
(609) 428-2300 or
(800) 257-8262
4-story hotel off I-295
near Garden State racetrack

Clark

$$$ RAMADA HOTEL
36 Valley Rd
(908) 574-0100
4-story hotel off
Garden State Pkwy
(excluding Dec 31)

Clifton

$$$ HOWARD JOHNSON
680 Rt 3 W
(201) 471-3800
4-story hotel off
Garden State Pkwy

$$$ RAMADA INN
265 Rt 3 E
(201) 778-6500 or
(800) 772-2816
4-story hotel off
Garden State Pkwy

East Brunswick

$$$ SHERATON INN
195 Rt 18
(908) 828-6900 or
(800) 688-4536
4-story hotel off NJ Tpk

East Hanover

$$$ RAMADA HOTEL
130 Rt 10 W
(201) 386-5622
5-story hotel off I-287

Elizabeth

$$$ HOLIDAY INN JETPORT
1000 Spring St
(908) 355-1700
10-story hotel off NJ Tpk
opposite Newark Airport
with luxury level rooms

$$$ **SHERATON NEWARK AIRPORT**
901 Spring St
(908) 527-1600
9-story hotel off
NJ Tpk near Newark Airport

Englewood

$$$ **RADISSON HOTEL**
401 S Van Brunt St
(201) 871-2020
9-story hotel near Fairleigh
Dickinson University with
luxury level rooms

Fairfield

$$$ **BEST WESTERN FAIRFIELD EXECUTIVE INN**
216-234 Rt 46 E
(201) 575-7700
4-story hotel off I-80

$$$$ **RADISSON HOTEL AND SUITES**
690 Rt 46 E
(201) 227-9200
5-story hotel off I-80

$$$ **RAMADA INN**
38 Two Bridges Rd
(201) 575-1742
Hotel off I-80 near
Willowbrook shopping center

Hazlet

$$ **WELLESLEY INN**
3215 Hwy 35 N
(908) 888-2800
3-story motel off
Garden State Pkwy

Iselin

$$$ **WOODBRIDGE HILTON**
120 Wood Ave S
(908) 494-6200
11-story hotel off Garden
State Pkwy with racquetball
court (excluding Dec 31)

Lawrenceville

$$ **HOWARD JOHNSON**
2991 Brunswick Pk
(609) 896-1100
Motel off I-295

Mahwah

$$$ **RAMADA INN**
180 Rt 17 S
(201) 529-5880
4-story hotel off I-87

$$$ **SHERATON INTERNATIONAL CROSSROADS**
1 International Blvd
(201) 529-1660
22-story hotel off I-87 at
base of Ramapo Mountains,
has luxury level rooms

Montvale

$$$ MONTVALE RAMADA INN
100 Chestnut Ridge Rd
(201) 391-7700
3-story hotel off Garden
State Pkwy with luxury level
rooms (max 3-night stay)

Morristown

$$$ HEADQUARTERS PLAZA HOTEL
3 Headquarters Plaza
(201) 898-9100 or
(800) 225-1942
16-story hotel off I-287 in
shopping/entertainment complex with luxury level rooms

$$$$ MADISON HOTEL
1 Convent Rd and Rt 124
(201) 285-1800 or
(800) 526-0729
4-story Georgian-style hotel
off I-287 with luxury level
rooms (excluding Dec 31)

Mt. Arlington

$$$ SHERATON MT. ARLINGTON
15 Howard Blvd
(201) 770-2000
5-story hotel off I-80
near Delaware Water Gap

Newark

$$$ HILTON GATEWAY HOTEL
Gateway Center-
Raymond Blvd
(201) 622-5000
15-story hotel off NJ Tpk

$$$ HOLIDAY INN NORTH
160 Holiday Plaza
(201) 589-1000
10-story hotel off
NJ Tpk near airport

$$$ NEWARK AIRPORT MARRIOTT HOTEL
Newark International Airport
(201) 623-0006 or
(800) 228-9290
10-story hotel off NJ Tpk

Paramus

$$$ RADISSON INN
601 From Rd
(201) 262-6900
Hotel off Garden State Pkwy
next to Paramus Park shopping
center, has volleyball courts

Parsippany

$$$ HOLIDAY INN
707 Rt 46 E
(201) 263-2000
4-story motel off I-80

Penns Grove

$$ **HOWARD JOHNSON**
10 Howard Johnson Ln
(609) 299-3800
Motel off NJ Tpk

Phillipsburg

$$ **HOWARD JOHNSON LODGE**
1315 Rt 22 W
(908) 454-6461
Motel on US 22 off I-78

Piscataway

$$$$ **WYNDHAM GARDEN HOTEL**
21 Kings Bridge Rd
(908) 980-0400
Near I-287

Plainfield

$$$ **THE PILLARS B AND B**
922 Central Ave
(908) 753-0922
Victorian B&B in Van Wyck
Brooks historic area

Princeton

$$$$ **THE SCANTICON-PRINCETON CONFERENCE CENTER AND HOTEL**
100 College Rd E
(609) 452-7800 or
(800) 222-1131
4-story 25-acre hotel off
US 1 (excluding May 23-30
and Dec 31)

Ramsey

$$ **WELLESLEY INN**
946 Rt 17 N
(201) 934-9250
3-story motel

Rochelle Park

$$ **RAMADA INN**
375 W Passaic St
(201) 845-3400
5-story hotel
off Garden State Pkwy

Rockaway

$$ **HOWARD JOHNSON**
14 Green Pond Rd
(201) 625-1200
Motel off I-80

Saddle Brook

$$$ **HOLIDAY INN AND CONFERENCE CENTER**
50 Kenney Pl
(201) 843-0600
12-story hotel off I-80
and Garden State Pkwy

$$$ **HOWARD JOHNSON PLAZA HOTEL**
129 Pehle Ave
(201) 845-7800
8-story hotel off I-80
and Garden State Pkwy
with luxury level rooms

Secaucus

$$$ COURTYARD BY MARRIOTT HOTEL
455 Harmon Meadow Blvd
(201) 617-8888
7-story hotel off NJ Tpk
near Meadowlands sports
complex and racetrack
(excluding Dec 31)

$$$ HOLIDAY INN HARMON MEADOWS
300 Plaza Dr
(201) 348-2000
8-story hotel off NJ Tpk
and I-95 in Harmon Meadow
shopping complex near
Meadowlands sports complex
and racetrack,

Somerset

$$$ HOLIDAY INN
195 Davidson Ave
(908) 356-1700 or
(800) 922-0645
6-story hotel off I-287

$$$ RAMADA INN OF SOMERSET
Weston Canal Rd and Rt 287
(908) 560-9880
5-story hotel off I-287

Summit

$$$ GRAND SUMMIT HOTEL
570 Springfield Ave
(908) 273-3000 or
(800) 223-1588
4-story Tudor-style hotel, all
rooms have four-poster beds

Tinton Falls

$$$ RESIDENCE INN BY MARRIOTT
90 Park Rd
(908) 389-8100 or
(800) 331-3131
All suite motel off Garden
State Pkwy near Monmouth
racetrack, many suites have
fireplaces

Wayne

$$ HOWARD JOHNSON
1850 Rt 23 and Ratzer Rd
(201) 696-8050
Motel off I-80

Whippany

$$$ HOWARD JOHNSON
1255 Rt 10
(201) 539-8350
Motel off I-287

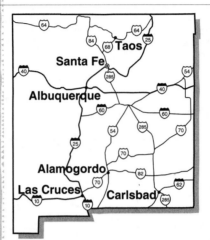

The scenery in New Mexico is as diverse as its peoples. Often likened to a colorful mosaic, the state comprises a fascinating collection of different cultures, including most prominently Native American, Spanish, and Anglo. To a landscape already highlighted by immense mesas, plunging canyons, dense forests, and towering mountains, these polyglot cultures have added their own distinctive marks—grandiose cliff dwellings, magnificent adobe buildings, and gleaming city skylines.

All three major cultures come together in **Albuquerque**, New Mexico's biggest city. Begin your exploration in the Old Town historic district, the Spanish heart of the city. Nearby, the Indian Pueblo Cultural Center has exhibits about the 19 tribes that first populated the area. Also worth visiting are the New Mexico Museum of Natural History,

Rio Grande Zoo, and the Sandia Peak Aerial Tramway, which takes riders on a spectacular trip to 10,000-foot Sandia Crest.

A strong sense of the past is also evident in **Las Cruces**, where you can clamber around an old frontier settlement (Fort Selden) and wander through a beautifully restored 19th-century Spanish community (Mesilla).

Taos offers yet more history: a picturesque pueblo—displaying a centuries old culture and a beautiful Plaza that still looks very much as it did well over 100 years ago.

A New Mexico itinerary should also include **Carlsbad**, home to a national park with one of the world's largest caves, and **Alamogordo**, site of the Space Center education and entertainment complex, as well as a massive crater where the first ever atomic bomb test took place.

Alamogordo

$$ BEST WESTERN DESERT AIRE MOTOR INN
1021 S White Sands Blvd
(505) 437-2110
Motel on US 54/US 70/
US 82 near downtown

Albuquerque

$$$ AMBERLY SUITE HOTEL
7620 Pan American Frwy NE
(505) 823-1300
3-story all-suite hotel off
I-25 (excluding Oct 1-11
and max 4-night stay)

$$ BEST WESTERN AIRPORT INN
2400 Yale Blvd SE
(505) 242-7022
Motel off I-25
(excluding Oct 1-15)

$$$ DOUBLETREE HOTEL ALBUQUERQUE
201 Marquette St NW
(505) 247-3344
16-story downtown hotel
off I-25 next to Convention
Center and near Old Town
(excluding Oct 5-15)

$$ HAMPTON INN
5101 Ellison NE
(505) 344-1555
3-story motel off I-25
(excluding International
Balloon Fiesta and max 5-
night stay)

$$$ LA POSADA DE ALBUQUERQUE
125 Second St NW
(505) 242-9090 or
(800) 777-5732
10-story 1939 downtown
hotel next to Convention
Center and near Old Town
with live jazz evenings, some
rooms have fireplaces
(excluding Oct 6-15)

$$ PLAZA INN ALBUQUERQUE
900 Medical Arts NE
(505) 243-5693 or
(800) 237-1307
5-story hotel off I-25 near
downtown and Convention
Center (max 5-night stay)

$$$ WYNDHAM GARDEN HOTEL
6000 Pan American Frwy NE
(505) 821-9451
Downtown hotel off I-25
with horseback riding nearby

Carlsbad

$$ QUALITY INN
3706 National Parks Hwy
(505) 887-2861
Hotel off US 62 and US 180

Las Cruces

$$ **BEST WESTERN MESILLA VALLEY INN**
901 Avenida de Mesilla
(505) 524-8603
Hotel off I-10 near
historic Mesilla and New
Mexico State University

$ **PLAZA SUITES**
301 E University Ave
(505) 525-5500 or
(800) 444-5250
All-suite hotel off I-10

Taos

$$$ **BEST WESTERN KACHINA LODGE**
413 N Paseo del Pueblo
(505) 758-2275 or
(800) 522-4462
Hotel on US 64 near Taos Plaza
and Taos Pueblo with Indian
dance performances daily

$$$ **HOLIDAY INN DON FERNANDO DE TAOS**
1005 Paseo del Pueblo Sur
(505) 758-4444 or
(800) 759-2736
Hotel off US 64 near Taos Plaza
with changing art displays,
some rooms have fireplaces

Tucumcari

$ **ECONOMY INN**
901 E Tucumcari Blvd
(505) 461-1340
Downtown motel on US 66

$ **RODEWAY INN EAST**
1023 E Tucumcari Blvd
(505) 461-0360
Motel on US 66 near
Convention Center

$$ **RODEWAY INN WEST**
1302 W Tucumcari Blvd
(505) 461-3140
Motel on US 66 near
Rodeo and Fairgrounds

New York

Lake Placid
Rochester
Buffalo
Syracuse
Albany
New York

Second only to California in terms of total population and industrial output, the state of New York ranks right at the top when it comes to cultural output, media and communications, and banking and commerce. The sheer diversity of the state makes it a big draw for visitors, whether it be the bright lights of the big city or the quiet serenity of a mountain lake.

At the very forefront of New York is its namesake city, one of the most cosmopolitan and exciting in the world. The nation's leading financial and artistic center, **New York** keeps up a frenetic pace for a full 24 hours each and every day of the year. Its major sights are almost too numerous to mention, although "must sees" include the Statue of Liberty, the Empire State Building, Central Park, the Metropolitan Museum of Art, St. Patrick's Cathedral, Lincoln Center for the Performing Arts, and the

American Museum of Natural History. Above all, New York is a city of neighborhoods—Greenwich Village, Soho, Wall Street, Chinatown, to name but a few—with some of the finest shopping anywhere on the globe.

The state capital of **Albany**, perched on the Hudson River, is dominated by Rockefeller Empire State Plaza, eight impressive blocks of government and cultural buildings.

Upstate New York is very different, with the Adirondack Mountains (site of **Lake Placid**) and the Finger Lakes providing wonderfully pastoral relief. Nevertheless, **Syracuse**, with its university and cultural pursuits, and **Rochester**, home to all kinds of scientific and technological endeavors, offer a full range of urban pleasures.

At the very western end of the state, **Buffalo** serves as the gateway to Niagara Falls, one of the great natural wonders of the world.

Albany

$$$ OMNI ALBANY HOTEL
State and Lodge Sts
(518) 462-6611
17-story downtown hotel at
Ten Eyck Plaza near State
Capitol and Rockefeller
Empire State Plaza

🕪 🍸 🚭 🛥 💪 🍽 🚌

Armonk

$$ RAMADA INN
94 Business Park Dr
(914) 273-9090
Hotel off I-684 in
Westchester Business Park

🕪 🍸 🖳 🚭 🛥 🍽 ✈
🚌 🎣

Batavia

**$$$ SHERATON INN AND
CONFERENCE CENTER**
8250 Park Rd
(716) 344-2100 or
(800) 323-5030 (NY)
5-story hotel off
NY State Thruway

🕪 🍸 🚭 🛥 🛥 💪
🍽 🎣

Binghamton

$$ HOJO INN
690 Old Front St
(607) 724-1341
Motel off I-81 near downtown

🚭 Ⓟ

$$$ HOLIDAY INN ARENA
2-8 Hawley St
(607) 722-1212
10-story downtown hotel
off I-81 on banks of
Chenango River

🕪 🍸 🚭 🛥 🛥 🍽 🚌 🎣

$$ RAMADA INN
65 Front St
(607) 724-2412
Downtown hotel off I-81
near Convention Center

🕪 🍸 🚭 🛥 💪 🎣

**$$ SUPER 8 UPPER COURT
STREET**
Rte 11, Upper Court St
(607) 775-3443
Motel off I-81 next to
Broome Industrial Park
(excluding Sats in May
and Oct)

🕪 🍸 🚭 🛥 💪 🚌 🎣

Brighton

**$$ WELLESLEY INN
ROCHESTER SOUTH**
797 E Henrietta Rd
(716) 427-0130
4-story motel off I-390

🖳 🚭 🎣

Buffalo

**$$$ BEST WESTERN INN
DOWNTOWN**
510 Delaware Ave
(716) 886-8333
5-story downtown motel
with luxury level rooms
(excluding Dec 31)

🚭 🍽

Cheektowaga

$$$ SHERATON INN BUFFALO AIRPORT
2040 Walden Ave
(716) 681-2400
8-story hotel off I-90 next to
Walden Galleria shopping center, has luxury level rooms

$$ WELLESLEY INN
4630 Genesee St
(716) 631-8966
4-story motel near Buffalo
International Airport

Colonie

$$$$ ALBANY MARRIOTT HOTEL
189 Wolf Rd
(518) 458-8444 or
(800) 228-9290
8-story hotel off I-87
near airport with luxury
level rooms

Cortland

$ DOWNES MOTEL
10 Church St
(607) 756-2856
Motel off I-81

East Elmhurst

$$$$ HOLIDAY INN CROWNE PLAZA
104-04 Ditmars Blvd
(718) 457-6300
7-story hotel opposite La
Guardia Airport and near Shea
Stadium, has luxury level rooms

East Syracuse

$$$ RESIDENCE INN BY MARRIOTT
6420 Yorktown Cir
(315) 432-4488 or
(800) 331-3131
All-suite motel off I-90

$$$$ SYRACUSE MARRIOTT HOTEL
6301 Rt 298
(315) 432-0200
7-story hotel off I-90
with luxury level rooms
(excluding Dec 31)

Elmsford

$$$ RAMADA INN
540 Saw Mill River Rd
(914) 592-3300
4-story hotel off I-287
with dinner theater

$$ SAW MILL RIVER MOTEL
25 Valley Ave
(914) 592-7500
Motel off I-287

Endicott

$$ BEST WESTERN HOMESTEAD INN
749 W Main St
(607) 754-1533
Motel off I-81

🔟 🍸 🚫 🛏 🏠

$ ENDICOTT INN
214 Washington Ave
(607) 754-6000
Hotel off I-81

🚫 🚌 🏠

$$ EXECUTIVE INN AND CONFERENCE CENTER
15 Delaware Ave
(607) 754-7570
Hotel off I-81

🔟 🍸 🚫 🏠

Fishkill

$$ WELLESLEY INN
2477 Route 9
(914) 896-4995
Off I-84

💻 🚫 🏠

Flushing

$$$$ SHERATON LAGUARDIA EAST HOTEL
135-20 39th Ave
(718) 460-6666
16-story hotel near US Tennis
Center and Shea Stadium

🔟 🍸 🚫 🍴 🚌

Fultonville

$$ THE POPLARS INN
Riverside Dr
(518) 853-4511
Motel on banks of Mohawk
River (excluding Dec 31)

🔟 🍸 🚫 🛌 P B

Glens Falls

$$ RAMADA INN
I-87 and Aviation Rd
(518) 793-7701
Hotel off I-87

🔟 🍸 🚫 🛌 🏠

Greece

$$$ MARRIOTT AIRPORT HOTEL
1890 W Ridge Rd
(716) 225-6880 or
(800) 228-9290
7-story hotel off I-390
with luxury level rooms

🚫 🛌 🍴 🏊 🚌 🏠

$$ WELLESLEY INN ROCHESTER NORTH
1635 W Ridge Rd
(716) 621-2060
4-story motel off I-390

🚫 ✈ 🏠

Henrietta

$$$$ ROCHESTER MARRIOTT THRUWAY
5257 W Henrietta Rd
(716) 359-1800 or
(800) 228-9290
5-story hotel off I-90 with
luxury level rooms

🔟 🍸 🚫 🍴 🍽 🚌

Ithaca

$$$ COLLEGETOWN MOTOR LODGE
312 College Ave
(607) 273-3542 or
(800) 745-3542
Motel near Cornell University
(discount on double rooms only)

Kingston

$$ RAMADA INN
Rt 28
(914) 339-3900
Hotel off I-87

Lake Placid

$$$ LAKESHORE MOTEL
54 Saranac Ave
(518) 523-2261
Motel on Lake Placid
with its own beach

Liberty

$$ LIBERTY MOTEL
204 S Main St
(914) 292-7272
Motel near downtown

New York City

$$$$ BEST WESTERN WOODWARD HOTEL
210 W 55th St
(212) 247-2000
14-story 1890 Midtown
hotel near Central Park

$$$$ CARLTON HOTEL
22 E 29th St
(212) 532-4100 or
(800) 542-1502
Midtown hotel near
Empire State Building

$$$$ DORAL PARK AVENUE HOTEL
70 Park Ave
(212) 687-7050
Midtown hotel near
Grand Central Station

$$$$ GORHAM NEW YORK
136 W 55th St
(212) 245-1800 or
(800) 735-0710
17-story 1929 Midtown
hotel near Radio City Music
Hall and Rockefeller Center
with luxury level rooms

$$$$ NEW YORK MARRIOTT MARQUIS
1535 Broadway
(212) 398-1900
48-story Midtown hotel
near Times Square with
luxury level rooms

$$$$ PARK CENTRAL HOTEL
870 7th Ave
(212) 247-8000
Midtown hotel near
Carnegie Hall and Central
Park (discount on double
room rate only)

$$$ TRAVEL INN HOTEL
515 W 42nd St
(212) 695-7171
7-story Midtown hotel near
Javits Convention Center
and Grand Central Station

North Syracuse

$$$ QUALITY INN NORTH
1308 Buckley Rd
(315) 451-1212
Hotel off I-90 and I-81

Norwich

$$ HOWARD JOHNSON LODGE
75 N Broad St
(607) 334-2200
3-story motel

Ossining

$$$ HUDSON RIVER INN
321 N Highland Ave
(914) 762-5600 or
(800) 825-5600
Hotel on Rt 9 (excluding
Dec 31)

Painted Post

$$ BEST WESTERN LODGE
ON THE GREEN
PO Box 150
(607) 962-2456
Hotel off US 15 near
Corning Glass Museum
and Rockwell Museum

Plattsburgh

$$$ HOLIDAY INN
412 Rt 3
(518) 561-5000
4-story hotel off I-87
near downtown (excluding
May 12-13)

Poughkeepsie

$$$ SHERATON CIVIC CENTER
HOTEL
40 Civic Center Plaza
(914) 485-5300
10-story downtown hotel off
US 44 overlooking Hudson
River with comedy club on
weekends

Rochester

$$$ HOLIDAY INN AIRPORT
911 Brooks Ave
(716) 328-6000
Hotel off I-390 near airport

$$$ **HOLIDAY INN GENESEE PLAZA**
120 E Main St
(716) 546-6400
15-story hotel next to
Convention Center
overlooking Genesee River
with comedy club

$$$ **HOWARD JOHNSON AIRPORT HOTEL**
1100 Brooks Ave
(716) 235-6030 or
(800) 544-9519
Hotel off I-390 at
airport entrance

$$ **MARKETPLACE INN**
800 Jefferson Rd
(716) 475-9190 or
(800) 888-8102
Hotel off I-90 with brewpub
and luxury level rooms

$$ **RAMADA INN ROCHESTER**
1273 Chili Ave
(716) 464-8800
Hotel off I-390 near airport

Ronkonkoma

$$$ **HOLIDAY INN MACARTHUR AIRPORT**
3845 Veterans Memorial Hwy
(516) 585-9500 or
(800) 422-9510
Hotel off I-495 near airport
with concierge level rooms

Saratoga Springs

$$$ **SHERATON SARATOGA SPRINGS HOTEL AND CONFERENCE CENTER**
534 Broadway
(518) 584-4000
5-story downtown hotel off
I-87 next to Civic Center

Smithtown

$$$ **SHERATON SMITHTOWN HOTEL**
110 Vanderbilt Motor Pkwy
(516) 231-1100
Hotel off I-495
(excluding Dec 31)

Suffern

$$ **WELLESLEY INN**
17 N Airmont Rd
(914) 368-1900
4-story motel off I-87

Syracuse

$$$ **HOLIDAY INN FAIRGROUNDS**
Farrell Rd
(315) 457-8700
Hotel off I-90 and I-690

$$ **HOLIDAY INN UNIVERSITY TOWER**
701 E Genesee St
(315) 479-7000
20-story downtown hotel off
I-81 near Convention Center
and Carrier Dome

$$	**RED CARPET INN**

6590 Thompson Rd
(315) 463-0202 or
(800) 251-1962
Motel off I-90

Utica

$$	**HOWARD JOHNSON LODGE**

302 N Genesee St
(315) 724-4141
Motel off I-90 near downtown

$$$	**RADISSON HOTEL-UTICA CENTRE**

200 Genesee St
(315) 797-8010
6-story downtown hotel
off I-90

Vestal

$$	**HOLIDAY INN AT THE UNIVERSITY**

4105 Vestal Pkwy E
(607) 729-6371
Hotel next to SUNY-
Binghamton with
luxury level rooms

Westbury

$$$	**ISLAND INN**

400 Old Country Rd
(516) 228-9500 or
(800) 228-8701
Hotel near Aqueduct and
Belmont racetracks

Woodbury

$$$$	**RAMADA INN WOODBURY**

8030 Jericho Tpk
(516) 921-8500
Hotel off I-495

North Carolina

From the snowy peaks of the Appalachian Mountains to the sun-drenched shores of the Atlantic, North Carolina offers all kinds of recreational opportunities. Throw in more than 400 years of recorded history (commencing with Sir Walter Raleigh's ill-fated Roanoke colony in 1585), as well as a surprisingly rich cultural heritage, and you have all the makings of a tourism bonanza.

Charlotte, the most populous metropolitan area in the Carolinas, is also one of the fastest growing cities in the country. Two of its biggest attractions are Discovery Place, featuring an OMNI-MAX theater, a planetarium, and a three-story rain forest, and Carowinds Theme Park, offering paddlewheeler trips, roller coasters, water rides, and musical shows. At Charlotte Motor Speedway, you can take a guided tour of the NASCAR facility and then a fast trip around the track.

Another booming part of North Carolina is the so-called "Research Triangle," at the apex of which lies **Raleigh**, the state capital. Among the city's many cultural and educational attractions are the North Carolina Museum of Art and the North Carolina Museum of History. Forming another major point on the triangle is **Durham**, home of Duke University and several major medical institutions.

Away to the west, **Winston-Salem** offers a masterful restoration of the old Moravian town of Salem, founded in 1766, as well as a notable performing arts center. Nearby **Greensboro** boasts a restored cotton mill, recalling the city's development as a major textile center more than a century ago.

Finally, don't overlook **Fayetteville**, a town full of historic houses and colorful gardens that is also the site of Fort Bragg, one of the nation's most important military installations.

Charlotte

$$$ DOUBLETREE CLUB HOTEL
895 W Trade St
(704) 347-0070
8-story downtown hotel
off I-77 in Gateway Center
complex

[icons]

$$$ EMBASSY SUITES
4800 S Tryon St
(704) 527-8400
8-story all-suite hotel off I-77

[icons]

$$ GOVERNMENT HOUSE HOTEL
201 S McDowell St
(704) 372-7550 or
(800) 762-1995
11-story downtown hotel
off I-277

[icons]

$$$ HILTON AT UNIVERSITY PLACE
8629 JM Keynes Dr
(704) 547-7444 or
(800) 462-5940
12-story hotel off I-85
near University of North
Carolina-Charlotte

[icons]

$$$ PARK HOTEL
2200 Rexford Rd
(704) 364-8220 or
(800) 334-0331
6-story hotel opposite
Southpark Mall shopping center with period furnishings
and original art

[icons]

$$ QUALITY INN AND SUITES CROWN POINT
2501 Sardis Rd N
(704) 845-2810
3-story motel off I-277

[icons]

$$$ RADISSON HOTEL AND SUITES EXECUTIVE PARK
5624 West Park Dr
(704) 527-8000 or
(800) 621-6410
7-story hotel off I-77 near
Carowinds theme park

[icons]

$$ RAMADA INN CENTRAL
515 Clanton Rd
(704) 527-3000
6-story hotel off I-77

[icons]

$$$ RESIDENCE INN BY MARRIOTT-NORTH
8503 N Tryon St
(704) 547-1122 or
(800) 331-3131
All-suite hotel off I-85 in
University Research Park
near University of North
Carolina-Charlotte, most
suites have fireplaces

[icons]

$$$ WYNDHAM GARDEN HOTEL
4200 Wilmount Rd
(704) 357-9100
3-story hotel off I-77
near Coliseum

[icons]

Durham

$$$$ GUEST QUARTERS SUITE HOTEL
2515 Meridian Pkwy
(919) 361-4660
7-story all-suite hotel off
I-40 in Research Triangle
Park with jogging trail

$$ HOLIDAY INN-WEST
3460 Hillsborough Rd.
(919) 383-1551
Hotel off I-85 near
Duke University

$$ HOWARD JOHNSON MOTOR LODGE
1800 Hillandale Rd.
(919) 477-7381
Hotel off I-85 near
Duke University

$$$ SHERATON INN UNIVERSITY CENTER
2800 Middleton Ave
(919) 383-8575 or
(800) 633-5379
4-story hotel off US 15 and
US 501 near Duke University
with luxury level rooms

Fayetteville

$$ RADISSON PRINCE CHARLES HOTEL
450 Hay St
(910) 433-4444 or
(800) 333-3333
8-story 1924 hotel in historic
downtown area off I-95 with
rooftop grand ballroom

Greensboro

$$$ GREENSBORO HIGH POINT MARRIOTT
Triad International Airport
(910) 852-6450 or
(800) 228-9290
5-story hotel off I-40
in airport complex

$$$ SHERATON GREENSBORO HOTEL
303 N Elm St
(910) 379-8000
11-story downtown hotel
off I-85

Maggie Valley

$$ MAGGIE VALLEY RESORT AND COUNTRY CLUB
340 Country Club Rd
(704) 926-1616 or
(800) 438-3861
Mountainside resort hotel
off US 19 (excluding
Jul 4 weekend)

Raleigh

$$$ HOLIDAY INN-NORTH
2815 Capital Blvd
(919) 872-7666
Hotel off US 1 with
luxury level rooms

$$$ NORTH RALEIGH HILTON
3415 Old Wake Forest Rd
(919) 872-2323 or
(800) 872-1982
6-story hotel off US 1
with luxury level rooms

$$$ **QUALITY SUITES HOTEL**
4400 Capital Blvd
(919) 876-2211 or
(800) 543-5497
3-story all-suite hotel
off US 1 and I-440

Winston-Salem

$$$ **THE RADISSON MARQUE HOTEL**
460 N Cherry St
(910) 725-1234 or
(800) 527-2341
9-story downtown hotel
next to Convention Center
with luxury level rooms

   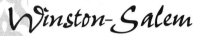

North Dakota

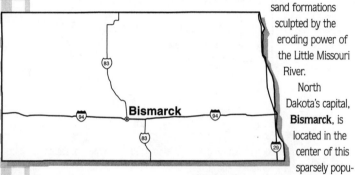

Despite the overwhelming amount of prairie in a state where agriculture reigns supreme, North Dakota is also the home of the Badlands, the spectacular clay and sand formations sculpted by the eroding power of the Little Missouri River.

North Dakota's capital, **Bismarck**, is located in the center of this sparsely populated state. The city, which sits on the banks of the tumultuous Missouri River, celebrates its native American, German, and Scandinavian heritage. The 19-story State Capitol, a fine example of art deco architecture, is often referred to as "the skyscraper of the prairie." Also highly recommended is a riverboat cruise aboard *Lewis and Clark*, a lovely old restored paddlewheeler.

Bismarck

| $$ | **RAMADA HOTEL**
1215 W Main St
(701) 223-9600
Hotel near downtown
and State Capitol |

Although much of the state is covered by farmland and forest, Ohio has the distinction of being the nation's third biggest industrial producer, bettered only by two other commercial giants, California and New York. This prolific output is explained by Ohio's superb transportation network and the long history and tradition of its major cities being associated with America's leading industries.

One of the best examples is the city of **Cleveland**, which from the end of the 19th century has been a major iron and steel center. In keeping with its industrial supremacy, the city has cultivated quite an artistic and recreational name for itself, too, as the home of the Cleveland Lakefront State Park, the Cleveland Orchestra, the Cleveland Museum of Art, and the Cleveland Museum of Natural History.

Much the same can be said for **Cincinnati**, which remains the com-

mercial capital of southern Ohio while continuing its long tradition as a bastion of the arts. Foremost among its many worthy attractions are the Museum Center at Union Terminal (the superbly restored train station), the Cincinnati Zoo, the Taft Museum, and the Cincinnati Art Museum.

The state capital of **Columbus** is another jewel, noted for the fine caliber of scientific and technological companies based there. Home of Ohio State University, the city also boasts an extraordinarily well restored downtown historic district, as well as a fine zoo and a stunning conservatory and botanical garden.

Other mandatory Ohio stops include **Dayton**, site of the United States Air Force Museum; **Toledo**, home to yet another acclaimed zoo and museum of art; and **Canton**, much celebrated for its Pro Football Hall of Fame.

Bedford Heights

$$$ RAMADA INN CLEVELAND SOUTHEAST
24801 Rockside Rd
(216) 439-2500
Hotel off I-271

[icons]

Canton

$$ COMFORT INN
5345 Broadmoor Cir NW
(216) 492-1331
3-story motel off I-77
(excluding Jul 27-29)

[icons]

$$ PARKE HOTEL CANTON
4343 Everhard Rd
(216) 499-9410 or
(800) 344-2345
Hotel off I-77 opposite
Belden Village shopping
center (excluding Hall of
Fame weekend)

[icons]

$$$ SHERATON INN CANTON
4375 Metro Cir NW
(216) 494-6494
6-story hotel off I-77 opposite
Belden Village shopping center

[icons]

Cincinnati

$$$ REGAL CINCINNATI HOTEL
150 W 5th St
(513) 352-2100
31-story downtown hotel
opposite Convention Center
and near Riverfront Stadium

[icons]

Cleveland

$$$ GLIDDEN HOUSE INN
1901 Ford Dr
(216) 231-8900
1910 Gothic-style hotel on Case
Western Reserve University
campus, listed on National
Register of Historic Places

[icons]

$$$ HOLIDAY INN LAKESIDE CITY CENTER
1111 Lakeside Ave
(216) 241-5100
18-story downtown hotel
near Convention Center and
City Hall

[icons]

$$$ RADISSON PLAZA SUITE HOTEL
1701 E 12th St
(216) 523-8000
13-story all-suite hotel near
Convention Center and
Gateway Stadium

[icons]

Columbus

$$ BEST WESTERN NORTH
888 E Dublin-Granville Rd
(614) 888-8230
Hotel off I-71
(excluding Dec 31)

[icons]

$$$ HARLEY HOTEL OF COLUMBUS
1000 E Dublin-Granville Rd
(614) 888-4300 or
(800) 321-2323
Hotel off I-71 with shuffleboard

[icons]

$$ HOJO INN EAST
5950 Scarborough Blvd
(614) 864-4670
Motel off I-270

$$$ HOLIDAY INN EAST I-70
4560 Hilton Corporate Dr
(614) 868-1380
12-story hotel off I-70

**$$$ HOLIDAY INN
CROWNE PLAZA**
33 Nationwide Blvd
(614) 461-4100
12-story downtown hotel off
US 23 next to Convention
Center and near State Capitol,
has luxury level rooms

$$ HOWARD JOHNSON NORTH
999 E Dublin-Granville Rd
(614) 885-4484
Motel off I-71

$$ PARKE UNIVERSITY HOTEL
3025 Olentangy River Rd
(614) 267-1111
3-story Tudor-style hotel
near Ohio State University

$$ RAMADA INN WEST
4601 W Broad St
(614) 878-5301
Hotel off I-270 and US 40

**$$$ RESIDENCE INN BY
MARRIOTT NORTH**
6191 W Zumstein Dr
(614) 431-1819
All-suite motel off I-71
next to French Market shop-
ping center, many suites have
fireplaces (discount on studio
suites only)

Curtice

$$ ECONO LODGE
10530 Corduroy Rd
(419) 836-2822 or
(800) 424-4777
Motel 5 miles from
Maumee Bay State Park

Dayton

**$$$ RADISSON HOTEL AND
SUITES**
11 S Ludlow St
(513) 461-4700
13-story 1898 downtown
hotel at Courthouse Square
in business district near
Convention Center

$$$ RADISSON INN
2401 Needmore Rd
(513) 278-5711
Hotel off I-75

**$$ RAMADA INN NORTH
AIRPORT**
4079 Little York Rd
(513) 890-9500
Hotel off I-75 and I-70

Defiance

$$ **DAYS INN**
1835 N Clinton St
(419) 782-5555
Motel off US 24 near downtown and Defiance College

Findlay

$$ **DAYS INN**
1305 W Main Cross St
(419) 423-7171
Hotel off I-75
(excluding Aug 7-15)

$$ **HOLIDAY INN**
820 Trenton Ave
(419) 423-8212
Hotel on US 224 off I-75

Independence

$ **RESIDENCE INN BY MARRIOTT**
5101 W Creek Rd
(216) 520-1450 or
(800) 331-3131
All-suite hotel off I-77,
most suites have fireplaces
(excluding Dec 31)

Mansfield

$$ **COMFORT INN NORTH**
500 N Trimble Rd
(419) 529-1000
Motel off I-71 near
downtown

Middleburg Heights

$$ **COMFORT INN**
17550 Rosbough Dr
(216) 234-3131 or
(800) 391-1112
3-story motel off I-71
(excluding May 26-29, Jul 1-4, Sep 1-4, Dec 31)

North Lima

$$ **SCOTTISH INNS**
10125 Market St
(216) 549-0440
Motel off I-76

North Olmsted

$$$ **RADISSON INN CLEVELAND AIRPORT**
25070 Country Club Blvd
(216) 734-5060
6-story hotel off I-480 at
Great Northern Corporate
Center and shopping complex
(excluding Dec 31)

Reynoldsburg

$ **ENVOY INN-REYNOLDSBURG**
6301 Oaktree Ln
(614) 866-8000
Motel off I-70

Sharonville

$$$ CINCINNATI MARRIOTT
11320 Chester Rd
(513) 772-1720 or
(800) 228-9290
14-story 23-acre hotel off
I-75 with luxury level rooms

$$$ HOWARD JOHNSON PLAZA HOTEL
11440 Chester Rd
(513) 771-3400
Hotel off I-75 and I-275
with volleyball court

$$ RAMADA INN
11029 Dowlin Dr
(513) 771-0300
Hotel off I-75

Springdale

$$$ SHERATON SPRINGDALE HOTEL
11911 Sheraton Ln
(513) 671-6600
10-story hotel off I-275 with
luxury level rooms

Strongsville

$$$ HOLIDAY INN STRONGSVILLE
15471 Royalton Rd
(216) 238-8800
6-story hotel off I-71
(excluding Dec 31)

Toledo

$$$ HILTON HOTEL
3100 Glendale Ave
(419) 381-6800
6-story hotel off I-80 and I-90

$$$ HOLIDAY INN CROWNE PLAZA
2 SeaGate
(419) 241-1411 or
(800) 289-1411
13-story downtown hotel

West Carrollton

$$ DAYS INN DAYTON SOUTH
3555 Miamisburg-Centerville Rd
(513) 847-8422
Motel off I-75

Westlake

$$$ HOLIDAY INN
1100 Crocker Rd
(216) 871-6000 or
(800) 762-7416
5-story hotel off I-90

Worthington

$$ COLUMBUS NORTH HILTON INN
7007 N High St
(614) 436-0700
3-story hotel off I-270 and I-71

Oklahoma

As the country's third largest supplier of natural gas and fifth leading producer of petroleum, Oklahoma literally helps to fuel the U.S. economy. Although the state has rebounded from the tragedy of the Dust Bowl to develop a sophisticated high tech economy, it has not repudiated its past as the home of the so-called Five Civilized Tribes—today more Native Americans live in Oklahoma than any other state except California.

The sprawling city of **Oklahoma City** has been the state capital since 1910. With one of the biggest cattle stockyards in the country, it has managed to balance its rural Western roots with the dynamic arrival of modern industries such as oil and aviation. Today, a trip to the National Cowboy Hall of Fame and Western Heritage Center can be contrasted with a visit to Enterprise Square, USA, a dramatic audiovisual presentation of the American free enterprise system. Other highlights include Oklahoma City Zoo and Myriad Botanical Gardens.

Tulsa, Oklahoma's second biggest city, not only boasts the greatest number of artificial lakes in the country, but it has also become one of the nation's prime inland ports, thanks to the 445-mile waterway that links it to the Gulf of Mexico. Nicknamed "Green Country" because of its profusion of parks, Tulsa can also proudly point to the Thomas Gilcrease Museum (with a magnificent Indian collection), the Philbrook Museum of Art, Oral Roberts University, and its much acclaimed zoo and living museum.

Other recommended sightseeing stops include **Lawton**, home of an historic frontier post, Fort Sill, and the Wichita Mountains Wildlife Refuge; and **Sand Springs**, where the outdoor Discoveryland amphitheater stages unique productions of "Oklahoma!"

Lawton

EXECUTIVE INN
$$
3110 Cache Rd
(405) 353-3104 or
(800) 241-3932
Motel off I-40 near Fort Sill

⬛ 🚫 🛗 🚌 🏋️

Oklahoma City

AIRPORT HOTEL AT WILL ROGERS AIRPORT
$
6300 Terminal Dr
(405) 681-3500
Hotel in airport complex

📺 🍸 🚫 🏊 🍽️ ✈️
🚌 🏋️

APPLETREE SUITES
$$
6022 1/2 NW 23rd
(405) 495-3881 or
(800) 234-3881
All-suite motel
off I-44 and I-40

🚫 🏊 🚌

ARBORS OF MACARTHUR SUITES
$$
1601 N MacArthur Blvd
(405) 495-1152
All-suite motel off I-40

🚫 🏊 🚌

HILTON INN NORTHWEST
$$$
2945 NW Expwy
(405) 848-4811 or
(800) 848-4811
9-story hotel in
business district

📺 🍸 🚫 🏊 🍽️ 🚌 🏋️

LEXINGTON HOTEL SUITES
$$$
1200 S Meridian Ave
(405) 943-7800
All-suite hotel off I-40

⬛ ✈️ 🚌

OKLAHOMA CITY MEDALLION HOTEL
$$$
1 N Broadway
(405) 235-2780
Downtown hotel next to
Convention Center and near
Myriad Botanical Gardens and
State Capitol

📺 🍸 ⬛ 🚫 🏊 🍽️ 🏋️

WALNUT GARDENS APARTMENTS/SUITES
$$
6700 NW 16th St
(405) 787-5151
All-suite hotel off I-40

🍸 🚫 🏊 🚌

Sand Springs

STRATFORD HOUSE INN
$
1110 E Charles Page Blvd
(918) 245-0283
Hotel off US 64
near Discoveryland

🚫 🛗 🏋️

Stillwater

BEST WESTERN STILLWATER
$$
600 E McElroy Ave
(405) 377-7010
4-story hotel near
Oklahoma State University

📺 🍸 🚫 🏊 🛗 🍽️ ✈️
🚌 🏋️

Tulsa

$$$ DOUBLETREE HOTEL DOWNTOWN TULSA
616 W 7th St
(918) 587-8000
17-story downtown hotel
next to Convention Center

$$$ RADISSON INN TULSA AIRPORT
2201 N 77th East Ave
(918) 835-9911
Hotel off I-244
at airport entrance

$$$ RESIDENCE INN BY MARRIOTT SOUTH
8181 E 41st St
(918) 664-7241 or
(800) 331-3131
All-suite motel off I-44,
many suites have fireplaces

$ STRATFORD HOUSE INN-RIVERSIDE
144 E Skelly Dr
(918) 743-2009
Hotel off I-44 near
Oral Roberts University

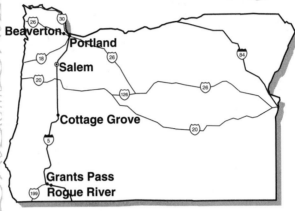

Oregon

Oregon is all about the great outdoors. From the snow-laden slopes of the Cascade Mountains to the lush green valleys of the Columbia River Gorge, from the golden sandy beaches of the Oregon coast to the raging waters of the Rogue River, this is a state that values its bountiful natural resources.

Oregon's principal city, **Portland**, is the West Coast's undiscovered gem—an energetic, compact city with a friendly, down-to-earth feel. Civic pride runs deep, and most of the residents have a fanatical devotion to outdoor pursuits. At Washington Park, you can savor the International Rose Test Gardens and the exquisite Japanese Gardens. Other highlights include the Oregon History Center, the Metro Washington Park Zoo, the Portland Art Museum, and the unusual (but quite fascinating) American Advertising Museum. Among a veritable cornucopia of shopping opportuni-

ties is the lovingly restored Yamhill Marketplace.

Nearby **Beaverton** is the birthplace of Nike, the popular footwear company, but today the town is equally famous for its abundance of wineries.

Downstate, most of the action centers around scenic **Grants Pass**, a resort town on the Rogue River with a delightfully restored central historic district and numerous riverside parks. Anglers come from far and wide to fish for Chinook salmon and steelhead trout. The main attraction, however—as it is in the waterfront community of **Rogue River** itself—continues to be white-water rafting and kayaking on the Rogue and nearby Umpqua and Klamath rivers.

Outdoor activity is also the name of the game in pretty **Cottage Grove**, nestled between two rivers in an area renowned for its historic connections.

Beaverton

$$$ RAMADA INN
13455 SW Canyon Rd
(503) 643-9100
3-story motel

▣ ⊗ ⇌ 🍴

Cottage Grove

$$ BEST WESTERN VILLAGE GREEN RESORT HOTEL
725 Row River Rd
(503) 942-2491 or
(800) 343-ROOM
16-acre resort hotel off I-5,
some rooms have fireplaces

▷ 🍸 ⊗ ♨ ✗ 🍴
✈ 🏋

Grants Pass

$$$ RIVERSIDE INN RESORT AND CONFERENCE CENTER
971 SE 6th St
(503) 476-6873 or
(800) 334-4567
Hotel off I-5 on banks of
Rogue River near downtown,
some rooms have fireplaces

▷ 🍸 ⊗ ⇌ ♨ 🚌
🏋 Ⓟ

Lake Oswego

$$$ HOLIDAY INN CROWNE PLAZA
14811 Kruse Oaks Blvd
(503) 624-8400
6-story hotel off I-5 with
luxury level rooms

▷ 🍸 ⊗ ⇌ ≈ 🍴 🏋

Portland

$$ BEST WESTERN HERITAGE INN
4319 NW Yeon
(503) 497-9044
Motel off I-405 near
Montgomery Park

▣ ⊗ ⇌ ♨ 🍴 🏋

$$$ DAYS INN CITY CENTER
1414 SW 6th Ave
(503) 221-1611
5-story downtown hotel
off I-5 near Oregon
Historical Society and
Portland Art Museum

▷ 🍸 ⊗ ⇌ 🚌

$$$ HOLIDAY INN EXPRESS
2323 NE 181st St
(503) 492-4000
Near I-84 and I-205

▣ ⊗ ⇌ ♨ 🏋

$$$ MARK SPENCER HOTEL
409 SW 11th Ave
(503) 224-3293 or
(800) 548-3934
Downtown hotel near
business district
(discount on suites only
and max 3-night stay)

⊗

$$$$ PORTLAND MARRIOTT HOTEL
1401 SW Front Ave
(503) 226-7600
15-story downtown hotel
off I-5 with luxury level
rooms, many rooms have
views of Willamette River

▷ 🍸 🚌 Ⓟ

$$$ RAMADA INN AIRPORT
6221 NE 82nd Ave
(503) 255-6511
Hotel off I-205 near airport

**$$$ RED LION
COLUMBIA RIVER**
1401 N Hayden Island Dr
(503) 283-2111 or
(800) 547-8010
3-story hotel off I-5 on
banks of Columbia River with
boat dock and luxury level
rooms (excluding Dec 31)

$$$ RIVERSIDE INN
50 SW Morrison St
(503) 221-0711 or
(800) 648-6440
5-story downtown hotel
off I-5 near Lloyd Center
and Yamhill shopping area,
many rooms have views of
Willamette River

Rogue River

**$$ BEST WESTERN INN
AT THE ROGUE**
8959 Rogue River Hwy
(503) 582-2200 or
(800) 238-0700
Motel off I-5 opposite
Rogue River with
hot-air ballooning nearby

Wilsonville

**$$ HOLIDAY INN
PORTLAND SOUTH**
25425 SW Boones Ferry Rd
(503) 682-2211
5-story hotel off I-5

Pennsylvania

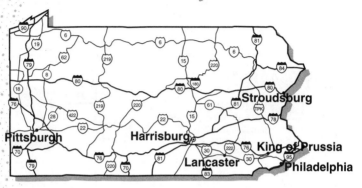

rom the moment William Penn founded his colony devoted to religious free-
dom in 1681, Pennsylvania has figured
prominently in the country's historical
development. In all three of the major
wars fought on American soil—French
and Indian, Revolutionary, and Civil—
Pennsylvania played a crucial role in
determining the final outcome. In
more recent years, the state has established itself as an industrial giant.

No American city can claim to have
spent more time in the historic spot-
light than **Philadelphia**, the nation's
capital during its rebellion against
British rule. Consequently, no
American city boasts more historic
landmarks: Independence Hall, the
Liberty Bell, Congress Hall, Christ
Church, the Betsy Ross House, and
the Second Bank of the United States,
among many others. The "City of
Brotherly Love" is also renowned as
the home of the Franklin Institute

Science Museum, the Philadelphia
Museum of Art, Temple University,
and the Philadelphia Symphony.

Pennsylvania's other big city,
Pittsburgh, is equally lively and interesting. From Point State Park and
Fort Pitt Museum, recalling the city's
frontier beginnings, to Schenly Park
and the Carnegie complex, loaded with
cultural and recreational attractions,
there is no shortage of things to do.

The same holds true for the rest of
the state: Pennsylvania's capital,
Harrisburg, has a fine state museum
and capitol building; **King of Prussia**
is the gateway to Valley Forge
National Park; **Lancaster** and sur-
roundings comprise the heart of
Pennsylvania Dutch Country, home to
Amish and Mennonite communities;
and **Stroudsburg** is the prime town
in the picturesque Pocono Mountains,
a noted ski area and summer resort.

Allentown

$$$ **ALLENTOWN HILTON**
904 Hamilton Mall
(215) 433-2221 or
(800) 999-7784
9-story downtown hotel

Altoona

$$ **HOLIDAY INN**
2915 Pleasant Valley Blvd
(814) 944-4581
Hotel on US 220
near downtown

Butler

$$ **DAYS INN CONFERENCE CENTER**
139 Pittsburgh Rd
(412) 287-6761
Hotel off US 422
near downtown

Camp Hill

$$$ **RADISSON PENN HARRIS HOTEL AND CONVENTION CENTER**
1150 Camp Hill By-Pass
(717) 763-7117 or
(800) 345-7366
3-story 26-acre hotel
on US 11 and US 15
with comedy club

Carlisle

$$ **EMBERS INN AND CONVENTION CENTER**
1700 Harrisburg Pike
(717) 243-1717 or
(800) 692-7315
Georgian-style hotel on US 11

$$ **HOWARD JOHNSON LODGE**
1255 Harrisburg Pike
(717) 243-6000
Motel on US 11

$$ **RODEWAY INN**
1239 Harrisburg Pike
(717) 249-2800
Motel on US 11

Clarks Summit

$$ **SUMMIT INN**
649 Northern Blvd
(717) 586-1211
Motel on US 6 and US 11

Coraopolis

$$ **DAYS INN PITTSBURGH AIRPORT**
1170 Thorn Run Rd
(412) 269-0990
Motel off I-79

**$$$ HOLIDAY INN
PITTSBURGH AIRPORT**
1406 Beers School Rd
(412) 262-3600 or
(800) 333-4835
Hotel off I-79 near airport

**$$$ ROYCE HOTEL
PITTSBURGH AIRPORT**
1160 Thorn Run Road
(412) 262-2400
9-story hotel off
US 60 near airport

Essington

**$$$ HOLIDAY INN
PHILADELPHIA
INTERNATIONAL AIRPORT**
45 Industrial Hwy
(215) 521-2400 or
(800) 685-6110
6-story hotel off I-95

Exton

$$ HOLIDAY INN
815 N Pottstown Pike
(215) 363-1100
4-story hotel off I-76

Harrisburg

**$$$ HARRISBURG HILTON AND
TOWERS**
One N 2nd St
(717) 233-6000
15-story downtown hotel
near State Capitol with
luxury level rooms

$$$ HARRISBURG MARRIOTT
4650 Lindle Rd
(717) 564-5511 or
(800) 228-9290
10-story hotel off I-283
with luxury level rooms

$$$ QUALITY INN RIVERFRONT
525 S Front St
(717) 233-1611
Downtown hotel off I-83
overlooking Susquehanna
River and near State Capitol

**$$$ RESIDENCE INN BY
MARRIOTT**
4480 Lewis Rd
(717) 561-1900 or
(800) 331-3131
All-suite motel off I-83,
most suites have fireplaces

Hermitage

$$ HOLIDAY INN
3200 S Hermitage Rd
(412) 981-1530
3-story hotel off I-80

Hidden Valley

$$$ HIDDEN VALLEY RESORT
1 Craighead Dr
(814) 443-6454 or
(800) 458-0175
Resort hotel in Laurel
Mountains

King of Prussia

$$$ **SHERATON PLAZA**
1150 1st Ave
(215) 265-1500
6-story hotel off I-76
near Valley Forge National
Park with dinner theater

$$$ **SHERATON VALLEY FORGE HOTEL**
1150 1st Ave
(215) 337-2000
15-story hotel off I-76
near Valley Forge National
Park with heliport

$$$ **VALLEY FORGE HILTON**
251 W DeKalb Pike
(215) 337-1200
9-story hotel off I-76 near
Valley Forge National Park

Lake Ariel

$$ **COMFORT INN**
RD 5
(717) 689-4148 or
(800) 523-4426
Motel off I-84 in
Pocono Mountains

Lancaster

$$$ **HOLIDAY INN EAST**
521 Greenfield Rd
(717) 299-2551
4-story hotel on US 30 in
Pennsylvania Dutch country

Levittown

$$ **LEVITTOWN ECONO LODGE**
6201 Bristol Pike
(215) 946-1100
Motel off I-276

Meadville

$$ **MEADVILLE DAYS INN**
240 Conneaut Lake Rd
(814) 337-4264
Hotel on US 6 and
US 322 near downtown

Middletown

$ **RODEWAY INN**
800 Eisenhower Blvd
(717) 939-4147
Motel off I-76 and I-283

Monroeville

$$$ **HOLIDAY INN**
2750 Mosside Blvd
(412) 372-1022
4-story hotel off I-76
near Monroeville Mall
shopping center

New Kensington

$$ **DAYS INN**
300 Tarentum Bridge Rd
(412) 335-9171
Hotel off Rt 28

Philadelphia

$$$$ **BEST WESTERN INDEPENDENCE PARK HOTEL**
235 Chestnut St
(215) 922-4443 or
(800) 624-2988
1856 downtown hotel
near Independence Mall

$$$ **BEST WESTERN NORTHEAST**
11580 Roosevelt Blvd
(215) 464-9500
Hotel off I-76 and I-95

$$$ **COMFORT INN AT PENN'S LANDING**
100 N Columbus Blvd
(215) 627-7900
10-story hotel off I-95
near Penn's Landing, many
rooms have riverside views
(excluding Dec 31)

$$$$ **GUEST QUARTERS SUITE HOTEL**
4101 Island Ave
(215) 365-6600
8-story hotel off I-95
in Gateway Center with
sand volleyball court

$$$ **HOLIDAY INN STADIUM**
900 Packer Ave
(215) 755-9500 or
(800) 424-0291
11-story hotel off I-76
and I-95 near Veterans
Stadium and the Spectrum

$$$$ **KORMAN SUITES HOTEL**
2001 Hamilton St
(215) 569-7000
24-story downtown hotel
near Franklin Institute and
Philadelphia Museum of Art

$$$$ **LATHAM HOTEL**
135 S 17th St
(215) 563-7474 or
(800) 528-4261
14-story downtown hotel
near Rittenhouse Square

$$$$ **PENN TOWER HOTEL**
Civic Center Blvd and 34th St
(215) 387-8333 or
(800) 356-7366
20-story downtown hotel
off I-76 next to Civic Center

$$ **TRAVELODGE STADIUM**
2015 Penrose Ave
(215) 755-6500 or
(800) 578-7878
Hotel near Veterans Stadium,
the Spectrum, and downtown

$$$ **WARWICK HOTEL**
1701 Locust St
(215) 735-6000 or
(800) 523-4210
20-story 1926 downtown
hotel near Rittenhouse Square

$$$$ **WYNDHAM FRANKLIN PLAZA HOTEL**
2 Franklin Plaza
(215) 448-2000
27-story downtown hotel
near Franklin Institute

Pittsburgh

$$$ HOLIDAY INN PARKWAY EAST
915 Brinton Rd
(412) 247-2700
Hotel off I-376 near
Kennywood Park
shopping center

$$$ HOLIDAY INN PITTSBURGH CENTRAL
401 Holiday Dr
(412) 922-8100
4-story hotel off I-279

$$$ HOLIDAY INN PITTSBURGH SOUTH
164 Fort Couch Rd
(412) 833-5300
7-story hotel on US 19 oppo-
site South Hills Village Mall

$$ HOWARD JOHNSON MOTEL
5300 Clairton Blvd
(412) 884-6000
3-story motel on Rt 51

$$$$ PITTSBURGH GREEN TREE MARRIOTT
101 Marriott Dr
(412) 922-8400 or
(800) 228-9290
5-story hotel off I-279
with luxury level rooms

Pottsville

$$ QUALITY HOTEL
100 S Center St
(717) 622-4600 or
(800) 777-8007
4-story downtown hotel

Reading

$$ HOLIDAY INN
2545 N 5th St Hwy
(215) 929-4741
Hotel on US 222 in
Pennsylvania Dutch country

Sayre

$$$ GUTHRIE INN AND CONFERENCE CENTER
255 Spring St
(717) 888-7711 or
(800) 627-7972
4-story hotel off Rt 17
with racquetball courts
(excluding Dec 31)

Selinsgrove

$ COMFORT INN
Rts 11 and 15
(717) 374-8880 or
(800) 627-7366
Motel on US 11 and
US 15 near Susquehanna
Valley Mall shopping center

Stroudsburg

$$ **SHERATON POCONO INN**
1220 Wt Main St
(717) 424-1930 or
(800) 777-5453
Hotel off I-80 in foothills
of Pocono Mountains

🔟 🍸 🚭 🛄 🛏 🏠

Trevose

$$$ **HOLIDAY INN BUCKS COUNTY**
4700 Street Rd
(215) 364-2000
6-story hotel off I-276

🔟 🍸 🚭 🏊

$$$ **RAMADA HOTEL AND CONFERENCE CENTER**
2400 Old Lincoln Hwy
(215) 638-8300
6-story hotel off I-276

🔟 🍸 🚭 🛄 🚭 🛏
🏊 🏠

Washington

$$$ **HOLIDAY INN MEADOW LANDS**
340 Race Track Rd
(412) 222-6200
7-story hotel off I-79

🔟 🍸 🚭 🛄 🛏 🏊 🕌
🚌 🏠

West Chester

$$ **BEECHWOOD MOTEL**
1310 Wilmington Pike
(215) 399-0970
Motel on US 202 and US 322

🚭

Wilkes Barre

$$ **BEST WESTERN GENETTI HOTEL AND CONFERENCE CENTER**
77 E Market St
(717) 823-6152 or
(800) 833-6152
4-story downtown hotel
off I-81 (excluding Dec 31)

🔟 🍸 🚭 🛄 ✈ 🏠

$$ **HOLIDAY INN WILKES BARRE**
800 Kidder St
(717) 824-8901
Hotel off I-81

🚭 🛄 🚌 🏠

Wyomissing

$$$ **SHERATON BERKSHIRE HOTEL**
422 W Papermill Rd
(215) 376-3811
4-story hotel off US 422
near factory outlet stores

🔟 🍸 🚭 🛄 🏊 🕌
🚌 🏠

$$ **WELLESLEY INN**
910 Woodland Ave
(215) 374-1500
4-story motel off US 422
near factory outlet stores

🚌 🚭 ✈ 🏠

York

$$ **YORKTOWNE HOTEL**
48 E Market St
(717) 848-1111
8-story 1925 downtown hotel
off I-83 in historic district

🔟 🍸 🚭 🛄 🚭 🏊
🚌 🏠

Rhode Island

America's tiniest state is just 37 miles wide, yet Rhode Island boasts a proud and distinguished history and provides an abundance of attractions for the most discerning of visitors.

Far and away the biggest city is **Providence**, which also serves as the state capital. A significant port, with a great seafaring heritage, the city is home to Brown University, and an excellent Museum of Art.

Although heavily industrialized, **Warwick** offers some 40 miles of beaches and shoreline along Narragansett Bay that provide welcome relief for summer visitors.

Cranston

| $$ | **DAYS INN**
101 New London Ave
(401) 942-4200
Motel off I-95 |

Providence

| $$$ | **HOLIDAY INN**
21 Atwells Ave
(401) 831-3900
14-story downtown
hotel off I-95 next to
Civic Center |

Warwick

| $$$ | **RESIDENCE INN BY MARRIOTT**
500 Kilvert St
(401) 737-7100 or
(800) 331-3131
Tudor-style all-suite
motel off I-95 |

| $$$ | **SHERATON TARA AIRPORT HOTEL**
1850 Post Rd
(401) 738-4000
5-story hotel off I-95
(discount on double
deluxe rooms only) |

South Carolina

Greenville · Spartanburg · Columbia · Aiken · Charleston · Hilton Head Island

The same grace and charm that marks so many of America's southern states is present in abundant supply in South Carolina. The state where America's tumultuous Civil War began—the first shot was fired at Fort Sumter in 1861—takes great pride in its historical past, although today South Carolina also sets its sights firmly in the future, spurred by the economic boom that has established it both as a prime tourist destination and an emerging industrial power.

At the heart of this growth is **Columbia**, South Carolina's state capital and primary city. Highly recommended among its many attractions are Riverbanks Zoo (where 2,000 animals are exhibited in a close simulation of their natural habitats), the South Carolina State Museum, the magnificent antebellum Hampton-Preston Mansion, and the State House, still pockmarked with Civil War shells fired by General Sherman's troops in 1865.

Genteel **Charleston** is the very embodiment of the Old South. Full of narrow, winding streets and hidden little alleys—with tiny gardens sprouting forth everywhere—this is a place to wander at will and make your own discoveries. Be sure to take a boat trip to see historic Fort Sumter. Nearby is Middleton Place, America's oldest landscaped garden.

In contrast, **Hilton Head Island** is a summer playground, with 25 golf courses, some 300 tennis courts, and mile upon mile of golden sandy beaches.

Other spots around the state worth visiting include **Aiken**, noted for its racetracks and equestrian museums; **Greenville**, beautifully situated in the Blue Ridge Mountains; and **Spartanburg**, a major textile center with a fine 18th-century plantation.

Aiken

$$ DELUXE INN
I-20 at Rt 19
(803) 642-2840
Motel off I-20
(excluding Masters golf
tournament)

$$ HOLLEY INN
235 Richland Ave
(803) 648-4265
Motel on US 1

$$ RAMADA INN
100 W Frontage Rd
(803) 648-4272
Hotel off I-20

Anderson

$ UNIVERSITY INN
3430 N Main St
(803) 225-3721
Motel off I-85

Charleston

$$$ CHARLESTON MARRIOTT
4770 Marriott Dr
(803) 747-1900 or
(800) 228-9290
9-story hotel off I-26

$$$ HOLIDAY INN RIVERVIEW
301 Savannah Hwy
(803) 556-7100
14-story hotel on US 17
near Citadel, many rooms
have views of Ashley River

$$$$ OMNI HOTEL AT CHARLESTON PLACE
130 Market St
(803) 722-4900 or
(800) THE-OMNI
8-story downtown hotel
near City Market (discount
on double room rate only)

$$$ PLANTERS INN
112 N Market St
(803) 722-2345 or
(800) 845-7082
4-story 1844 B&B in
downtown historic district
at City Market

$$$ SHERATON CHARLESTON HOTEL
170 Lockwood Dr
(803) 723-3000
13-story hotel on US 17
on banks of Ashley River
near downtown

Columbia

$$ COMFORT INN
2025 Main St
(803) 252-6321
Downtown motel on US 76

$$ HOLIDAY INN COLISEUM
630 Assembly St
(803) 799-7800
9-story hotel off US 21
opposite University of
South Carolina and near
State Capitol

Fort Mill

$$ **RAMADA INN CAROWINDS**
225 Carowinds Blvd
(704) 334-4450
Multistory hotel off I-77
opposite Carowinds theme park

Gaffney

$ **DAYS INN**
136 Peachoid Rd
(803) 489-7172
Motel off I-85 near
shopping outlets

Greenville

$$ **GREENVILLE RAMADA**
1001 S Church St
(803) 232-7666
6-story hotel near downtown
on US 29 (excluding Dec 31)

Hilton Head Island

$$$$ **CRYSTAL SANDS CROWNE PLAZA RESORT**
130 Shipyard Dr
(803) 842-2400 or
(800) 334-1881
5-story 800-acre oceanfront
resort hotel off US 278 with
its own beach

$$$ **HAMPTON INN**
1 Airport Rd
(803) 681-7900 or
(800) 752-3673
Motel off US 278 near
Charleston International Airport

$$$ **PLAYERS CLUB, A COLONY INTERNATIONAL RESORT**
35 DeAllyon Ave
(803) 785-8000
Off US 278

North Charleston

$$ **COMFORT INN-AIRPORT**
5055 N Arco Ln
(803) 554-6485
Motel off I-26

$$ **HOLIDAY INN AIRPORT**
6099 Fain St
(803) 744-1621
3-story hotel off I-26

$$$ **RESIDENCE INN BY MARRIOTT**
7645 Northwoods Blvd
(803) 572-5757
Off I-26 (discount on
studio suites only)

Spartanburg

$$ **RAMADA INN**
1000 Hearon Cir
(803) 578-7170
Hotel off I-85

South Dakota

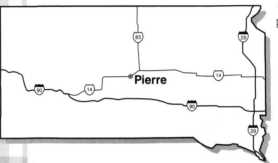

_T_he Missouri River splits South Dakota neatly in two: to the east stretches fertile prairie, the agricultural lifeblood of the state, while to the west, rising dramatically from the flat plains, are the bizarrely eroded Badlands and the mineral-laden Black Hills. The state's most familiar icon, however, is Mount Rushmore, the monumental granite carving of presidents Washington, Jefferson, Lincoln, and Roosevelt.

Appropriately, the South Dakotan capital of **Pierre** lies in the virtual geographic center of the state. From its vantage point on the Missouri River, the city has become a recreational hub, noted for its fine Capitol building.

Pierre

| $$ | **STATE MOTEL**
640 N Euclid Ave
(605) 224-5896
Motel on US 14 and
US 83 near downtown

Tennessee

*T*ennessee holds great appeal for visitors. From the scenic wonders and recreational delights of the Great Smoky Mountains to the urban pleasures and cultural diversions of its major cities, this attractive state continues to be a magnet for tourists.

Perhaps nowhere is the pull greater than **Nashville**, capital to both Tennessee and the country music industry. Each year hundreds of thousands of fans come to the Grand Ole Opry, which has been putting on its legendary shows without missing a beat since 1925. The success of this American institution has spawned Opryland USA, a slew of complementary attractions, including a theme park showcasing the nation's musical heritage. But Nashville offers a lot more than just music—not only is it the headquarters of the Southern Baptist Convention, but the city has also been acclaimed for its architecture, including most notably a full-size replica of the Parthenon.

Musical roots run deep, too, in **Memphis**, the home of blues great W.C. Handy and rock 'n' roll "king" Elvis Presley, whose Graceland mansion is now almost a shrine. Additional attractions include the National Civil Rights Museum and Mud Island, a 52-acre entertainment complex in the middle of the Mississippi River.

Don't leave Tennessee without paying visits to **Chattanooga**, where Lookout Mountain and several Civil War battlefield parks are the prime attractions; **Knoxville**, host to the 1982 World's Fair and headquarters of the Tennessee Valley Authority; **Gatlinburg**, gateway to the Great Smoky Mountains National Park; and **Oak Ridge**, the country's premier research and development center, with its excellent American Museum of Science and Energy.

Athens

$ | HOMESTEAD INN
1827 Holiday Dr
(615) 744-9002
Near I-75 and Hwy 30

Bucksnort

$ | BUCKSNORT MOTEL
Rt 1
(615) 729-5450
Motel off I-40

Buffalo

$$ | DAYS INN AT HURRICANE MILLS
Rt 1, Box 53A,
Hurricane Mills
(615) 296-7647
Motel off I-40

Chattanooga

$$ | RAMADA INN I-75 SOUTH AIRPORT
6639 Capehart Ln
(615) 894-6110
Hotel off I-75 with jogging
track and fishing pond

Donelson

$$$ | GUEST QUARTERS SUITE HOTEL
2424 Atrium Way
(615) 889-8889
3-story all-suite hotel near
Memphis International Airport

$$$ | WYNDHAM GARDEN HOTEL
1112 Airport Center Dr
(615) 889-9090
7-story hotel off I-40 near
Memphis International Airport

Gatlinburg

$$$ | EDGEWATER HOTEL
402 River Rd
(615) 436-4151 or
(800) 423-9582
8-story downtown hotel
off US 441, some rooms
have fireplaces

Knoxville

$$$ | KNOXVILLE HILTON
501 W Church Ave
(615) 523-2300
18-story downtown hotel
off I-40 and I-75 near
University of Tennessee
with luxury level rooms

$$$ | RAMADA INN CEDAR BLUFF
323 Cedar Bluff Rd
(615) 693-7330
Hotel off I-40 and I-75

Memphis

$$$ ADAM'S MARK HOTEL
939 Ridge Lake Blvd
(901) 684-6664 or
(800) 44-ADAMS
27-story lakeside hotel
off I-240 with jogging
course (discount on double
room rate only)

$$ BEST WESTERN AIRPORT HOTEL
2240 Democrat Rd
(901) 332-1130
Hotel off I-240 near
airport with jogging track

$$ COMFORT INN
100 N Front St
(901) 526-0583
Downtown hotel off I-40 and
I-55 opposite Mud Island and
near Convention Center

$$$ HOLIDAY INN AIRPORT
1441 E Brooks Rd
(901) 398-9211
4-story hotel off I-55 near
airport and Graceland
(excluding Aug 8-15)

$$$ MEMPHIS MARRIOTT HOTEL
2625 Thousand Oaks Blvd
(901) 362-6200 or
(800) 627-3587
Hotel off I-240 in Thousand
Oaks Business Center with
luxury level rooms

$$ WELCOME INN AMERICA
939 Getwell Rd
(901) 452-7275
Off I-240

Nashville

$$$ DOUBLETREE HOTEL NASHVILLE
315 4th Ave N
(615) 244-8200
Downtown hotel next to State
Capitol and near Convention
Center, has luxury level rooms

$$$$ OPRYLAND HOTEL
2800 Opryland Dr
(615) 889-1000
Hotel next to Grand Ole Opry
and Opryland USA with tropi-
cal gardens and waterfall

$$$ REGAL MAXWELL HOUSE
2025 Metro Center Blvd
(615) 259-4343 or
(800) 457-4460
Hotel off I-265 in
Metro Center Office Park
near downtown

$$$ RESIDENCE INN BY MARRIOTT
2300 Elm Hill Pike
(615) 889-8600
All-suite motel off I-40
near airport, many suites
have fireplaces

$$$$ **UNION STATION HOTEL**
1001 Broadway
(615) 726-1001 or
(800) 331-2123
7-story circa 1900 hotel
(originally a train station)
off I-40 near Convention
Center, Music Row, and
Vanderbilt University

Oak Ridge

$$ **HOLIDAY INN**
420 S Illinois Ave
(615) 483-4371
Hotel on Rt 62 near
American Museum of
Science and Energy

Only

$$ **BUDGET HOST INN**
PO Box 689
(615) 729-5450 or
(800) 742-6715
Motel off I-40

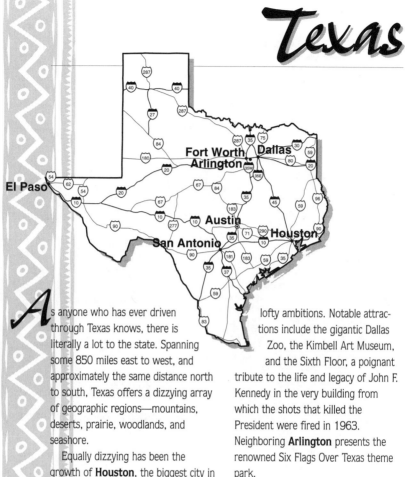

Texas

As anyone who has ever driven through Texas knows, there is literally a lot to the state. Spanning some 850 miles east to west, and approximately the same distance north to south, Texas offers a dizzying array of geographic regions—mountains, deserts, prairie, woodlands, and seashore.

Equally dizzying has been the growth of **Houston**, the biggest city in a very big state—and now the fourth largest city in the nation. Unrestrained, Houston sprawls in every direction, although its many cultural and recreational attractions have enjoyed unfettered growth, too. Any trip to the city should include stops at NASA's Johnson Space Center, the Astrodome (America's first domed stadium), and the stunning Menil Collection of art.

Dallas and its sister city of **Fort Worth** are the very epitome of the state—grandiose modern cities with lofty ambitions. Notable attractions include the gigantic Dallas Zoo, the Kimbell Art Museum, and the Sixth Floor, a poignant tribute to the life and legacy of John F. Kennedy in the very building from which the shots that killed the President were fired in 1963. Neighboring **Arlington** presents the renowned Six Flags Over Texas theme park.

Texas' capital is **Austin**, an urbane and engrossing city with lots to see, including the LBJ Library and Museum, the National Wildflower Research Center, and a handsome State Capitol.

Also not to be missed is **San Antonio**, an American national treasure forever famous as the site of the Alamo and the tranquil Riverwalk.

Last but not least, there's **El Paso**, on the border with Mexico, where the state's Hispanic heritage takes center stage.

Addison

$$$ DALLAS MARRIOTT QUORUM
14901 N Dallas Pkwy
(214) 661-2800 or
(800) 228-9290
12-story hotel off I-635
with luxury level rooms and
basketball court (discount on
double rooms only)

Amarillo

$$ BUDGET HOST LA PALOMA INN
2915 I-40 E
(806) 372-8101
Motel off I-40 near American
Quarter Horse Museum

$ TRAVELODGE EAST
3205 I-40 E
(806) 372-8171
Motel off I-40 near downtown

Arlington

$$$ ARLINGTON HILTON
2401 E Lamar Blvd
(817) 640-3322 or
(800) 527-9332
16-story hotel off I-30
next to Six Flags Over
Texas theme park

$$$ ARLINGTON MARRIOTT
1500 Convention Center Dr
(817) 261-8200 or
(800) 442-7275
19-story hotel off I-30 next
to Convention Center and
Arlington Stadium with
luxury level rooms

$$ FLAGSHIP INN
601 Ave H East
(817) 640-1666
Resort complex off I-30
near Six Flags Over
Texas theme park

$$$ RADISSON SUITE HOTEL
700 Ave H East
(817) 640-0440 or
(800) 333-3333
7-story all-suite hotel off
I-30 near Six Flags Over
Texas theme park with
luxury level rooms

Austin

$$$$ DOUBLETREE HOTEL
6505 I-35 N
(512) 454-3737
6-story hotel off I-35
near Highland Mall with
luxury level rooms

$$$ HABITAT SUITES HOTEL
500 E Highland Mall Blvd
(512) 467-6000 or
(800) 535-4663
All-suite hotel off I-35
near Highland Mall, most
rooms have fireplaces

HAWTHORN SUITES SOUTH `$$$`
4020 I-35 S
(512) 440-7722
All-suite motel off I-35,
most suites have fireplaces

HOLIDAY INN `$$$`
3401 I-35 S
(512) 448-2444
5-story hotel off I-35

HOLIDAY INN AUSTIN AIRPORT `$$$`
6911 I-35 N
(512) 459-4251
Hotel off I-35

HOLIDAY INN TOWN LAKE `$$$`
20 I-35 N
(512) 472-8211
14-story hotel off I-35
near downtown with
jogging trails and bike paths

Baytown

HOLIDAY INN BAYTOWN `$$`
300 S Hwy 146
(713) 427-7481
Hotel off I-10
(excluding Mar 4-7)

Bedford

HOLIDAY INN DFW AIRPORT WEST `$$$`
3005 Airport Frwy
(817) 267-3181
5-story hotel

Corpus Christi

CHRISTY ESTATES SUITES `$$$`
3942 Holly Rd
(512) 854-1091
All-suite hotel with some
individually decorated rooms

EMBASSY SUITES `$$$`
4337 S Padre Island Dr
(512) 853-7899
3-story all-suite hotel off I-37

Dallas

BEST WESTERN MARKET CENTER `$$`
2023 Market Center Blvd
(214) 741-9000
3-story hotel off I-35 near
Market Center and historic
West End Marketplace

CLARION HOTEL DALLAS `$$$`
1241 W Mockingbird Ln
(214) 630-7000 or
(800) 442-7547
13-story hotel off I-35
at Stemmons Corporate
Headquarters Center
(no reservations more than
14 days in advance)

DALLAS GRAND `$$$`
1914 Commerce St
(214) 747-7000 or
(800) 421-0011
20-story downtown hotel
near Convention Center

$$$ DALLAS PARK CENTRAL HOTEL
7750 LBJ Frwy
(214) 233-4421
Hotel off I-635 (excluding
Feb 10-14, May 8-10,
Sep 11-14)

$$$ DOUBLETREE HOTEL AT CAMPBELL CENTRE
8250 N Central Expwy
(214) 691-8700
21-story hotel off US 75 near
North Star shopping center

$$$ DOUBLETREE HOTEL AT LINCOLN CENTER
5410 LBJ Frwy
(214) 934-8400 or
(800) 528-0444
18-story hotel off I-635
opposite Galleria shopping
center with luxury level rooms

$$$$ EMBASSY SUITES DALLAS LOVE FIELD
3880 W Northwest Hwy
(214) 357-4500
8-story all-suite hotel
near Love Field Airport

$$ HOLIDAY INN NORTH PARK PLAZA
10650 N Central Expwy
(214) 373-6000 or
(800) 322-ROOM
Hotel near North Park
shopping center

$$$ QUALITY HOTEL MARKET CENTER
2015 Market Center Blvd
(214) 741-7481
11-story hotel off I-35
near Market Hall with l
uxury level rooms

$$$ RADISSON HOTEL
6060 N Central Expwy
(214) 750-6060 or
(800) 527-1808
Hotel opposite Southern
Methodist University

$$$ RADISSON HOTEL AND SUITES
2330 W Northwest Hwy
(214) 351-4477
8-story hotel off I-35
near Texas Stadium with
luxury level rooms

$$$ RADISSON MOCKINGBIRD HOTEL
1893 W Mockingbird Ln
(214) 634-8850
8-story hotel off I-35
near Love Field Airport

$$$ SOUTHLAND CENTER HOTEL
400 N Olive St
(214) 922-8000 or
(800) 272-8007
29-story downtown hotel
in Southland Center with
Southwestern art gallery
and luxury level rooms

$$$$ STONELEIGH HOTEL
2927 Maple Ave
(214) 871-7111 or
(800) 255-9299
1923 hotel near downtown
and Market Center

Del Rio

$ REMINGTON INN
3808 Hwy 90 W
(210) 775-0585
Motel on US 90

El Paso

$$ BEST WESTERN AIRPORT INN
7144 Gateway E
(915) 779-7700
Hotel off I-10 near airport

$$$ CLIFF INN
1600 E Cliff Dr
(915) 533-6700 or
(800) 333-CLIF
Downtown hotel off I-10

$$$ EL PASO MARRIOTT
1600 Airway Blvd
(915) 779-3300
6-story hotel off I-10 near
airport with luxury level rooms

Farmers Branch

$$$ DALLAS PARKWAY HILTON
4801 LBJ Freeway
(214) 661-3600 or
(800) 356-3924
15-story hotel off I-635
next to Galleria shopping center with luxury level rooms

Fort Worth

$$$ RAMADA FORT WORTH DOWNTOWN
1701 Commence St
(817) 335-7000
12-story downtown hotel
opposite Convention Center

$$ REMINGTON HOTEL AND CONFERENCE CENTER
600 Commerce St
(817) 332-6900
12-story downtown hotel
near Convention Center

Galveston

$$$ VICTORIAN CONDO HOTEL
6300 Seawall Blvd
(409) 740-3555
3-story condo hotel off I-45,
many rooms have Gulf views

Houston

$$ DAYS INN EAST
10155 E Frwy
(713) 675-2711
Hotel off I-10

$$$ DOUBLETREE AT ALLEN CENTER
400 Dallas St
(713) 759-0202
20-story downtown hotel
next to Sam Houston Park
and near Convention Center

$$$$ GUEST QUARTERS SUITE HOTEL
5353 Westheimer Rd
(713) 961-9000 or
(800) 424-2900
26-story all-suite hotel
off I-610 at Galleria
shopping center

$$$ HILTON SOUTHWEST
6780 Southwest Frwy
(713) 977-7911
12-story hotel off US 59 near
Sharpstown shopping center

$$ HOLIDAY INN I-10 WEST AT LOOP 610
7611 Katy Frwy
(713) 688-2221
6-story hotel off I-10 near
Galleria shopping center

$$$ HOLIDAY INN INTERCONTINENTAL AIRPORT
15222 JFK Blvd
(713) 449-2311
5-story hotel near airport
with volleyball court and
jogging track

$$ HOLIDAY INN WEST LOOP
3131 W Loop S
(713) 621-1900
Hotel off I-610 next to
Galleria shopping center

$$$ HOUSTON MEDALLION
3000 N Loop W
(713) 688-0100 or
(800) 688-3000
10-story hotel off I-610
with luxury level rooms

$$$ MARRIOTT ASTRODOME
2100 S Braeswood
(713) 797-9000 or
(800) 228-9290
3-story hotel off I-610
near Astrodome and
Texas Medical Center

$$$ MARRIOTT HOTEL GREENSPOINT
255 E North Belt
(713) 875-4000 or
(800) 228-9290
12-story hotel off I-45

$$$$ OMNI HOUSTON HOTEL
Four Riverway
(713) 871-8181 or
(800) THE-OMNI
11-story hotel off I-610
in Riverway complex near
Galleria shopping center

$$$$ PLAZA HILTON
6633 Travis
(713) 524-6633
Hotel off I-610 near
Rice University and
Texas Medical Center

$$ PREMIER INNS
2929 SW Frwy
(713) 528-6161
Motel off I-610 at Greenway
Plaza shopping center

$$ RAMADA HOTEL-GALLERIA
7787 Katy Frwy
(713) 681-5000 or
(800) 822-8373
11-story hotel off !-10

$$ RAMADA INN SOUTH/NASA
1301 Nasa Rd One
(713) 488-0220
Hotel off I-45 next to
Johnson Space Center

$$$$ RESIDENCE INN BY MARRIOTT HOUSTON-CLEAR LAKE
525 Bay Area Blvd
(713) 486-2424 or
(800) 331-3131
All-suite motel off I-45,
many suites have fireplaces

$$$ RESIDENCE INN BY MARRIOTT-GALLERIA
2500 McCue
(713) 840-9757
All-suite motel off I-610
near Galleria shopping center

$$$ SHERATON CROWN HOTEL
15700 JFK Blvd
(713) 442-5100
10-story hotel off I-45
near airport with luxury level
rooms (excluding Jan 25-28)

$$$$ SOFITEL HOTEL HOUSTON
425 N Sam Houston Pkwy E
(713) 445-9000
8-story French-style hotel
off I-45 near Greenspoint
shopping center

$$ TRAVELODGE GREENWAY PLAZA
2828 Southwest Frwy
(713) 526-4571
9-story hotel off US 59

Irving

$$$ HOLIDAY INN DFW AIRPORT SOUTH
4440 W Airport Frwy
(214) 399-1010
4-story hotel next to airport

$$$ WYNDHAM GARDEN HOTEL
110 W Carpenter Frwy
(214) 650-1600
3-story hotel near
Texas Stadium

Littlefield

$$ **CRESCENT PARK MOTEL**
2001 Hall Ave
(806) 385-4464 or
(800) 658-9960
Motel off US 84

🚭 🏊 🚐 🏠

Lufkin

$$ **RAMADA INN**
2011 S 1st St
(409) 639-1122
Hotel off US 59

📶 🍸 🚭 🏊 🍽 🚐
🏠 🅿

McAllen

$$ **CASA DE PALMAS/DOUBLETREE HOTEL**
101 N Main St
(210) 631-1101 or
(800) 274-1102
5-story Spanish-style hotel
off US 83 near downtown

📶 🍸 🚭 🏊 🍽 🏃 🚐
🅿 🅱

Round Rock

$ **TRAVELERS INN**
1400 I-35 N
(512) 255-4437
Motel off I-35

🍸 🚭 🏊 🏠

San Antonio

$$$ **HAWTHORN SUITES**
4041 Bluemel Rd
(210) 561-9660
All-suite motel off I-10 near
San Antonio Medical Center,
many suites have fireplaces

💻 🚭 🏊 🍽 🚐 🏠

$$$$ **PLAZA SAN ANTONIO**
555 S Alamo St
(210) 229-1000 or
(800) 421-1172
7-story downtown hotel
opposite Convention Center
and Hemisfair Park near the
Alamo (max 5-night stay)

📶 🍸 🚭 🏊 🐾 🍽
🏃 🏠

San Marcos

$$$ **HOLIDAY INN**
1635 Aquarena Springs Dr
(512) 353-8011
Hotel off I-35 near Aquarena
Springs and downtown

📶 🍸 🚭 🏊 🅿

Seminole

$ **SEMINOLE INN**
2200 Hobbs Hwy
(915) 758-9881 or
(800) 658-9985
Motel on US 62 and US 180

📶 🚭 🏊 🏃 🚐

Temple

$ | **RAMADA INN**
400 SW Dodgen Loop 363
(817) 773-1515
Hotel off US 190
next to Medical Center

🕩 🍸 🚭 🛍 🚌 🏠

Texarkana

$ | **RAMADA INN**
2005 Mall Dr
(903) 794-3131
Off I-30

🕩 🍸 🚭 🛍 🍴 🚌 🏠

$$ | **SHERATON INN**
5301 N Stateline Ave
(903) 792-3222
6-story hotel off I-30
with midweek comedy club

🕩 🍸 🚭 🛍 🍴 🚌 🏠

Wichita Falls

$$ | **SHERATON WICHITA FALLS**
1000 Central Frwy
(817) 761-6000
6-story hotel off I-44
opposite 90 Foot Falls
and near downtown, has
luxury level rooms

🕩 🍸 🚭 🛍 🏊 🍴

🚌 🏠

Utah

With five national parks—Arches, Bryce Canyon, Canyonlands, Capitol Reef, and Zion—to its name, Utah would appear to have more than its allotment of natural wonders, but when you add seven national forests, six national monuments, and two national recreation areas, it's obvious that this most scenic of states boasts a veritable embarrassment of riches.

Utah's capital, **Salt Lake City**, is spectacularly situated at the base of the Wasatch Mountains. Off to the west lies the Great Salt Lake, an immense yet shallow body of water with one of the highest salinity levels in the world. Founded by Brigham Young in 1847 as the headquarters of the fledgling Mormon community, Salt Lake City has firmly established itself as the denomination's ecclesiastical center. Right in the center of the city sits Temple Square, incorporating the Tabernacle, with its huge domed roof,

and the Mormon Temple, completed in 1893 but open only to Mormons. You can also see Beehive House, the restored home of Brigham Young, as well as his grave and a memorial to the great man. Genealogists flock to the Family History Library to research birth, marriage, and death records extending back to 1550.

Mormon pioneers were also responsible for the establishment of **Ogden**, although the city's primary importance is as a rail center. At nearby Promontory two railway tracks were ceremonially joined in 1869 to signal the opening of America's first transcontinental railroad.

Two other Utah destinations should also be considered: **Price**, with its Dinosaur Prehistoric Museum containing dinosaur skeletons and Indian artifacts; and **St. George**, site of Utah's first Mormon temple and the winter home of Brigham Young.

Ogden

$$ **HOLIDAY INN**
3306 Washington Blvd
(801) 399-5671 or
(800) 999-6841
Hotel off I-15 near downtown

$$ **OGDEN PARK HOTEL**
247 24th St
(801) 627-1190 or
(800) 421-7599
8-story hotel off I-15

Price

$$ **GREEN WELL MOTEL**
655 E Main St
(801) 637-3520 or
(800) 666-3520
Motel off US 191 near
Dinosaur Prehistoric Museum

Salt Lake City

$$ **BEST WESTERN OLYMPUS**
161 W 600 South
(801) 521-7373 or
(800) 426-0722
13-story downtown hotel
near Salt Palace and
Temple Square

$$$ **COMFORT INN AIRPORT**
200 N Admiral Byrd Rd
(801) 537-7444 or
(800) 535-8742
4-story motel off I-80
in Salt Lake International
Center near airport

$$$ **DOUBLETREE HOTEL SALT LAKE CITY**
215 W South Temple
(801) 531-7500 or
(800) 528-0444
15-story downtown hotel
next to Salt Palace and near
Temple Square

$$$$ **MARRIOTT HOTEL**
75 S West Temple
(801) 531-0800 or
(800) 228-9290
16-story downtown hotel
connected to Crossroads
shopping center opposite
Salt Palace and near
Temple Square, has
luxury level rooms

$$$ **SALT LAKE HILTON**
150 W 5th South
(801) 532-3344
10-story downtown hotel
near Salt Palace with luxury
level rooms

$$$ **UNIVERSITY PARK HOTEL**
480 Wakara Way
(801) 581-1000 or
(800) 637-4390
7-story hotel at foot of
Wasatch Mountains in
University of Utah's Research
Park with luxury level rooms,
some rooms have mountain
views

Vermont

*F*ew parts of the United States offer such a colorful change of seasons as the little state of Vermont. Most familiar of all, of course, is the fall when the leaves produce a shower of different colors—rich maroons, bright oranges, golden yellows, and the like. Then comes the pure white snow of winter, followed by the pastel flowers of spring and, finally, the deep blue skies of summer.

All of these colors are on display in **Burlington**, the largest city in the state, which looks out across Lake Champlain. First settled in 1775, the city has preserved many of its oldest neighborhoods, including Battery Street along the lakefront. You can also see the Ethan Allen Homestead, where Vermont's Revolutionary War hero once owned a farm. At nearby Shelburne, some 37 historic New England buildings have been re-erected and filled with art and artifacts from Colonial times in the unique Shelburne Museum.

From Burlington, a scenic drive south takes you to **Chittenden**, nestled high in the picturesque Green Mountains that form the backbone of the state.

Not far away is the famous resort town of **Killington**, which offers a welter of varied activities all year round. In winter most of the attention focuses on the snowy slopes of Killington and Pico Peaks, but during the summer there are water slides and nature trails to cool everyone down.

Nearby **Rutland** has become known as the "Marble City," for this is where most of Vermont's most precious stone is quarried and then finished. The town is also the home of the Norman Rockwell Museum, where more than 2,000 of the famous American illustrator's works are exhibited.

Burlington

$$$ **RADISSON HOTEL BURLINGTON**
60 Battery St
(802) 658-6500
7-story downtown hotel
with weekend comedy club,
many rooms overlook Lake
Champlain and Adirondack
Mountains

Killington

$$$$ **CORTINA INN**
HC 34, Box 33
(802) 773-3331 or
(800) 451-6108
Resort hotel on US 4
near Killington and Pico ski
areas with guided mountain
bike trips, some rooms have
fireplaces

Chittenden

$$$$ **MOUNTAIN TOP INN AND RESORT**
Mountain Top Rd
(802) 483-2311
3-story 1,300-acre resort
lodge in Green Mountains off
US 7 with horsedrawn sleigh
rides in winter, many rooms
have fireplaces

Rutland

$$$ **HO JO INN**
378 S Main St
(802) 775-4303
Motel on US 7
near downtown

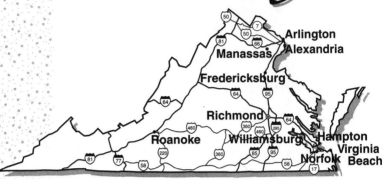

Virginia

uch of America's history has been shaped by events that took place in Virginia. As early as 1607 the first permanent European settlement in North America was established in Jamestown. At nearby Yorktown the British surrendered to end the Revolutionary War. And the Civil War came to a finale at Appomattox Courthouse with Robert E. Lee's capitulation to U.S. Grant.

In fact, Virginia's capital, **Richmond**, also served as the capital of the Confederacy. The story of this bitter period is well told at the Museum of the Confederacy and the various sites that make up Richmond National Battlefield Park. The city also proudly cossets its historic buildings, including Maymont, John Marshall House, Agecraft Hall, the Poe House, and the State Capitol.

Among Virginia's many other prominent Civil War battlefields are **Manassas**, site of the first major

encounter, and **Fredericksburg**, where George Washington's boyhood home and James Monroe's law office can also be visited.

History is well preserved, too, in **Williamsburg**, where a mile-long section of the old Colonial city has been faithfully restored; nearby Busch Gardens offers fun for all the family.

Also close at hand are **Hampton**, another very old Virginia settlement; **Norfolk**, the world's largest naval base; and **Virginia Beach**, a major summer resort area.

Much of northern Virginia is part of suburban Washington, including **Alexandria**, famous for its Old Town historic area, and **Arlington**, where America's war dead (and other heroes such as John F. Kennedy) are buried at Arlington National Cemetery.

Finally, **Roanoke**, in southwestern Virginia, is the gateway to the Shenandoah Mountains.

Alexandria

$$$ BEST WESTERN OLD COLONY INN
625 First St
(703) 548-6300
4-story hotel in Old Town

$$ COMFORT INN MOUNT VERNON
7212 Richmond Hwy
(703) 765-9000
Motel on US 1

$$ COMFORT INN VAN DORN
5716 S Van Dorn St
(703) 922-9200
9-story motel off I-95
and I-495

$$ ECONO LODGE-MOUNT VERNON
8849 Richmond Hwy
(703) 780-0300
3-story motel on US 1

$$$ EXECUTIVE CLUB SUITES
610 Bashford Ln
(703) 739-2582
All-suite hotel near
Old Town and Washington
National Airport

$$$$ GUEST QUARTERS SUITE HOTEL
100 S Reynolds St
(703) 370-9600
9-story all-suite hotel off
I-395 with jogging track

$$$ HOLIDAY INN
2460 Eisenhower Ave
(703) 960-3400
10-story hotel off I-95
and I-495 near Old Town

$$$ HOWARD JOHNSON
5821 Richmond Hwy
(703) 329-1400
7-story hotel on US 1
near Old Town

$$$ THE TOWERS HOTEL SUITES
420 N Van Dorn St
(703) 370-1000 or
(800) 368-3339
All-suite hotel off I-395 near
Landmark shopping center

Arlington

$$$ COMFORT INN BALLSTON
1211 N Glebe Rd
(703) 247-3399
3-story motel off I-66
near Ballston Commons
shopping center

$$$$ DOUBLETREE HOTEL NATIONAL AIRPORT
300 Army Navy Dr
(703) 416-4100 or
(800) 848-7000
15-story hotel off I-395
opposite Pentagon and
near airport and downtown
Washington, has luxury
level rooms

$$ **ECONO TRAVEL MOTOR HOTEL**
3335 Lee Hwy
(703) 524-9800
Motel off I-66 near
downtown Washington

$$$$ **EXECUTIVE CLUB SUITES**
108 S Courthouse Rd
(703) 522-2582
All-suite hotel next to Fort
Myer and near Pentagon

$$$ **HOWARD JOHNSON HOTEL NATIONAL AIRPORT**
2650 Jefferson Davis Hwy
(703) 684-7200
17-story hotel on US 1
near airport and Crystal City
shopping center

$$$ **QUALITY HOTEL ARLINGTON**
1200 N Courthouse Rd
(703) 524-4000
10-story hotel on US 50 near
Arlington National Cemetery
with luxury level rooms

Chesapeake

$$ **WELLESLEY INN**
1750 Sara Dr
(804) 366-0100
4-story motel off I-64

Chester

$$ **HOLIDAY INN**
2401 W Hundred Rd
(804) 748-6321
Hotel off I-95 near John
Tyler Community College

Fairfax

$$ **WELLESLEY INN**
10327 Lee Hwy
(703) 359-2888
Hotel on US 50

Fredericksburg

$$$ **DUNNING MILLS INN**
2305C Jefferson Davis Hwy
(703) 373-1256
Motel off I-95 with
luxury level rooms

$$ **HOLIDAY INN SOUTH**
5324 Jefferson Davis Hwy
(703) 898-1102 or
(800) 465-4329
Hotel off I-95

$$ **RAMADA INN SPOTSYLVANIA MALL**
PO Box 36
(703) 786-8361
Motel off I-95 near
Spotsylvania Mall,
Civil War battlefield, and
Mary Washington College,
has luxury level rooms

$$$ **SHERATON INN**
2801 Plank Rd
(703) 786-8321 or
(800) 682-1049
3-story hotel off I-95
with private pond

Hampton

$ **ARROW INN**
7 Semple Farm Rd
(804) 865-0300 or
(800) 833-2520
3-story motel off I-64

Manassas

$$ **RAMADA INN**
10820 Balls Ford Rd
(703) 361-0221
Hotel off I-66 near
Civil War battlefield

Norfolk

$$ **HOWARD JOHNSON HOTEL**
700 Monticello Ave
(804) 627-5555 or
(800) 682-7678
Downtown hotel opposite
Convention Center and
near Waterside Festival
Marketplace

$$$ **NORFOLK AIRPORT HILTON**
1500 N Military Hwy
(804) 466-8000 or
(800) 422-7474
6-story hotel off US 13
near airport with luxury
level rooms

$$$ **OMNI NORFOLK**
777 Waterside Dr
(804) 622-6664
Downtown hotel next to
Convention Center and
Waterside Festival
Marketplace with luxury
level rooms, many rooms
have river views

Richmond

$$ **HOLIDAY INN CROSSROADS**
2000 Staples Mill Rd
(804) 359-6061
8-story hotel off I-64 near
University of Richmond with
luxury level rooms

$$$ **HOLIDAY INN HISTORIC DISTRICT**
301 W Franklin St
(804) 644-9871
16-story downtown hotel
off I-95 near State Capitol
and Richmond Centre

$$ **HOLIDAY INN KOGER CENTER SOUTH**
1021 Koger Center Blvd
(804) 379-3800
8-story hotel off I-95
with luxury level rooms

$$ **RAMADA INN SOUTH**
2126 Willis Rd
(804) 271-1281
Hotel off I-95

🔲 🚭 ➰ 🏃

$$$ **RICHMOND MARRIOTT HOTEL**
500 E Broad St
(804) 643-3400 or
(800) 228-9290
18-story downtown hotel
off I-95 next to Convention
Center and near State Capitol,
has luxury level rooms

🔲 🍸 🚭 ➰ 🛏 🍴 🐾

$$$ **SHERATON INN PARK SOUTH**
9901 Midlothian Tpk
(804) 323-1144 or
(800) 525-9538
7-story hotel off I-195
with jogging path

🔲 🚭 ➰ ➰ 🛏 🍴 🐾

$$$ **SHERATON INN RICHMOND AIRPORT**
4700 S Laburnum Ave
(804) 226-4300 or
(800) 628-7601
4-story hotel off I-64
near airport

🔲 🍸 🚭 ➰ 🛏 🍴 ✈
🚌 🐾

Roanoke

$$ **HOLIDAY INN AIRPORT**
6626 Thirlane Rd
(703) 366-8861
Hotel off I-581 near airport

🔲 🍸 🚭 ➰ 🍴 ✈
🚌 🐾

$$ **HOLIDAY INN CIVIC CENTER**
501 Orange Ave
(703) 342-8961
Hotel off I-581 opposite Civic
Center and near downtown

🔲 🍸 🚭 ➰ 🐾

Rosslyn

$$$ **EXECUTIVE CLUB**
1730 Arlington Blvd
(703) 525-2582
Near Georgetown
and Foggy Bottom in
Washington, D.C.

🍸 🖥 🚭 🛏 🍴 🚌 🐾

Springfield

$$ **WASHINGTON-SPRINGFIELD RAMADA LIMITED**
6868 Springfield Blvd
(703) 644-5311 or
(800) 456-4683
4-story motel off I-95

🖥 🚭 🛏 🐾

Sterling

$$ **HAMPTON INN WASHINGTON-DULLES AIRPORT**
45440 Holiday Dr
(703) 471-8300
Motel off Rt 28 near airport

🖥 🚭 ➰ 🛏 ✈ 🚌 🐾

$$$ **HOLIDAY INN WASHINGTON-DULLES**
1000 Sully Rd
(703) 471-7411
Hotel on Rt 28 near airport

🔲 🍸 🚭 ➰ 🛏 🍴 ✈
🚌 🐾

Vienna

$$ | **COMFORT INN TYSONS CORNER**
1587 Springhill Rd
(703) 448-8020
3-story motel off I-495

Virginia Beach

$$$ | **CLARION HOTEL-PEMBROKE CORPORATE CENTER**
4453 Bonney Rd
(804) 473-1700
8-story hotel off I-44
on boardwalk

$$$ | **RADISSON HOTEL VIRGINIA BEACH**
1900 Pavilion Dr
(804) 422-8900
Downtown hotel next
to Convention Center
and near ocean

Williamsburg

$$ | **COLONIAL AMERICA INN**
216 Parkway Dr
(804) 253-6450
Motel off I-64 near
Colonial Williamsburg
and Busch Gardens

$$$ | **WILLIAMSBURG HILTON**
50 Kingsmill Rd
(804) 220-2500
6-story hotel on US 60
near Busch Gardens and
Colonial Williamsburg
(excluding Dec 31)

$$$ | **WILLIAMSBURG HOSPITALITY HOUSE**
415 Richmond Rd
(804) 229-4020 or
(800) 932-9192
Multistory hotel on US 60
opposite William and Mary
College and near Colonial
Williamsburg

Washington

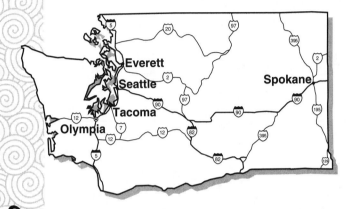

ashington is very much a state of extremes. Parts of the Olympic Peninsula, in the northwestern corner of the state, receive more rainfall than anywhere else in the country, yet barely 200 miles to the east is some of America's most arid desert. This startling contrast is caused by the Cascade Range, a series of immense mountain peaks, many of which are volcanic in origin (including the infamous Mount St. Helens)—on one side the climate is mild and temperate, on the other it is dry and volatile.

Washington's dominant city is **Seattle**, a cosmopolitan place with a lively sense of fun that's almost completely surrounded by water. In fact, one of the best places to appreciate the city is on the waterfront, especially at Pike Place Market, a Seattle institution since 1907. A short walk away lies Pioneer Square, a fascinating turn-of-the-century neighborhood, and the

Seattle Art Museum. Other highlights include the 605-foot Space Needle, a relic of the 1962 World's Fair, and the first-rate Museum of Flight.

Since Seattle is synonymous with the aircraft industry, a visit to suburban **Everett** to tour the Boeing 747-767 Division is highly recommended.

Seattle's near neighbor to the south, **Tacoma**, is also well worth a trip. The Washington State Historical Society Museum contains excellent exhibits about the native peoples of the Pacific Northwest, while Point Defiance Park features a zoo, a fort, a theme park, and a museum about logging.

For a complete change of pace, head east to **Spokane**, Washington's second biggest city, which has retained its proud pioneering spirit. Riverfront Park, the site of Expo '74, is a real delight, as is Manito Park, with its myriad of different gardens.

Bellevue

EMBASSY SUITES
$$$$
3225 158th Ave SE
(206) 644-2500
5-story all-suite hotel
off I-90 near Bell Square
shopping center

**RED LION INN/
BELLEVUE CENTER**
$$$
818 112th Ave NE
(206) 455-1515 or
(800) 547-8010
3-story hotel off I-405

Bellingham

RAMADA INN
$$$
215 Samish Way
(360) 734-8830 or
(800) 272-6232
3-story motel off I-5
near downtown and Western
Washington University

Blaine

**INN AT SEMI-AH-MOO,
A WYNDHAM RESORT**
$$$$
9565 Semiahmoo Pkwy
(360) 371-2000
4-story waterfront resort
hotel off I-5 with its own
beach and marina, many
rooms have fireplaces

Bothell

**WYNDHAM GARDEN
HOTEL**
$$$
19333 N Creek Pkwy
(206) 485-5557
Hotel off I-405

Des Moines

NENDEL'S BY VALUE INN
$
22246 Pacific Hwy S
(206) 878-8427 or
(800) 547-0106
Near SEA-TAC airport

Everett

HOLIDAY INN
$
101 128th St SE
(206) 745-2555 or
(800) 221-9839
4-story hotel off I-5

**WESTCOAST EVERETT
PACIFIC HOTEL**
$$$
3105 Pine St
(206) 339-3333
7-story art deco-style
hotel off I-5

Kirkland

CLARION INN
$$$
12233 NE Totem Lake Way
(206) 821-2202
All-suite lakeside motel
off I-405

Renton

$$$ HOLIDAY INN RENTON
800 Ranier Ave S
(206) 226-7700 or
(800) 521-1412
6-story hotel off I-405
near Longacres racetrack
and Southcenter Mall

Sea-Tac

$$$ HOLIDAY INN SEA-TAC
17338 International Blvd
(206) 248-1000
12-story hotel off I-5 near
airport, some rooms have
views of Mount Rainier
(excluding Mar 31-Apr 4)

$$$ RED LION HOTEL SEATTLE AIRPORT
18740 International Blvd
(206) 246-8600 or
(800) 547-8010
13-story hotel off I-5
opposite airport

$$$ WYNDHAM GARDEN HOTEL
18118 International Blvd
(206) 244-6666
6-story hotel off I-5
opposite airport

Seattle

$$$ DAYS INN TOWN CENTER
2205 7th Ave
(206) 448-3434 or
(800) 225-7169
4-story downtown hotel
near Seattle Center, Space
Needle, and waterfront

$$$ HILTON HOTEL
1301 6th Ave
(206) 624-0500
14-story downtown hotel

$$$ MEANY TOWER HOTEL
4507 Brooklyn Ave NE
(206) 634-2000 or
(800) 648-6440
14-story octagonal hotel
off I-5 near University of
Washington (excluding
Mar 30-Apr 3)

$$$ RAMADA INN DOWNTOWN
2200 5th Ave
(206) 441-9785
4-story downtown hotel near
Seattle Center, Space Needle,
and waterfront

$$$$ WARWICK HOTEL
401 Lenora St
(206) 443-4300 or
(800) 426-9280
19-story downtown hotel
with free shuttle service
to major attractions

Spokane

$$ **BEST WESTERN TRADE WINDS DOWNTOWN**
907 W 3rd Ave
(509) 838-2091
4-story motel off I-90
near downtown

$$$$ **QUALITY INN VALLEY SUITES**
8923 E Mission Ave
(509) 928-5218 or
(800) 777-7355
4-story hotel off I-90,
some suites have fireplaces
(discount on suites only)

$$ **WESTCOAST RIDPATH HOTEL**
515 W Sprague Ave
(509) 838-2711 or
(800) 426-0670
13-story downtown hotel

Tacoma

$$$ **DAYS INN-CLOVER PARK**
6802 S Sprague Ave
(206) 475-5900
Hotel off I-5 near Tacoma
Dome and downtown

$$ **HOWARD JOHNSON**
8702 S Hosmer St
(206) 535-3100
Motel off I-5 near Tacoma
Dome and Tacoma Mall

Tukwila

$$$ **DOUBLETREE INN**
205 Strander Blvd
(206) 575-8220 or
(800) 528-0444
Hotel off I-5 next to
Southcenter Mall

$$$ **DOUBLETREE SUITES HOTEL**
16500 Southcenter Pkwy
(206) 575-8220 or
(800) 528-0444
8-story all-suite hotel
off I-5 opposite Southcenter
Mall with racquetball courts
and helipad

$$$ **EMBASSY SUITES SOUTHCENTER**
15920 W Valley Hwy
(206) 227-8844
8-story all-suite hotel off
I-405 next to Longacres
racetrack and near
Southcenter Mall

$$$ **HOMEWOOD SUITES**
6955 Southcenter Blvd
(206) 433-8000
3-story all-suite hotel off
I-405 near Southcenter Mall,
some suites have fireplaces

Tumwater

$$ **THE TYEE HOTEL**
500 Tyee Dr
(360) 352-0511 or
(800) 648-6440
Hotel off I-5, some
rooms have fireplaces

West Virginia

Triadelphia
Fairmont
Clarksburg
Martinsburg
Huntington
Charleston

ost visitors to West Virginia expect to see signs of heavy industry wherever they go. In reality, things are quite different. Although the state is unquestionably dependent on its iron and steel plants, its chemical works, and, above all, its coal fields, West Virginia remains delightfully rural, an attractive mix of rugged mountains, plunging river valleys, dense forests, and rolling hills.

The two different faces of West Virginia are both very much on display in the town of **Fairmont**. Picturesquely set on the banks of the Monongahela River with steep hills rising on all sides, this flourishing community is nevertheless located in one of the state's principal coal mining areas.

The same dichotomy, on a much larger scale, can be seen in **Huntington**, West Virginia's second biggest city and one of its principal industrial centers. Yet amid all the heavy manufacturing is a lovely rose garden that boasts almost 100 different varieties. And the Huntington Museum of Art is a cultural delight.

At **Martinsburg**, far to the east near the historic town of Harpers Ferry, apple and peach orchards blanket the surrounding countryside. This was the home of the famous Confederate spy Belle Boyd.

Another revered Southerner, Thomas "Stonewall" Jackson, was born in **Clarksburg**, which served as a Union supply depot for most of the Civil War.

Last but not least, in the northern sliver of the state, there's **Triadelphia**, just outside Wheeling, which features Oglebay Park, a 1,500-acre recreational area incorporating gardens, a glass museum, and a superb children's zoo.

Bridgeport

$$ **HOLIDAY INN-CLARKSBURG**
100 Lodgeville Rd
(304) 842-5411
Hotel off I-79 near
downtown Clarksburg

Fairmont

$ **HOLIDAY INN**
I-79 and Old Grafton Rd
(304) 366-5500
Hilltop hotel off I-79
near downtown

Huntington

$$$ **RADISSON HOTEL**
1001 3rd Ave
(304) 525-1001
11-story downtown hotel
off I-64 near Civic Center
with luxury level rooms,
many rooms have river views

Martinsburg

$$$ **HOLIDAY INN**
301 Foxcroft Ave
(304) 267-5500
5-story hotel off I-81

Triadelphia

$ **DAYS INN**
I-70 and Dallas Pike
(304) 547-0610
Hilltop hotel off I-70

Wisconsin

Wisconsin truly is America's "dairyland." This state of gently rolling uplands, fertile prairie, and nearly 15,000 lakes leads the nation in the production of milk, cheese, and butter. But another American staple, beer, is also produced in large quantities; and with almost half of the state covered by forest, lumbering has become an important industry, too.

Wisconsin's biggest city, **Milwaukee**, still has many small town traits and offers a vibrant mix of old-world tradition and modern razzle-dazzle. Among its many highlights are Milwaukee County Zoo, Mitchell Park Horticultural Conservatory, and Milwaukee Public Museum. But don't leave without enjoying its lakefront location by taking a harbor cruise, or its beer-making tradition by taking a tour of one of Milwaukee's many breweries.

The state capital of **Madison** is America's only city located on an isthmus. The downtown skyline is dominated by the majestic State Capitol, with its huge white granite dome. A short walk away lies the University of Wisconsin campus, with many cultural attractions.

Pigskin fans won't want to miss an opportunity to visit **Green Bay**, home of the Packers, the oldest club in the National Football League. At the Green Bay Packer Hall of Fame, soak up all the history going back to 1919. Then take a look at the historic locomotives in the National Railroad Museum.

Transportation is also the big draw in nearby **Oshkosh**, which contains one of the country's best aviation collections, the EEA Adventure Museum, with almost 100 historically significant aircraft on display. The town is a great place to shop, thanks to Manufacturers Marketplace, an enormous outlet mall.

Brookfield

$$$ RESIDENCE INN BY MARRIOTT
950 S Pinehurst Ct
(414) 782-5990 or
(800) 331-3131
All-suite motel off I-94
on golf course

$$$ WYNDHAM GARDEN HOTEL
18155 Bluemound Rd
(414) 792-1212
3-story hotel off I-94

Green Bay

$$ DAYS INN
406 N Washington St
(414) 435-4484
5-story downtown hotel
on US 141

$$$ RADISSON INN
2040 Airport Dr
(414) 494-7300
Hotel opposite airport

Madison

$$$ HOWARD JOHNSON PLAZA HOTEL
525 W Johnson St
(608) 251-5511
7-story downtown hotel next
to University of Wisconsin
and near State Capitol

Milwaukee

$$ HOTEL WISCONSIN
720 N 3rd St
(414) 271-4900
1913 downtown hotel
near Grand Avenue Mall
and Performing Arts Center

$$$ MARC PLAZA HOTEL
509 W Wisconsin Ave
(414) 271-7250
24-story 1928 art deco-style
downtown hotel off I-794

$$$$ WYNDHAM MILWAUKEE CENTER HOTEL
139 E Kilbourn Ave
(414) 276-8686
10-story downtown hotel
off I-794 connected to
Milwaukee Center and near
Bradley Sports Center

Oshkosh

$$ HOLIDAY INN HOLIDOME
500 S Koeller Rd
(414) 233-1511
Hotel on US 41 near downtown

Wauwatosa

$$$ SHERATON MAYFAIR
2303 N Mayfair Rd
(414) 257-3400
8-story hotel off
US 45 opposite Mayfair
shopping center

Wyoming

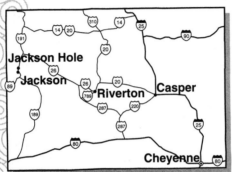

With two of America's most spectacular national parks, Yellowstone (which was also the nation's first) and Grand Teton, as well as a host of national monuments, national historic sites, and national forests, Wyoming is an outdoor paradise.

To get yourself firmly in the Western mood, head for **Jackson**, which serves not only as a major skiing center (for Snow King) but also as a terminus for numerous whitewater rafting trips. A few miles away lies **Jackson Hole** valley in Grand Teton National Park.

Casper, the biggest city in the state, is famed for its annual five-day fair and rodeo in late July, early August.

Casper

| $$ | **WESTRIDGE MOTEL** |

955 Cy Ave
(307) 234-8911
Motel off I-25

Jackson

| $$$ | **ANGLERS INN** |

265 N Millward St,
(307) 733-3682
Hotel next to Flat Creek
near downtown

Jackson Hole

| $$$ | **JACKSON HOLE LODGE** |

420 W Broadway
(307) 733-2992
Downtown hotel
near Snow King
(max 5-night stay)

Riverton

| $ | **EL RANCHO MOTEL FRIENDSHIP INN** |

221 S Federal Blvd
(307) 856-7455
Motel on US 26

About the Author

Neil Saunders

*N*eil Saunders has spent most of his career writing about travel. Since moving to the United States in 1977 from his native Britain, Neil has lived in Chicago, Los Angeles, and Baltimore and has traveled extensively throughout the country. His most recent book, **Soccer Access**, was published by HarperCollins in conjunction with the 1994 World Cup tournament held in the United States. He is also the author of **London Confidential** and **Cheers! The Best of British Pubs**. For six years Neil worked as the editor of **British Travel Letter**, a monthly newsletter for Anglophiles he founded in 1988.

QUALITY
SERVICES
INTERNATIONAL®

Detach card along perforation

*U*sing this travel guide will save you money on your hotel stays. If you wish to save hundreds of additional dollars each year on all your travel needs — both business and pleasure, simply call **1-800-355-1833** for more information on receiving a trial membership in one of the nation's largest preferred travel clubs.

Learn how you can
- obtain deep discounts on special vacation packages and cruises

SAVE 20-50%
- at hundreds of restaurants
- receive discounted rates and extra value coupons from nationally known car rental companies, renowned theme parks, and attractions
- enjoy one-call airline reservations that guarantee the lowest available airfare
- **plus**…a variety of other exclusive savings and privileges.

Administered by QSI®/ENCORE®

_____
                                      Signature